P9-AOU-039

THE PSYCHOLOGY OF LAUGHTER & COMEDY

THE PSYCHOLOGY OF LAUGHTER AND COMEDY

BY

J. Y. T. GREIG, M.A.

Registrar, Armstrong College, in the University of Durham

Si Mimnermus uti censet, sine amore jocisque
Nil est jucundum ; vivas in amore jocisque.
HORACE.—*Epist.*, I, 6, 65—66.

Mieulx est de ris que de larmes escrire,
Pour ce que rire est le propre de l'homme.
RABELAIS.—Prologue to *Gargantua*.

COOPER SQUARE PUBLISHERS, INC.
NEW YORK
1969

Originally Published 1923
Published by Cooper Square Publishers, Inc.
59 Fourth Avenue, New York, N. Y. 10003
Standard Book Number 8154-0295-3
Library of Congress Catalog Card No. 72-79198

Printed in the United States of America

PREFACE

When this book was all but completed, I mentioned it to a candid friend, a philosopher by profession. He gazed at me with sad eyes. "The only people who have the cheek to write on laughter," said he, "are those with no sense of humour."

I dare say he was right. At any rate, this is certainly not a jest-book. It might be better if it were. There are still many men alive—and perhaps a few women too, though they are more difficult to find—who have made it their business to stir the world to laughter, and who have succeeded therein. Charlie Chaplin is one such, Grock the clown is another, Stephen Leacock is a third. I do not know if they have a 'sense of humour': probably not. But if I had the gifts to be of their fraternity, I would. As it is, I have had to be content to lumber after them, a long way behind, loaded with the abstract terms of a science, psychology, which is still in the astrological stage of its development.

And while I am about it, I may as well confess how this book came to be written at all. It is the fulfilment of a vendetta. Some ten, or it may be more years ago, I dropped in upon a fellow-undergraduate, in the small, grey hours of a summer morning. What I wanted from him was a belated drink, to cheer me home to my own lodgings and so to bed: what I got from him was a dissertation on 'Theories of Comedy,' the reading of which aloud lasted some two hours. As I left him, with a dry throat and sleepy eyes, I vowed to be revenged on him, by writing a better dissertation myself on the same subject. This book will show him, if he ever reads it, how long I can cherish malice in my heart.

I do not know how much I owe to unconscious memory of his work; but my indebtedness to other writers, who have the advantage over him in that their books have been published and can be read at leisure, will be obvious to anyone with a working knowledge of such books. Above all, I wish to put on record how much I have learned from the writings of two men, very different one from another—Professor James Sully and Professor Sigmund Freud.

For the loan of books, and for friendly encouragement and help in other ways, I am greatly indebted to my present Principal, Sir Theodore Morison, and to my colleagues in the University of Durham, Professors Arthur Robinson, J. Wight Duff, R. F. A. Hoernlé, and W. L. Renwick. The College librarian, Dr. Frederick Bradshaw, has stinted neither time nor labour in helping me to come by books and references. The whole of the proofs have been read by Mr. Norman Wood, to whom I wish to extend my thanks.

J. Y. T. G.

ARMSTRONG COLLEGE,
NEWCASTLE-UPON-TYNE,
January, 1923.

CONTENTS

The Psychology of Laughter and Comedy

CHAPTER I

INTRODUCTION

MOST of the philosophers and psychologists who have addressed themselves to the subject of laughter, have dashed boldly into the midst of it, and there dealt about them manfully with the weapons that came to hand. I am, I confess it, of a fainter heart, and would lay out and take the measure of the weapons to be used in the fray. For in truth the subject of laughter is a battle-ground, strewn with the bodies of heroes and encumbered with the debris of many a brave system of philosophy. It is prudent to reconnoitre the field before adventuring.

INSTINCTIVE BEHAVIOUR.

It is wiser to make a beginning with instinctive behaviour rather than with instinct. Instinct is a dangerous word. Too many psychologists have hypnotized themselves with its aid and slipped away dreamily into metaphysics. A useful term, too useful a term to discard altogether, its value in psychology is nevertheless descriptive and classificatory, not explanatory. It shortens our labour in describing the *how* of human and animal behaviour: it is as useless as its companion term 'diathesis' in attempts to explain the *why*.[1]

[1] Psychologists are not more apt to hypostatize instinct than biologists to perform the same pious office for diathesis. Mr. W. P. Pycraft reverently announces that "Horns are the witness of a horn-producing diathesis."—*The Courtship of Animals*, p. 51.

Of instinctive behaviour Professor Lloyd Morgan has provided a definition that is fast becoming classical. "Instinctive behaviour is that which is, on its first occurrence, independent of prior experience; which tends to the well-being of the individual and the preservation of the race; which is similarly performed by all members of the same more or less restricted group of animals; and which may be subject to subsequent modification under the guidance of experience."[1] Though this definition appears to have found more favour with the biologists than with the psychologists,[2] it is difficult to improve upon it.

Examination of instinctive behaviour leads to its classification under three main headings, in order of decreasing specificity. These may be called the reflex-instincts, the instincts (without qualification), and the instinctive tendencies.

Behaviour of the first class—of the reflex-instincts—is highly specific as to stimulus and response, sufficiently well co-ordinated on its first occurrence to serve practical needs, approximately equal throughout one animal species, and comparatively unmodifiable by subsequent experience. It is the characteristic behaviour of the 'little brain type' of animals, the hackneyed example being that of the Yucca moth. The human reflex-instincts, like sucking, and grasping with the hand, are much less complicated, and though they are interesting enough, they do not become really important for psychology until they are enlisted into the service of behaviour of the second class—of the instincts.

Behaviour of the instincts is much less specific as to stimulus and response; it fumbles at first; though universal in an animal species, it is subject to considerable variations within that species; and, above all, it is highly sensitive to the guidance of experience. Happily it is not necessary, in a study of laughter, to compile an authentic, inclusive,

[1] *Instinct and Experience*, p. 5.

[2] Professor Arthur Thomson quotes it with approval (*The System of Animate Nature*, vol. i, p. 202), while Dr. James Drever seems dissatisfied (*Instinct in Man*, passim).

and exclusive list of the human instincts. I suggest that we agree to include feeding, love, and fighting, and perhaps curiosity and hunting as well. Many of the other supposed instincts given, for instance, by Professor McDougall and Dr. Drever, appear to me still doubtful.

Still less specific than the instincts is the behaviour of the instinctive tendencies. Indeed, these are so general, so formal or constitutive of behaviour as such, that psychologists have hesitated to apply the adjective 'instinctive' to them at all, and it has remained for Professor Graham Wallas to insist that some of them at least must be projected on to the same plane as McDougall's dispositions to be angry, to be curious, and to be afraid. Graham Wallas maintains that "we are born with a tendency, under appropriate conditions, to think, which is as original and independent as our tendency, under appropriate conditions, to run away."[1] No more than in the case of the instincts do I propose to pledge my credit on an exhaustive list of the instinctive tendencies. Those of immediate importance are: feeling behaviour as pleasant or unpleasant, memory, thinking, continuing behaviour felt as pleasant, seeking similar behaviour in future, discontinuing behaviour felt as unpleasant, avoiding similar behaviour in future, and suggestibility.

FORCE.

All these psychological notions turn upon the idea of force, which is the central idea in modern psychology. This idea masquerades under different names. The Freudian school speaks of the *wish*, a sufficiently misleading term; the Zürich school writes learnedly—and pompously—of the *libido*; Bergson has immortalized the phrase *l'élan vital*. Some recent psychologists have taken to using the term *horme*. The term to be used does not greatly matter. The least committal is probably *psycho-physical energy*, the hyphen leaving us free to

[1] *The Great Society*, p. 40.

drop either half of the compound word, according to whatever solution may eventually be found for the Body-Mind problem.

Each individual may be assumed, then, to be dowered with an indefinite but not unlimited amount of psycho-physical energy, to be spent in behaviour. The general directions of this expenditure are laid down inexorably in the instinctive tendencies. No man, by taking thought, can eliminate thought, except he die. More specific lines of direction are laid down in the instincts, and in view of results achieved in psychotherapy it would seem justifiable to assume that varying amounts of energy are actually hypothecated to the instincts. This is only another way of saying that each instinct must be exercised somehow, or the whole organism suffers. Again, the amount of energy so hypothecated varies with age and other conditions; the instinct of love, for instance, gathers its charge gradually in the early years, increasing till about the age of five or six, remaining fairly constant or decreasing in importance from then until shortly before puberty, and then rapidly increasing again until it reaches its maximum. We may suppose also, if we like, that besides hypothecated energy there is a general reserve to be called upon at need, or, since the behaviour of one instinct is not distinct in all respects from that of others, —it is, after all, one organism that behaves—we may prefer to assume that energy normally intended for one instinct can be drawn off to the service of another, if and when the need arises.

The proof of all these assumptions is pragmatic. They *work* in psychotherapy, an art followed by some of the greatest living psychologists. Thus M. Pierre Janet, one of the most distinguished of these artists, writes: "La plupart des névropathes sont des déprimés, des épuisés, leurs troubles mentaux tirent leur origine de cette faiblesse même. Si l'on me permet d'employer une comparaison empruntée au langage de la finance, toutes ces maladies ne sont au fond que diverses manières de faire faillite et de tomber dans la misère, mais cette ruine, cette misère, ne semble pas avoir chez tous le même point de départ."[1]

"Every instinct is an impulse," said James,[2] and it makes a great deal of difference in psychology whether we read this to mean 'an impulse *from*' or 'an impulse *to*.' One may be driven from behind or attracted from in front. The intellectualist psychology which is slowly going out of favour, thought of an impulse as attracted *to* or *by* an object; man pursued 'ends,' which he was able to conceive more or less clearly for himself. Modern psychology, on the other hand, thinks of an impulse as a direction of energy *away from*, and is less concerned about the 'ends' that are supposed to be pursued. Professor Freud, still dominated, linguistically at least, by the older point of view, distinguishes, for instance, between the sexual aim and the sexual object,[3] but the whole effect of his work is to emphasize the distinction between what may be called the sexual urge and the sexual aim. To hit the aim may not satisfy the urge, that is to say, may not *put a stop to the urge*. For it is only from the stoppage of the urge that we can conclude the 'end' or purpose. When the urge ceases, the behaviour-cycle of which it is the centre is closed, and from this conclusion in time we can go on to infer, with varying degrees of accuracy, the aim, purpose, or 'end' towards which the given instinct is directed. There is no pretending that this inference is always easy to draw, but we generalize from a large number of observations, and our mistakes do not invalidate the method. Besides, in the observation of human behaviour we can enlist the co-operation of the person who behaves. A man's thoughts may be far enough away from what he is doing, may be, as the Behaviorist has it, "a mere irrelevance, a surface embroidery on action." [4] But not invariably. They may be brought back to focus on his behaviour, and then they deserve consideration, though not necessarily belief.

[1] *Les médications psychologiques*, tome ii, p. 303.
[2] *Principles of Psychology*, vol. ii, p. 385.
[3] *Three Contributions to the Theory of Sex*, passim.
[4] E. B. Holt, *The Freudian Wish*, p. 87.

Observation of what men do, eked out by what the men themselves have to say about it, does enable us to determine with approximate accuracy the immediate 'ends' which behaviour serves.

The Instinctive Tendencies.

The activity of the instincts is not continuous, but intermittent. The activity of the instinctive tendencies is unremitting.

1. *Memory.*

The law of mnemic causation has been stated by Mr. Bertrand Russell, thus : "If a complex stimulus A has caused a complex reaction B in an organism, the occurrence of a part of A on a future occasion tends to cause the whole reaction B."[1] The operation of this law makes it very difficult, and sometimes almost impossible, to determine exactly what are the original stimuli of the instincts of man. To be sure of an instinct one must catch it *in flagrante* the very first time, in a large number of different persons, and then, after analysing out the accidents in the different situations, decide what is the essential element common to all. If the very first time is allowed to pass unnoticed, the supposedly original stimulus on the second or third occasion may turn out not to be the original one after all, but to be one of the 'accidents,' to be, in fact, a substituted stimulus. It may be only a part of the original stimulus, or it may only resemble the original stimulus in some comparatively unimportant detail. Patient observation and experiment have already eliminated some supposedly original stimuli of human instincts.[2]

[1] *The Analysis of Mind*, p. 86.

[2] Fear is real enough, though I doubt if we are justified in speaking of a human instinct of fear. What is certain is that we are no longer justified in speaking of an inborn fear in the human infant of darkness, or small furry animals, or snakes. Cf. the experiments of Mr. John B. Watson, recorded in *Psychology from the Standpoint of a Behaviorist*, pp. 199 ff.

2. *Feeling and Emotion.*

In popularizing the idea that emotions are indissolubly linked to instincts, McDougall performed a great service for English psychology, though I suspect that in his insistence on qualitative differences between one emotion and another he performed an almost equivalent disservice. In his opinion emotion is 'the central part' of the whole process of instinct, which includes cognition, emotion, and impulse or conation. Drever, who follows him in the main, breaks away from his lead at this point, offering the alternative hypothesis that emotion arises only when the satisfaction of the instinct is suspended or checked, when "interest passes into tension"[1]

Drever has certainly divined the weak spot in McDougall's armour, though in thrusting at it he has failed to thrust home. Starting innocently with the threefold division of cognition, feeling, and conation, which is a commonplace in all text-books on psychology, McDougall none the less uses the middle term, feeling, in a double sense. On the one hand he uses it to indicate that behaviour is felt as pleasant or unpleasant by the subject who behaves, on the other, to indicate a supposed special quality in the feeling apart from its pleasantness or unpleasantness. An instinct, he says, "determines its possessor . . . to experience an emotional excitement of a particular quality" upon his perceiving an object of a particular class.[2] It is this idea of qualitative difference in emotion which is so misleading. Instincts differ in three respects, and in three respects only—in the situations which evoke them, in the responses, explicit and implicit, evoked, and in quantitative combinations of pleasure and displeasure felt by the subject during the responses. In so far as these differences amount, *in the aggregate*, to a difference in quality, it is convenient to speak as though emotions differed in quality. But it is important to remember that by no process of analysis can we discover any qualitative differences in feeling as

[1] *Instinct in Man*, p. 157.

[2] *Social Psychology*, p. 29.

such, except differences of pleasure and displeasure. Dr. Wohlgemuth has carried out a series of most exhaustive experiments on this problem, and concludes: "There are only two feeling-elements, viz: Pleasure and Unpleasure. Any differences except intensity, duration, and extensity, are apparent only, and are found to belong to sensations, or to other cognitive or conative processes."[1]

The law of feeling can be simply stated. Behaviour is felt as pleasant which is in a fair way to reach its appropriate end-result; behaviour is felt as unpleasant which is being prevented from reaching its appropriate end-result. In the limiting cases in both directions feeling disappears altogether. Neither behaviour which is wholly unopposed nor behaviour which is wholly arrested is felt at all, but both limits are outside life, as it is known to us. The behaviour of every organism is opposed to some extent, if it is only by the force of gravity; but only to some extent, else the organism dies. Pleasure and displeasure are therefore truly correlative: without some degree of displeasure no pleasure can be felt, and vice versa. Pleasure is the feeling equivalent of (relatively) uninterrupted behaviour, displeasure the feeling equivalent of (relatively) interrupted behaviour.

It is necessary to notice briefly whence come interruptions. On the one hand, clearly, interruption may have its source in external opposing forces. An organism may be attempting something which, for wholly physical reasons, it is difficult or even impossible for it to perform. On the other hand, interruptions may have their source internally; the organism may be divided against itself. Such interruptions are by far the more important psychologically.

It is plain from the operation of the law of mnemic causation that any element which is constantly recurring in different situations tends to become linked to a variety

[1] *Pleasure—Unpleasure*, p. 235. This appears also to be, in substance, the opinion of Dr. James Ward, the *doyen* of English psychologists. Cf. *Psychological Principles*, chaps. x and xi.

of different instincts. Two or more instincts may thus be excited simultaneously by the same situation, or the same instinct may be impelled in more than one direction. Some degree of strain or tension is thus set up. It may be either short-lived, or violent and prolonged. Remembering these prolonged internecine conflicts, an individual does what he can to avoid them in future by organizing his instincts, and if he succeeds, is said to have set up a 'sentiment.' A sentiment is a system of organized instincts, having their common centre in some object, and not conflicting seriously with any other organized system in the same individual; the whole process being carried out more or less consciously and the individual being well aware of what he is doing. The individual wittingly prepares his behaviour beforehand in relation to some object or series of objects of common occurrence. A 'complex,' on the other hand, is a sentiment of which the individual has either never been, or has ceased to be, conscious. It indicates either that the organization of instincts has gone on without the individual himself being aware of what he is doing, or that a sentiment has come into violent collision with another sentiment, and instead of being honestly and deliberately broken up, has been pushed out of the focus of attention, has been repressed, and is now dissociated.

Opposition to behaviour, then, may arise from either external or internal sources. Purely physical opposition of some kind there must always be, but it is, on the whole, less important than the civil wars provoked within behaviour itself. One instinct may tug one way, another another way, one sentiment may paralyse another, one complex may twist the whole conduct of an individual awry. Whatever the source of the opposition may be, with it enters the feeling of displeasure; and as soon as displeasure ceases to be minimal, the complete feeling in the behaviour, combining both pleasure and displeasure, becomes sufficiently noticeable to be called *emotion*.

The intensity of the emotion is proportional to the intensity of the struggle between the combatants. If the force of an external obstruction is slight in comparison with the psycho-physical energy which an individual mobilizes against it, the resulting emotion is correspondingly slight. We do not usually feel any emotion in the activities of walking a hundred yards. But walking three steps across the room once caused all of us wild joy, walking the last lap of thirty miles, in the gathering dusk of a winter day, will probably induce mixed feelings in most amateur pedestrians, and, if we are recovering from a broken leg, walking up or down a flight of ten steps will certainly be an emotional experience. If the external obstruction is powerful and the individual makes no more than a feint of struggling against it, again the emotion is slight. Many a soldier in the European War scrambled over the parapet and marched forward in an attack to what he fully believed to be certain death, with more equanimity than he showed four days earlier in rest billets when a flight of enemy bombing planes was heard overhead. And this principle, which holds for external obstruction, holds equally when the friction is internal : if the opposing forces are out of all proportion to one another the resulting emotion is negligible. It is when the internal forces in contraposition are, or seem to be, about equally matched, that emotion is at its most intense. When the course of true love does, for once, run smooth, it is quite properly looked on as a dull affair ; no novelist could get a thrill out of it.

An objection must be met. It may be that a struggle, violent enough while it lasts, endures only for an instant of time, though the emotion which we say results from it, persists for hours or even days. Feeling, in short, does appear to have some sort of independent existence, and not to depend wholly upon the observable behaviour which is going on simultaneously. This objection works hardly against the hypothesis of qualitative differences in emotion, but not, I submit, against the position I have taken up. It is admittedly difficult to tell with certainty when any given struggle, A, is concluded ; the implicit behaviour started may, as the researches of Mr. W. B.

Cannon[1] and others have shown, continue for a considerable time after all explicit signs of the struggle have passed away. But even supposing struggle A to be definitely ended, there have followed hard upon it struggles B, C, D, . . . Z, no one of which is wholly independent either of the one that went before or of the one that followed after. Behaviour, which for convenience of observation we split up into sections, is continuous; the past gnaws into the present and the present into the future. Feeling, which is in behaviour, is continuous also, and its two elements, pleasure and displeasure, are subject to continuous quantitative adjustment according as behaviour is functioning smoothly or encountering obstacles. Emotion A is a cross section of feeling; so is emotion B; if pleasure predominates in A and displeasure in B no one would suggest that emotion A persists beyond the term set by the conclusion of the struggle out of which it arose. It is only when the proportions of pleasure and displeasure in A and B are approximately the same that we speak of the enduring of an emotion after all the rest of the associated behaviour has ceased.

Four laws of emotion may be stated:

1. Emotion arises when behaviour is appreciably hindered.
2. Such hindrance may have its source either externally or internally.
3. The intensity of an emotion depends upon the relative strength of the opposing forces, the greatest intensity being reached when they are almost equal.
4. Success in overcoming the hindrance is felt as pleasant, failure as unpleasant.

3. *Suggestibility.*

Contrary to general usage I have proposed the inclusion of suggestibility under the constitutive instinctive tendencies, rather than under the instincts. The activity of an instinct is intermittent, the tendency to be suggestible is continuous.

[1] *Bodily Changes in Pain, Hunger, Fear, and Rage.*

McDougall offers us three 'pseudo-instincts,' namely, sympathy, imitation, and suggestion; though he notes that the three are closely allied as regards their effects. In point of fact, these three supposed instincts are so closely allied that there is no justification for separating them at all; it is simplest and most accurate to speak only of one tendency, suggestibility. This tendency can be described as follows: The behaviour of an individual X tends to provoke similar behaviour in an individual Y of the same animal species, as soon as Y becomes aware of what X is doing, and without Y being necessarily stimulated directly by what provoked the behaviour of X: Y does not need to infer the stimulus of X's behaviour, but responds directly to a response.[1]

Suggestibility is a compulsive instinctive tendency in man no less than in other animals. It is never completely inhibited; all we can do is to arrest the suggested behaviour the moment it begins, or crowd it out with other behaviour that takes up our full attention. The whole of art is built on the foundation of this tendency.

[1] I cannot agree with M. Baudouin (*Suggestion et autosuggestion*) that auto-suggestion is prior to hetero-suggestion.

CHAPTER II

THE LAUGHTER OF INFANTS

I GATHER, chiefly from the work of M. Raulin entitled *Le rire et les exhilarants,* that laughter was at one time a vexed question among the anatomists and the physiologists, the activity, or inactivity, of the diaphragm being the chief matter in dispute ; and I acknowledge a certain malign satisfaction in the thought that the philosophers have not had a monopoly in the controversies which laughter has provoked. But I propose to leave it there, and not to be drawn into any anatomical or physiological discussion. It is more important psychologically to make sure what laughter looks like and sounds like.

THE EXPLICIT BEHAVIOUR.

"During laughter the mouth is opened more or less widely, with the corners drawn much backwards, as well as a little upwards, and the upper lip is somewhat raised." [1] Wrinkles form under and at the outer corners of the eyes, and the eyes brighten. This is all that is needed to produce the appearance of a genuine smile. In addition, however, the nose may be wrinkled, and the nostrils slightly distended. According to an opinion expressed by Raulin, for which there is much to be said, this wrinkling of the nose gives to the face the appearance of lascivious enjoyment ; and Raulin adds, "Ce rire gaillard et égrillard . . . est très usité ches les comédiens

[1] Charles Darwin, *The Expression of the Emotions*, p. 208.

et les bouffes." [1] Wrinkling of the forehead may also occur, but this is adventitious.

The smile should be bilateral. A slight, one-sided contraction of the facial muscles puzzles the wits of the spectator to interpret.[2]

In its early stages the laugh is identical with the smile; later, sounds are added. The orthodox opinion on these sounds is that women and children use chiefly the vowels 'ee' and 'eh,' (French 'i' and 'é'), and adult men the vowels 'ah' and 'oh,' (more frequently perhaps 'aw').[3] Obviously fashion and convention alter the natural sounds very considerably.

The 'good laugh' is no niggard of its effects. Teufelsdröckh, it will be remembered, "burst forth like the neighing of all Tattersall's—tears streaming down his cheeks, pipe held aloft, foot clutched into the air—loud, long-continuing, uncontrollable; a laugh not of the face and diaphragm only, but of the whole man from head to heel." [4] Untrained observers have stated, and trained psychologists have recorded,[5] that the activity of laughter may begin with the lips, the eyes, the ears, the cheeks, the head, or the shoulders, and one wonders why the trunk, arms, and legs should have been omitted. The outward behaviour of violent laughter has been many times described. "During excessive laughter the whole body is often thrown backwards and shakes, or is almost convulsed; the respiration is much disturbed; the head and face become gorged with blood, with the veins distended; and the orbicular muscles are spasmodically contracted in order to protect the eyes. Tears are freely shed. Hence . . . it is scarcely possible to point out any

[1] *Op. cit.*, pp. 50–51. Cf. the gesture of the comic man on the music-hall stage and in the club smoke-room—laying the forefinger along the nose.

[2] Cf. the enigmatic smile (?) of La Gioconda.

[3] It is interesting to note that in Chinese (Pekingese Mandarin form) the word for *laugh* is *hsiao*, which contains three out of the four vowel sounds.

[4] Carlyle, *Sartor Resartus*, Bk. I, ch. iv.

[5] *Vide* the returns to the questionary sent out by G. Stanley Hall and Arthur Allin, summarized in *The Psychology of Tickling, Laughter, and the Comic*.

difference between the tear-stained face of a person after a paroxysm of excessive laughter and after a bitter crying fit."[1] Other more remote and implicit effects have been suggested by the learned.[2]

From these effects, real or imaginary, I propose to consider only one, and that very briefly for the moment. It is common knowledge that laughter 'takes away one's breath.' The result of this is that prolonged laughter narrows down all behaviour of an explicit kind. Before jumping a gate, pulling the trigger of a rifle, or performing any other act that requires muscular strain either to produce or to inhibit outward movements, one takes a long breath and holds it. For laughter, one takes a long breath and then vents it in short, sharp explosions of sound.

DATES.

The dates of the first laughter of children have been recorded by many psychologists, famous in their generation. According to Pliny, laughter does not begin before the fortieth day of life.[3] Modern science has overturned so many of Pliny's pleasant fictions that it would be some satisfaction to find this statement at the least confirmed, and indeed, if we confined ourselves to the observations of Darwin, we might make shift to pass it. Darwin's children are reported by him to have smiled for the first time on the forty-fifth and forty-sixth days, respectively.[4] Yet, for all my wish to confirm Pliny's chronology, truth compels me to admit that other observers have recorded dates considerably earlier. Perez assures us that children often smile when only a month old.[5] Preyer pushes the date further forward still, to the tenth

[1] Darwin, *op. cit.*, p. 214.

[2] *Vide* especially Burton, *The Anatomy of Melancholy*, Part II, Sect. 2, Mem. 6, Subsect. 4, on *Mirth and Merry Company*.

[3] "Has (lacrymas) protinus vitæ principio; at hercules risus, præcox et celerrimus ante quadragesimum diem nulli datur."—*De Natura Rerum*, Bk. vii, ch. i.

[4] Darwin, *op. cit.*, p. 217.

[5] Bernard Perez, *Les trois premières années de l'enfant*, pp. 48–9.

day: [1] while two other infants, too precocious for this slow world, are stated by their admiring parents to have smiled on the fifth [2] and sixth [3] days, respectively, of their eager young lives.

On the whole, the first laugh, properly so called, is reported to occur later than the first smile. Darwin's elder child began his laughing career on the fifty-third day with "a little bleating noise," though his father, with admirable restraint, hesitates to call this noise unmistakable laughter. His younger child laughed on the sixty-fifth day.[4] The twenty-sixth day was eventful in the biography of Preyer's child, for on that day (as ever was), he accompanied a smile with "some sounds not before heard, which were appropriate to his happy mood." [5] Miss Shinn, however, heard no genuine laughter from her niece before the hundred and eighteenth day.[6]

All these records may be accepted without prejudice. The only safe conclusions that can be drawn from them are: that neither the smile nor the laugh are manifest immediately after birth, that the smile precedes the laugh, and—happiest conclusion of all—that children vary.

All the psychologists I have quoted insist upon a distinction, which they regard as important, between mechanical smiling and expressive smiling. Preyer, for example, says: "The first smiling is the movement most often misunderstood. Every opening of the mouth whatever, capable of being interpreted as a smile, is wont to be gladly called a smile even in the youngest child. But it is no more the case with the child than with the adult that the mere contortion of the mouth fulfils the idea of the smile. There is required for this either a feeling of satisfaction or an idea of an agreeable sort." [7] In

[1] W. Preyer, *The Mind of the Child*, Part I, "The Senses and the Will," pp. 157, 295.

[2] Tiedemann's son, quoted by Raulin, *op. cit.*, p. 75.

[3] Mrs. Moore's child, quoted by James Sully, *An Essay on Laughter*, p. 165.

[4] Darwin, *op. cit.*, p. 218.

[5] Preyer, *op. cit.*, p. 296.

[6] *Notes on the Development of a Child*, vol. i, p. 202.

[7] Preyer, *op. cit.*, p. 294.

conformity with this general principle, Preyer considers the supposed smile of his own child on the tenth day of life as a wholly mechanical phenomenon, and dates the first true smile from the twenty-sixth day, when, as he startles us by remarking, "the child could better discriminate between his sensations and the feelings generated by them."[1] Substantially the same distinction between mechanical or reflex laughter and expressive or mimetic laughter is made, in different words, by Perez, Sully, Miss Shinn, Raulin, and other writers.

Passing over the astonishing, and doubtless Teutonic, precocity of the young Preyer in introspecting his own behaviour, I suspect that psychologists of the twentieth century would be less confident of their ability to distinguish automatic from expressive behaviour in an infant of a few weeks old. We are less enamoured of intellectual theories in psychology than were our predecessors of the nineteenth century, and we tend to find just as much *meaning* in automatic as in conscious activities. We must therefore decline to be side-tracked by Preyer's warning, and must pay as much attention to early mechanical laughter as to that which is said to have become mimetic.

The Occasions of Infants' Laughter.

The smiles of Darwin's two children, on the forty-fifth and forty-sixth days, "arose chiefly when looking at their mother."[2] The smile of Preyer's child on the tenth day occurred during sleep after he had taken a full meal.[3] The smile on the twenty-sixth day also followed feeding; "he smiled, opening his eyes, and directed his look to the friendly face of his mother."[4] The same child, Preyer informs us, began to laugh "in the period from the sixth to the ninth week, as a sign of joy at a familiar pleasing impression, his eyes being fixed on his

[1] Preyer, *op. cit.*, p. 295.
[2] Darwin, *A Biographical Sketch of an Infant*, p. 288.
[3] Preyer, *op. cit.*, pp. 157, 295.
[4] *Ibid.*, p. 296.

mother's face. But the laugh at the friendly nodding to him, and singing, of the members of the family, was then already much more marked, and was later accompanied by rapid raisings and dropping of the arms as signs of the utmost pleasure (sixth month)."[1] At one hundred and ten days one of Darwin's children "was exceedingly amused by a pinafore being thrown over his face and then suddenly withdrawn; and so he was when I suddenly uncovered my own face and approached his."[2] Three or four weeks earlier he received slight pinches on the nose and cheek "as a good joke." On the one hundred and thirty-seventh day he was puzzled by his father's approaching him with his back turned. "He looked very grave and much surprised, and would soon have cried had I not turned round; then his face instantly relaxed into a smile."[3] Miss Shinn's little niece Ruth, of whom I shall have much to say in these early chapters, was a merry child. On the thirty-second day she began to smile on looking at faces,[4] and on the same day "smiled repeatedly when her mother was rubbing a speck from her lip."[5] In the latter part of the second month "a smile could almost always be coaxed by rubbing the lip or touching the cheek with a finger tip."[6] She laughed at a grimace on the one hundred and thirtieth day,[7] and about the end of the fourth month "smiles, or even laughter and joyous movements, could be coaxed at almost any time, in these sunny moods, by a few caressing words or touches."[8] "At three months old, she liked to be tossed in her father's arms, and during the fourth month became very fond of a frolic, and would crow and smile in high glee when she was tossed in the air, slid down one's knees, or otherwise tumbled about; the first true laughter I heard from her was over such a frolic in the last week of this month (one hundred and eighteenth day); and in the first six months this was almost the only cause of laughter. . . . Thus on the

[1] Preyer, *op. cit.*, p. 298. [2] Darwin, *op. cit.*, p. 289. [3] *Ibid.*, p. 283.
[4] Shinn, *op. cit.*, p. 79. [5] *Ibid.*, p. 136.
[6] *Loc. cit.* [7] *Ibid.*, p. 16. [8] *Ibid.*, p. 239.

one hundred and thirty-third day, seated on her mother's foot and danced up and down (held by the arms), she wore an expression of rapt delight, and whenever her mother stopped she would set up a little cry of desire. . . . In the twenty-fourth week her father began another play that was very delightful to her—swinging or tossing her into her mother's arms, or mine, to be swung back into his; sometimes the three of us passed her thus from one to another. This excited great hilarity; she reached her arms from one to another and laughed aloud; and when the frolic was stopped and she was taken from the room, she set up a remonstrant whine. I have a number of notes afterward of merriment over this play and desire for it."[1] At three and a half months Marie, of whom Perez writes, "est très sensible aux caresses, elle rit et joue avec quiconque rit et joue avec elle."[2] In the period from the eighth to the tenth weeks Professor Sully's boy, C., "expressed his pleasure at seeing his father's face, not only by a bright smile, but by certain cooing sounds. At the same date a playful touch on the child's cheek was sufficient to provoke a smile."[3] When ten weeks old C. "would still greet new faces with a gracious smile.[4] . . When between four and five months old he was accustomed to watch the antics of his sister, an elfish being, given to flying about the room, screaming, and other disorderly proceedings, with all the signs of a sense of the comicality of the spectacle. So far as the father could judge, this sister served as a kind of jester to the baby monarch. He would take just that distant, good-natured interest in her foolings that Shakespeare's sovereigns took in the eccentric and unpredictable ways of their jesters. The sense of the droll became still more distinctly marked at six months. About this date the child delighted in pulling his sister's hair, and her shrieks would send him into a fit of laughter. Among other provocatives of laughter at this time were sudden movements of one's

[1] Shinn, *op. cit.*, pp. 202–3. [2] Perez, *op. cit.*, p. 42.
[3] James Sully, *Studies of Childhood*, p. 407. [4] *Ibid.*, p. 410.

head, a rapid succession of sharp staccato sounds from one's vocal organ (when these were not disconcerting by their violence), and, of course, sudden reappearances of one's head after hiding in a game of bo-peep."[1] Mr. Rasmussen records that when his little girl, S., was one hundred and sixty-two days old he could always make her laugh by asking: 'Can you laugh a little at father?' pitching his voice on high notes.[2] My own boy was first observed to smile during sleep, after a meal, at about three weeks old: some three weeks later he is reported, on what I admit to myself is rather meagre evidence, to have smiled while awake, and while his grandfather was talking to him in caressing tones.

It will be noticed that all the above examples have a common element in the situation that is said to call out the smile or the laugh: some person is near, and is apparently noticed by the infant. Preyer solemnly warns his readers against regarding this as in any way significant,[3] but having already decided to disregard one of his warnings, I take courage to disregard this one also. It is true that instances of early laughter may be cited where the situation does not explicitly contain the presence of a second person, or where such a person appears unimportant. Thus Preyer's own child is stated to have laughed as early as the twenty-third day at a bright curtain, and Sully's boy, when seven weeks old, seemed to interest himself in a cheap, brightly coloured card. "When carried to the place where it hung," says his father, "above the glass over the fireplace, he would look up to it and greet his first-love in the world of art with a pretty smile."[4] It is somewhere stated also (I have lost the reference), that Darwin's children laughed first at tassels. None of these examples weigh heavily against the rule that the earliest laughter of infants is a response to some person. Preyer tells us next to nothing of the curtain situation, and even Sully's example, though more fully described,

[1] Sully, *op. cit.*, p. 411.
[2] Vilhelm Rasmussen, *Child Psychology*, Part I.
[3] Preyer, *op. cit.*, p. 296.
[4] Sully, *op. cit.*, p. 403.

is not convincing. One would like to be sure that it was really the showy card on the wall that aroused C.'s amusement the first time he was carried to it, and not some much more personal element in the situation—a caressing tone in his father's voice, for instance. I think it is indisputable that the coloured cared must have been a 'substituted' stimulus of laughter, and not an original one, though it is impossible, on the information given by Sully, to hazard a guess from what primary situation the substitution was first effected.

Tickling.

It is most convenient to consider all the facts of tickling together, whether they relate to infants, to animals other than man, or to human adults.

Tickling is generally said to consist of light and intermittent touches applied to the surface of the body. For reasons which will appear in the course of the discussion I think undue importance has been given to the quality of lightness, but this question may be deferred for the present. It is more important to notice at once the variety in the reactions to the stimulus of tickling: these may be laughter, vomiting, or all sorts of avoiding, defensive, or offensive movements. There is opportunity for confusion here, and in the hope of avoiding it I would be understood, in the sequel, to mean by tickling (except when otherwise stated) only such tactual stimuli as normally occasion laughter.

It has been generally concluded that one cannot tickle (in the special sense given) a very young infant. Darwin tested his elder child for the plantar reflex at seven days old; the foot was jerked away, and the toes curled, but no smile occurred.[1] The indefatigable Preyer seems hardly to have waited till the child was born before carrying out the same test; he obtained the same result. Dr. Louis Robinson, an authority on ticklishness, wrote to Sully, "I have never been able to succeed in eliciting

[1] Darwin, *op. cit.*, p. 285.

laughter from young infants under three months old by means of tickling, *unless one also smiled and caught their attention in some such way*." [1] Though the available evidence is not very comprehensive, it suggests that the laughter of ticklishness is not, properly, a reflex of a simple kind, but rather a reflex gathered up and modified within the behaviour of an instinct, or instincts, much less specific and automatic.

This conclusion is apt to be obscured by the seeming inevitability of ticklish laughter in older children and in adults. But such inevitability is rather the result of habit. Once the habit is set, control over laughter is undoubtedly almost lost; but loss of control comes only with time. Children who are just beginning to be shy with strangers cannot be successfully tickled by them, and in young children also ticklishness may completely disappear during illness.

It has been said also that one cannot tickle oneself. This has been modified into the form: 'One can tickle oneself only by means of some foreign body, such as a feather'; and it has been assumed that it is the double touch in self-titillation which destroys ticklishness. I believe that this assumption has been too hastily made, and have tested and disproved it several times with my own child. I take hold of one of his wrists, tell him to raise the opposite arm, and then, still holding his wrist, I direct it towards the exposed axilla, taking care not to touch any part of his person, other than the wrist held, with my own person. The moment his own hand, as directed by mine, reaches the axilla, he laughs heartily, his laughter on these occasions not being any different, so far as I can tell, from that which follows when I tickle him with my own fingers. Nor is his laughter to be adequately explained as arising from expectation of a good game, for he laughed the very first time I tried the experiment, though he did not know what I was about to do before I began. I do not wish to pretend that these experiments are conclusive, but only to throw doubt

[1] Quoted by Sully, *An Essay on Laughter*, p 178 (italics in text).

on the statement so often made that one cannot tickle oneself with one's own fingers. I know no instance of *spontaneous* self-tickling, and my attempts to induce my own child to tickle himself, without my intervention, have all failed; whether he used his own fingers or a foreign body, he remained quite indifferent, to all appearance, to such tactual stimuli. It seems that the truth lies somewhat short of the statement that one cannot tickle oneself. It is safer to say: one can tickle oneself only with difficulty, and, probably, only with the help of someone else.

The point is of some importance. Darwin and Sully, arguing from the impossibility of self-tickling maintain that some element of the unknown is essential to ticklishness. It may be suspected that both jumped to this conclusion because the idea of the unknown is a familiar point of departure in theories of laughter. Darwin, indeed, makes no secrecy about it. In tickling, he says, "it seems that the precise point to be touched must not be known; so with the mind, something unexpected—a novel or incongruous idea which breaks through an habitual train of thought—appears to be a strong element in the ludicrous."[1] A strong element it undoubtedly is, but it does not follow that something of the unknown is actually necessary for ticklishness. Localization of the sensations of touch is never very exact in children, specially in those parts of the body seldom touched or difficult to see. But within the usual limits of epicritic sensibility it does not, in some circumstances, make any appreciable difference in the laughing response whether the child knows beforehand or is left guessing where he is going to be tickled. If I ask my boy where he would like to be tickled, he will sometimes answer 'Anywhere' and sometimes choose some special place. His favourite spot is just above the knee, presumably because he can watch it so easily. At the time when I began these experiments on him he was apparently not yet old enough for the habit of ticklish laughter to be completely established—

[1] *Expression of the Emotions*, p. 207.

he was four and a half years old—for, if I purposely missed the chosen spot, he did not laugh, but insisted on my repeating the attack accurately. And when I touched the precise spot he was so carefully watching, he laughed immediately.

The stock examples of ticklishness in animals have been many times quoted. Darwin observed that young chimpanzees and young orangs made a chuckling sound, similar to laughter, when tickled, and that in the former the armpits were especially sensitive in this respect.[1] It is common knowledge that a dog seems to enjoy gentle scratching behind the ears, on certain parts of the back, and elsewhere, and it has been stated that under such stimulation he will retract the corners of the mouth and show something that can, by a stretch of fancy, be called an incipient smile.[2] Robinson, besides confirming Darwin's observations by experiments upon young anthropoid apes, alleges that horses and pigs are ticklish in parts roughly corresponding to the specially ticklish parts of the human body.[3] There is no doubt that certain parts of the skin in a horse are unusually sensitive to light touches, the ears, the flanks, and the nose perhaps most of all. But all the evidence goes to show that horses dislike having such parts 'tickled.' Never having been on tickling terms with pigs I have nothing to say about them.

The results for all animals except the anthropoid apes are too doubtful to be worth much, but it seems legitimate to conclude that some at least of the anthropoid apes are ticklish, in the strict sense of the word.

Both general ticklishness and the relative ticklishness of different parts of the human body vary widely from time to time in the same individual. On the whole, general ticklishness decreases with increasing age or with a fall in the level of health. Among different individuals the variations are still wider; some can hardly be

[1] Darwin, *op. cit.*, p. 134. [2] Hall and Allin, *op. cit.*, p. 33.
[3] Article on "Ticklishness," in Tuke's *Dictionary of Psychological Medicine.*

made to laugh at all, others are "so loosely put together that a wink will shake them."[1] Nor can any two people be made to agree on the most ticklish part of the body, though tables of averages can be, and have been, compiled. Robinson[2] arranges the parts of the body in the following order of decreasing ticklishness: region in front of the neck, the ribs, the axillæ, bend of the elbow, junction of the ribs and abdominal muscles, flanks, region of the hip joint, upper anterior part of the thigh. This list is rather surprising; it leaves out, for instance, the sole of the foot, generally regarded as a very ticklish spot. Hall and Allin give the following similar table, compiled from their returns: Soles of the feet (117), armpits (104), neck (86), under the chin (76), waist and ribs (60), cheeks (58), knees (25), down the back (19), behind the ears (15), all over the body (15), palms of the hands (14), corners of the mouth (8), breast (8), nose (7), legs (5), elbows (3), and lips (3). This list also is full of surprises, besides being sometimes delightfully vague. And there is a notable omission from both lists, an omission less easy to forgive in Robinson than in the proper, well-brought-up American citizens who answered the questionary of Hall and Allin. The genital organs are undoubtedly ticklish in a high degree, especially in children and adolescents, though such evidence as can be obtained goes to show that their ticklishness diminishes greatly after full sexual relationships have been established.

I provisionally accepted the definition of tickling as light and intermittent tactual stimuli applied to the surface of the body, but it is important to notice that laughter may be provoked by touch that is not light. In the case of my own child the sole of the foot is not very sensitive to feather-weight titillation, but he responds at once with laughter and defensive movements when I scrub it with a hard scrubbing brush. Similarly, it would appear that in many persons the epidermis is much

[1] George Meredith, *An Essay on Comedy*, p. 10.

[2] *Op. cit.*, and information supplied privately to Sully, and quoted by him in *An Essay on Laughter*.

less ticklish than the underlying muscles. To 'squeeze' the ribs of the flirtatious maiden is an effective way of stimulating her laughter, even though in so doing the pain centres are aroused simultaneously, and she complains, through her giggles, that the fingers of her amorous swain 'hurt.' Facts like these suggest that so far as concerns laughter the essential stimulus is touch, and not specially light touch.

The feeling aroused by being tickled varies within wide limits, from wild pleasure to acute displeasure; but after what was said on feeling in the previous chapter this variation should present no difficulty. If a child, in good health and not otherwise occupied, is tickled for a few seconds by his mother on some part of his body normally ticklish, the experience seems to be pleasant: at any rate, he will probably ask for it to be repeated. If he is not in good health, or if his attention is devoted to something else, the experience seems to be unpleasant; even though he laugh, he will protest against it as an interruption. Continued tickling becomes quickly unpleasant and then intolerable: it is recorded of Simon de Montfort, I do not know with what truth, that he put the Albigenses to death by tickling, and it is said that a certain sect of Anabaptists, unwilling to shed blood, used the same means to execute offenders against their laws. Being tickled is always an emotional experience, and it is only by special efforts, calling up and expending considerable reserves of psycho-physical energy, that an individual can maintain his ascendancy over the disturbing factors and continue to feel the experience as pleasant.[1]

[1] I cannot resist quoting from an absurd book by a modern Puritan, a would-be Philip Stubbes of the nineteenth century, yet without the inexhaustible vigour of Stubbes. "The physiological fact is that coughing and laughing are both performed by the same important organs, and they both have a very similar influence on the lungs and brain, and that influence is always of a painful and injurious character. . . . The conclusion is unavoidable that the absurd habit of laughing is entirely occasioned by the unnatural and false associations which have been forced upon us in early life," the worst of which are produced, we are told, by tickling and fairy tales!—George Vasey, *The Philosophy of Laughter and Smiling*, pp. 35 and 58.

Some Theories.

I have set out the facts, baldly; it remains to consider certain theories induced from the facts.

1. '*Laughter is the Expression of Pleasure.*'

In one form or another this generalization meets us in the pages of nearly every writer on the subject of laughter. Darwin says: "Laughter seems primarily to be the expression of mere joy or happiness,"[1] and it is clear from the context that he does not attach to the term 'Joy' any of the refinements of meaning which, thanks chiefly to the work of McDougall and Shand, it is now coming to have in English psychology. Sully follows Darwin: "The laugh," he says, "like the smile which is its beginning, is in general an expression of a pleasurable state of feeling."[2]

Now it seems impossible to derive this conclusion from a study of infants without something uncommonly like circular reasoning. It is generally admitted that the so-called *expressive* signs of pleasure in infants are less marked than those of pain or displeasure. Wide opening of the eyes has been supposed to be the earliest sign of pleasure. Yet this movement is also assigned by some to the supposed emotion of surprise, which, presumably, is not invariably pleasant. Kicking with the legs and raising of the arms have also been thought to indicate pleasure.[3] But Watson, whose observations of children, so far as they go, are unsurpassed, whatever may be thought of his Behaviorism, writes, definitely enough, "*Kicking with the legs and slashing with the arms are almost continuous during active moments from a few minutes after birth,*"[4] and again, asserts that drawing up and down of the legs and slashing with the hands and arms are *rage* responses.[5] If all these supposed expressive signs of pleasure are ruled out as uncertain, one seems left with

[1] *Op. cit.*, p. 203. [2] *Op. cit.*, p. 39.
[3] *Vide.*, e.g. quotation from Preyer on p. 28 above.
[4] *Op. cit.*, p. 238 (italics in text).
[5] *Op. cit.*, p. 200.

very little except crowing and chuckling sounds (incipient laughter), and the smile itself. But, obviously, one has no right to argue from laughter to the pleasure it is said to express, and then argue back again from the pleasure to laughter. None the less, a movement of thought very like this may be suspected in Darwin, when he says of his elder child that "being at the time in a happy frame of mind" he smiled, [1] and in Preyer and Sully also when they use the criterion of pleasure to distinguish the earliest expressive smile from the still earlier unexpressive or mechanical smile.

Nor does inference from the laughter of older children and adults justify us in supposing that in infants it is primarily the expression of pleasure. For, in the first place, we know that in adults it may be highly unpleasant. One instance has already been given, namely the laughter which continues to follow tickling long after the experience has become intensely unpleasant. Another, more striking, example may be cited from the article by Hall and Allin to which reference has already been made more than once. They tell how "a frontiersman, in a well-authenticated case, came home to find his dearly beloved wife and children all lying dead, scalped, and mutilated by Indians. He burst out into a fit of laughter, exclaiming repeatedly, 'It is the funniest thing I ever heard of,' and laughed on convulsively and uncontrollably till he died from a ruptured blood-vessel." [2] Such behaviour may be highly abnormal, but it is none the less relevant; we are becoming accustomed in modern psychology to look in the abnormal for clues to the normal, and with certain safeguards, the method is sound. Without, however, going outside normal behaviour at all, we shall each be able to put forward a score of instances from our own experience where the feeling of the whole behaviour which included as one of its elements laughter, was distinctly unpleasant.

'The feeling of the whole behaviour' gives the key to the situation. A wholly fictitious importance is ascribed to isolated movements when they are selected for *expressive*

[1] *Op. cit.*, p. 217. [2] *Op. cit.*, p. 7.

purposes. Behaviour comprises more than gestures which can be seen or heard ; but even if we confine our attention only to these outward forms of behaviour it is essential that each separate gesture should be considered *in its place* and not in lonely grandeur. Each can be interpreted only in relation to those that precede, accompany, and follow it. In the last resort the only indubitable sign that behaviour is felt as pleasant is that it is continued when the individual who is behaving has, so far as the observer can judge, full power in himself to stop it. And conversely the only unmistakable sign of displeasure is that some clearly defined behaviour-cycle is broken off.

On this basis we may speak elliptically of certain movements as being expressive of pleasure or displeasure. Thus, sucking and swallowing may be called movements expressive of pleasure in the behaviour-cycle of feeding: they contribute directly towards the satisfaction of the instinct, and it is on that account that they are expressive of pleasure. If this behaviour-cycle is abruptly broken off, and the child screws up his eyes and screams, the screwing up of his eyes and the screaming are taken to be gestures of displeasure ; but their expressive character is strictly contingent, being derived from the behaviour-cycle (feeding) which they have interrupted. Both might, in other circumstances, be expressive of pleasure. It is probable, for example, that when a spoiled child (older, of course, than the suckling) screams, not because he has been balked in what appear to him his lawful endeavours, but because he believes that by screaming he will attract attention to himself or coerce an indulgent parent, the noisy gesture is actually expressive of pleasure for a time, though, being physically exhausting, it will no doubt soon cease to be a part of pleasant behaviour and become, to the screamer as to other people, disorderly, interruptory, and unpleasant. Be that as it may, the general rule holds : contributory movements are expressive of pleasure, interruptory of displeasure.

This, taken in its nakedness, leads to the astonishing conclusion that the laugh, so far from being expressive of pleasure, is really expressive of displeasure. And so, in effect, if we persist in isolating particular gestures, we are compelled to say. For the laugh in its beginnings is manifestly disorderly, in that it does not contribute towards the end of any behaviour of which a very young child can be supposed capable ; and it retains this character in most of the behaviour of later life. It is generally interruptory and can only be regarded as contributory when it is deliberately *used* by the laugher.

It is necessary to make this point, once and for all, but now that it is made, it is wise to return to what was said earlier, namely that it is the whole behaviour at any given moment that is really expressive of pleasure or displeasure. The smile and the laugh are seldom more than mere flashes in behaviour, and though they always indicate emotion, and therefore, on the view maintained in this book, some degree of pleasure, the interruption by which they are caused, and the interruption they cause themselves, may well be almost negligible when measured against the force that is working towards definite conclusions.

2. *Theories of Tickling.*

The theories offered to account for tickling are mostly biological.

Robinson allows us the choice of three.

On the ground that the most ticklish parts of the body are also those most vulnerable to attack in serious warfare, he suggests, as his first explanation, that ticklishness has been evolved because it is useful to the young animal in mimic warfare, by which he is trained for what will occupy a great part of his adult life. How far this theory was developed in independence of that proposed by Professor Karl Groos to acount for play, I do not know. The two theories have close affinities, and are open to most of the same objections. It is not my business at present to enter into any biological disputes, and I would therefore merely suggest two objections that occur to me. There is good reason, in the first place, to believe that girls and women are more ticklish on the average than boys and men,[1] but I know of no evidence to support the opinion that at any period during the evolution of the human race fighting was not pre-eminently a male occupation. In the second place, there is admittedly such wide divergence of opinion on what actually are the most ticklish parts of the body that it is unwise to assume that they coincide with the most vulnerable. Robinson, it will be remembered, left the sole of the foot out of his list altogether, though Hall and Allin placed it at the top of their list. If it is to be reckoned a very ticklish place—and I think common sense would reckon it so—Robinson's parallel between the most ticklish and the most vulnerable parts of the body breaks down rather seriously; for by no stretch of reasoning can it be maintained that the sole of the foot can ever have been specially liable to attack in any kind of warfare, human or pre-human.

Robinson's second explanation is certainly more attractive. He suggests that ticklishness may recall the time when parasites were more numerous and more troublesome on the surface of the human body than they are in this our hygienic twentieth century. Ticklishness would then be much the same as itchiness, and the theory might be irreverently called 'the bug theory of tickling.'

It will be noted that neither of the above explanations of ticklishness really explains what at present we wish to have explained, namely the connection between tickling and laughter. There is no self-evident reason why a child should laugh when it is being trained for war, or why a child or an adult should laugh when being pestered by a bug.

Robinson's third explanation, though by far the most promising, is merely suggested by him, without elaboration. He says that agreeable ticklishness may represent "vestigial relics of the caresses of courtship referable to some out-of-date methods of making love."[2] I do not know why he should have called the methods out-of-date. It seems to me that tickling is quite an up-to-date

[1] Cf. Havelock Ellis, *Man and Woman*, 5th edition, p. 405.
[2] *Op. cit.*, p. 1295.

method of making love, which is practised daily in every secluded lane.

Before dealing with the suggested connection of ticklishness and sex, which has been worked out in more detail by Mr. Havelock Ellis, passing notice must be taken of the theory outlined by Hall and Allin. It is very similar to the first of Robinson's explanations. According to these two writers, since primitive organisms had only the sense of touch by which danger in any form could be announced, minimal sensations of touch form the oldest strata of psychic life, and are most marked in those parts of the body which are the most vulnerable to painful wounds that take a long time to heal. To this I have little to say. It may be so, though I am sceptical about explanations that have to be fetched from the protozoa; but whether it is so or not, it does not seem to have much relevance to laughter, about which Hall and Allin were ostensibly writing.

Sully, after recommending to the further consideration of psychologists both the 'preparation for war' and the 'bug' theories of Robinson—he is strangely reticent about the sex explanation, mentioning it only casually in a footnote—develops on his own account a 'play' theory of tickling. "Tickling," he says, "pretty obviously finds a fitting place among the simpler forms of playful combat which have a teasing-like character. . . . If play —pure, good-natured play—was to be developed out of teasing attacks it would become a matter of the highest importance that it should be clearly understood to be such." Laughter is the means to such understanding. It is "an admirable way of announcing the friendly playful mood."[1]

At first glance such a hypothesis is very attractive, but a little cold thinking dims its lustre. We are entitled to demand what meaning Sully precisely attaches to 'play'; and this demand is not really met in his otherwise most illuminating book on laughter. Again and again he makes use of phrases like 'the play impulse,' 'the

[1] *Op. cit.*, pp. 182–3.

play attitude,' 'the play mood,' as though they were self-explanatory. Unfortunately they are, if anything, more provocative of controversy than laughter itself. To explain the laughter of ticklishness—and laughter in general also, for Sully extends the theory—in terms of play is only to push the difficulty further back.

In a later chapter I shall attempt to give some psychological meaning to the term 'play,' and to show the inadequacy of the play theory of laughter. For the present the matter must be left undecided.

In one of the volumes of his monumental *Studies in the Psychology of Sex,* Mr. Havelock Ellis deals at some length with ticklishness. He compares the explosion of laughter to the sexual orgasm. "There is more than an analogy," he says, "between laughter and the phenomena of sexual tumescence and detumescence."[1] "Before coitus the sexual energy seems to be dissipated along all the nerve channels and especially along the secondary sexual routes—the breasts, nape of the neck, eyebrows, lips, cheeks, armpits, and hair thereon, etc.—but after marriage the surplus energy is diverted from these secondary channels and response to tickling is diminished."[2] After this promising beginning, however, Ellis continues with a suggestion which seems strangely weak. Ticklishness, he says, may well be Nature's method of defence against premature sexual advances. He quotes from 'a medical correspondent'; "The young girl instinctively wishing to hide the armpits, breasts, and other ticklish regions, tucks herself up to prevent these parts being touched."[3] That may be true, but again one is driven to ask, what place in this scheme can be found for laughter? What part does it play in the defence?

I am convinced that ticklishness and sex are closely related. To show the nature of this relationship and how it comes about will be one of the tasks of the next chapter.

[1] *Sexual Selection in Man*, p. 14. [2] *Ibid.*, p. 18. [3] *Loc. cit.*

CHAPTER III

LOVE AND LAUGHTER

A NUMBER of threads have been left dangling, and must now be caught again. It was found that the smile and the laugh do not begin until some time after birth, and that the situations which call them forth all contain as an important element the presence of some second person who attracts the child's attention by some performance. Tickling, again, is almost always performed by someone else ; it can be carried out on oneself only with the direct help of someone else ; and it is the opinion of an expert that it can be carried out on a child under the age of three months only when the child's attention is caught and held by some other means. For a time, also, after the laughing response of ticklishness has been once elicited, and until it has become set into a habit, it remains largely subject to the child's own control. To be successfully tickled he must be in the mood for it, and he is not likely to be in the mood for it if his tender mind is otherwise occupied, or if the aggressor is a person of whom he has learned to be shy.

These facts point to the hypothesis that laughter, in its beginnings at least, is somehow associated with the instinct of love. Let us see where this hypothesis takes us.

THE INSTINCT OF LOVE.

I have chosen the term 'love' with some misgiving, and only because no better suggests itself. 'Sex' is an alternative—a term used by the Freudians in a very wide, not to say vague, sense; but unfortunately 'sex' is a heavily loaded term in ordinary speech, and the attempts of the Freudians to weaken and extend its connotation for scientific purposes have resulted in some confusion, both in their own minds and in the minds of those who dispute with them. It is better to reserve 'sex' to denote certain fairly specific directions which the instinct of love may take. The psychological school of McDougall postulates two instincts; the parental, with 'tender emotion' as its specific feeling, and the sexual, with lust as its specific feeling. This dualism certainly commends itself to the popular mind—in England and America at least, where propriety must be satisfied. Yet, having separated the two instincts, and thereby saved appearances, McDougall is compelled to unite them again, as in holy, though eugenic, matrimony. Of the sexual instinct he says: "One point of interest is its intimate connection with the parental instinct. There can, I think, be little doubt that this connection is an innate one, and that in all (save debased) natures it secures that the object of the sexual impulse shall become also the object in some degree of tender emotion."[1] What is meant by an *innate* connection between one instinct and another? According to the passage quoted, it would seem to mean that the stimulus of one is also the stimulus of the other, debased natures, of course, being always carefully excepted. McDougall might have gone on to add that the responses of the one instinct are essentially the same as the responses of the other, both being designed to bring the person who behaves into ever closer *contact* with the stimulus. Now if two supposed instincts are identical in respect to both stimulus and response, it is surely wiser to give up speaking of two, and be content with one.

I do not wish to dispute indefatigably about words. In the end it makes very little difference whether we start with two instincts which have afterwards to be joined together, or start with one which afterwards appears to split into two. For my part I prefer to act on the principle of economy, presupposing one instinct only, to be called 'love.'

[1] *Op. cit.*, p. 82.

Love and Touch.

Touch elicits, and touch expresses love, in animals, in children, in grown men and women.

On animals I would recall the examples of ticklishness already cited; these are easily supplemented. The dog in a 'loving' mood asks unmistakably to be patted and stroked, gently beaten and pushed about, and in reply he nuzzles into your hand, paws you, licks you, and it may be bites you gently. Darwin records having seen dogs licking cats with whom they were on friendly terms, and adds, significantly: "This habit probably originated in the females carefully licking their puppies—the dearest object of their love—for the sake of cleansing them. They also often give their puppies, after a short absence, a few cursory licks, apparently from affection."[1] I have myself watched a kitten, some months old, hold down with her paws a puppy of about the same age, while she indefatigably licked his chops with her rough little tongue. Of cats in such a mood of affection Darwin says: "The desire to rub something is so strong . . . that they may often be seen rubbing themselves against the legs of chairs or tables, or against door-posts. This manner of expressing affection probably originated through association, as in the case of dogs, from the mother nursing and fondling her young; and perhaps from the young themselves loving each other and playing together. Another and very different gesture, expressive of pleasure, has already been described, namely, the curious manner in which young and even old cats, when pleased, alternately protrude their fore-feet, with separated toes, as if pushing against and sucking their mother's teats. This habit is so far analogous to that of rubbing against something, that both apparently are derived from actions performed during the nursing period."[2]

For the child, as for the kitten or the puppy, the earliest stimulus of love is the close touch brought about by the nursing embrace, and the instinct is at first canalized

[1] *Expression of the Emotions*, p. 120. [2] *Ibid.*, p. 129.

by way of the lips and cheeks and tongue. In this connection Miss Shinn's *Notes* are very full. Ruth first 'noticed' touch when it was applied to her upper lip (twenty-ninth day). "In the ninth week when she was held close to anyone's cheek, if hungry, she would lay hold on it and suck, but if not hungry would apply her lips to it and lick it. From this time she developed a peculiar delight in putting her lips to someone's face and mouthing it, which lasted throughout the year. . . . As she became able to discriminate between people, she confined this mouthing to her favourites, and kissing appeared to be developed from it; but it was also done a great deal with no appearance of affection, merely rompingly; she would seize on a face that she could reach . . . and would mouth it with demonstrations of gaiety. It was like a dog's desire to lick one's face, in caress or in frolic. . . . After she could grasp, everything went to her mouth for a time, during the sixth month and on into the seventh; but the habit declined perceptibly in the seventh, and thereafter gradually disappeared."[1] How sensitive the mouth and lips remain always in love needs no words; kissing is evidence enough. And even among those races in which the kiss (between adults) is not customary, it is replaced, as Darwin reminds us, by other forms of intimate contact.[2] Along with the kiss must be considered the 'love-bite.' At some stage in their development all children tend to fall into this trick. With Ruth it was intermittent; her aunt notes it every month from the twelfth to the sixteenth, and again in the twenty-first, twenty-eighth, and thirtieth. It recurred for the last time (apparently) in the thirty-fifth.[3] But it never disappears altogether from human behaviour, and at times of strong sexual excitement the most civilized of adults are apt to revert to this childish way of making love.

From the nursing embrace, as original stimulus, it is possible to derive all later stimuli of love, and I am

[1] Shinn, *op. cit.*, pp. 136–7. [2] Darwin, *op. cit.*, p. 223.
[3] Shinn, *op. cit.*, p. 390.

inclined to adopt this view. But it is more usual, perhaps, to assume that touch upon other parts of the body may be equally original stimuli of the instinct, and it does not greatly matter which opinion is maintained. The erotogenic zones[1] (whether original or not) seem to correspond roughly to those parts showing more or less clearly marked secondary sexual characters, that is, characters not actually necessary to the sexual act but in some measure varying with sex ; in addition to those parts with primary sexual characters, the genital organs.

From its tactual beginnings, the instinct of love irradiates to the other senses. The vision of the mother's face, vague though it be, and the sound of her voice, in soothing tones, occur simultaneously with the tactile sensations of the nursing embrace, and the child, breaking up and redintegrating the presentational continuum (to use the technical though cumbrous phrase), comes to react with love to faces, if well lighted up, and to sounds that are not too harsh in quality. The first steps having been taken, progress is rapid, and may continue almost indefinitely. From the mother who touches and caresses the child, suckles him, sings to him, smiles to him, moves about in his line of vision, and is for ever disappearing and reappearing, substitution passes easily to other persons, to moving, well-lighted, bumping, sounding, bo-peeping objects, like domestic animals, curtains, swinging lamps, tassels, pictures, rattles, pianos, toys, to anything associated with such objects, and so to the images and ideas of them.

The practical checks to this process of substitution are two-fold.

On the one hand, the same objects and classes of objects become linked, mnemically, to other instincts, the impulses of which may be stronger than, and are often antagonistic to, that of the instinct of love. Similarly, the object to which the child's love goes out, may fail to respond, or may respond too violently. The small dog that licks his face to-day may to-morrow knock him over, and so break

[1] Less accurately called the *erogenous* zones.

up again the behaviour pattern that was slowly being fashioned.

On the other hand, substitution is restricted by the very responses of the instinct. Love must be able to 'keep in touch.' An object that is wholly intangible is out of love's reach. The tiny infant loves what is, or can be, brought into contact with his hypersensitive mouth; the older child loves things that he can kiss, handle, hug, or at the least *bump*. And the adult, for all the complexity of his behaviour, does no otherwise. If, besides his love for persons and animals and books and engines, he professes a devotion to some cause—be it that of party, church, class, or nation—towards which his instinct has been 'sublimated,' it will be found that the strength of his devotion, as measured not by his words only but by all his actions, is ever in need of renewal through personal contact with things tangible, usually persons, which embody for him the cause to which he is devoted.

The Genesis of Laughter.

Preyer's observation of the first smile of his own child, at ten days of age, after a full meal, is typical, except that it sets the date unusually early. Preyer, as we saw, considered this smile as wholly mechanical, and therefore paid no great attention to it; the popular belief about such smiling, occurring during sleep or immediately before sleep, is that it betokens a mild degree of stomach-ache! For my own part, I am quite willing to fall in with the popular belief. What is certain is that the smile begins, whether mechanically or not makes no matter, as a kind of feeble and vacillating continuation of the behaviour of feeding. It is clearly similar to the behaviour of sucking, at all events; many of the same facial muscles are involved. This similarity has been noted by more than one writer, by Professor Freud, for example, in a footnote,[1] and by Mr. Arthur Allin at greater length. In a review of Sully's *Essay on Laughter*, Allin, no longer in

[1] *Wit and its Relation to the Unconscious*, p. 226.

double harness with Stanley Hall, throws out the suggestion that the smile betokens an attitude of the whole organism in which the inception of food is the most striking characteristic.[1] This is a valuable hint, for which I wish to make due acknowledgment; but it is a hint that takes us no distance towards an explanation of the smile so long as we continue to occupy ourselves with the behaviour of the feeding instinct. The functioning of the feeding instinct is similar in the young of most mammals, but the smile is peculiar to man and the anthropoid apes; nor does the smile persist in man in any close relation to the behaviour of feeding. The primary result of sucking is the inception of food, and Allin stops there; the secondary result is the stimulation of the instinct of love, by the situation 'nursing embrace,' and to give a true account of the smile we must pass on to this secondary result. The same situation is the primary stimulus of both instincts, and at the beginning there is much in behaviour that is common to both; but with growth and experience the responses of the two are more clearly differentiated, though their common origin can still be traced. In the infant, the impulse of the feeding instinct is necessarily strong and impatient, drawing off the greater part of his psycho-physical energy at frequent and regular intervals. It is tiring behaviour, and after it he normally goes to sleep. In such heavily charged behaviour all the responses are soon sharpened to a point, just so many being made as are required for the strict business of feeding. The ancestors, human and pre-human, of the twentieth-century child have learned in a hard school to cut out the frills from such behaviour, and *his* earliest actions are determined accordingly: he, too, cuts out the frills, and goes straight ahead with the business of feeding himself. And so the smile, which is just such a frill, a non-contributory movement in relation to feeding, is dropped out of the behaviour of this instinct. On the other hand, in its beginnings, and indeed for many years to come, the instinct of love is but lightly charged

[1] In *Psychological Review*, vol. x, May 1903.

with energy, and its behaviour is diffuse, loosely co-ordinated, and divagant. It is, so to speak, in no great hurry, and it does not point imperiously in one direction. Within the behaviour of such an instinct there is room for frills, even if, to all appearance, they are quite useless. Love retains the frills that feeding dispenses with, and among them retains the smile.

The addition to the smile of the sounds which turn it into a laugh, presents greater difficulties. Havelock Ellis suggests that the disturbance of respiration may have much the same biological utility as the coyness of the female, because it heightens the sexual excitement of the male. He calls attention to the connection between love and strangling, a connection which may not be very generally recognized, but which seems to have the support of facts. One may recall Browning's poem, *Porphyria's Lover,* and especially the following lines :

> Be sure I look'd up at her eyes
> Happy and proud ; at last I knew
> Porphyria worshipp'd me ; surprise
> Made my heart swell, and still it grew,
> While I debated what to do.
> That moment she was mine, mine, fair,
> Perfectly pure and good : I found
> A thing to do, and all her hair
> In one long yellow string I wound
> Three times her little throat around,
> And strangled her.

If, as we believe now, the abnormal is only the exaggeration of the normal, and not something *sui generis,* it is conceivable that the wild desire of Porphyria's lover to strangle her is the witness of a connection, innate in us all, though kept in control by most, between love and disturbances of breathing. Ellis says : " We have to remark that respiratory excitement has always been a conspicuous part of the whole process of tumescence and detumescence, of the struggles of courtship and its climax, and that any restraint upon respiration, or indeed any restraint upon muscular and emotional activity generally, tends to heighten the state of sexual excitement associated with such activity."[1] I would not be thought to push this suggestion too far. Ellis's statement is exactly in accord with what we found to be true of emotion in general, namely that in the conflicts which go on in behaviour, of which emotion is the feeling equivalent, the more nearly balanced the opposing sides are, the more intense is the emotion. But this does not help us very much towards understanding the genesis of laughter, except in so far as it calls attention to the close relation which exists between love in its extremer forms and disturbances of respiration. What we have to discover is the relation between love in its milder forms and similar, though also slighter, disturbances of respiration.

I am inclined to think that a modification of the opinion put forward by Herbert Spencer in his essay on *The Physiology of Laughter* will best serve our purpose here. We may suppose an indeterminate amount of the psycho-physical energy of an infant to be working itself out in the behaviour of love, and the smile to be already established in the way I have attempted to describe, among the ill-co-ordinated responses of this instinct. Now suppose this behaviour to be suddenly opposed or obstructed in some way. One of two courses is open to the infant. He may divert his attention altogether from the end he was striving to reach, or he may persist as against the opposition or obstruction, exerting himself more. The respiratory equivalent of such exertion (or bracing up) is the taking of a deeper breath. If the block in behaviour continues, and he cannot overcome it, however he may try, his gathering psycho-physical energy will vent itself in gestures which we say express displeasure—jerky movements of the body and crying. But if for any reason at all, the block or obstruction suddenly gives way, vanishes, or is so weakened as to become negligible, the surplus energy which is no longer required to push against it may be either *used* in other ways or simply allowed to escape in various non-contributory movements. The smile is one possible channel of escape, and if this

[1] *The Sexual Impulse Love and Pain, etc.*, p. 121.

channel is not adequate, another must be found. But it will be remembered that a marked feature of the previous bracing up was the taking of a deeper breath. This has to be expired in any case, and the expiration has only to be made a little more noisy and explosive than normal breathing, and to be linked up with the smile which has already been established in behaviour, for most of the unexpended, surplus energy to be carried off easily. Once the trick has been learned, it is rapidly improved by practice, and from " the little bleating noise " of Darwin's child we soon arrive at the clear, shrill, unmistakable laugh.

This is the outline of a hypothesis. It remains to fill it in.

Tickling Again.

The discussion on tickling in the last chapter was broken off somewhat abruptly, and two theories of ticklishness —the sex theory and the play theory—were reserved for further consideration. The play theory must be postponed still further, for we can give no psychological meaning yet awhile to the term 'play.' But we are clearly in a better position now to discuss the sex theory.

Tickling may now be described as intermittent tactual stimulation of an erotogenic zone. The stimulus need not necessarily be a light touch, though obviously it is more likely to be intermittent if it is light than if it is heavy. Intermittence of stimulation is essential. In general, the erotogenic zones are those parts of the body showing primary, or more or less clearly marked secondary, sexual characters, but in certain circumstances—when a woman is violently 'in love,' for instance—the whole body may become erotogenic in respect to some person of the opposite sex.

The growth of ticklishness may be schematically set out as follows. The very first erotogenic zone in the infant includes the mouth, lips, chin, and cheeks, and the earliest response to touch on this zone is an attempt to suck. At this very early stage the behaviour of love is not differentiated from that of feeding. Later, when this differentiation has begun, when the smile is being evolved out of the original sucking movements, it will depend on whether the infant is hungry or not, what response touch on the lips or chin will elicit. If he is hungry, he will try as before to suck ; if he is not hungry, he may only smile. Later still, other parts of the body gradually become erotogenic, and the child is, so to speak, weaned from his early concentration on the mouth. But he is not weaned from the response he has developed—the smile—which may still be the answer to gentle touches on the ribs or the neck or the legs. As soon as the child is old enough to recognize in the person who touches him a *something* that *may* hurt as well as soothe, a new element has crept into his behaviour. He is no longer quite sure about this touch. If, in addition, the stimulus recurs more rapidly than the normal rhythm of nervous conduction, it may be actually painful, or become so very quickly. The stimulus on the erotogenic zone still touches off love behaviour, but this behaviour is no longer simple or smoothly flowing. It is obstructed by pain, and by fear—which is the apprehension of pain. So long as the obstructions are overcome from moment to moment and do not overbalance the erotic sensations which the touch provokes, the child will probably continue to laugh ; and in the end, the habit of laughter in such situations having taken firm hold, the child or the man may continue to laugh when tickled, even although the experience is highly unpleasant on the whole, that is to say, even although the obstructions *do* heavily overbalance the erotic and pleasurable sensations. The whole behaviour takes place on a comparatively low psycho-physical level, and remains relatively uncontrolled by the higher centres.

Peep-bo.

The game of peep-bo has been mentioned by both Darwin and Sully as an easy way of evoking the laughter of their children. In this situation it obviously matters very little whether the father's or the child's head is the one to be covered; what happens in either event is that the object of attention, the father, disappears; and such disappearance for an infant is equivalent to going out of existence. The child, responding with love, in however fumbling and weak a manner, to an object which has become a substituted stimulus of that instinct—the father's eyes, or beard, or nose, or whatever feature happens to have caught the child's fancy—is suddenly balked in his activities by the object vanishing. For a moment he stops all overt behaviour, the next moment the face reappears, and his previous behaviour may continue. But matters are not exactly as they were before. The disappearance of the face was an interruption, to meet which energy has been instinctively called up, and it is this energy, or some of it, which slips out in the chuckle or the laugh.

This peep-bo situation is for ever recurring in the early years of a child. All manner of objects which arouse his affection mysteriously disappear and reappear the moment after. And every time this happens, a trace is left in memory, with this important result, among others, that sooner or later the child realizes that disappearance is not equivalent to going out of existence. Once this knowledge has been gained, laughter may be advanced somewhat in time; the mere disappearance of the object may excite it, as when a child playing with a ball throws it accidentally over his head out of sight. As with tickling also, habit gradually secures that the laughter shall become almost automatic in all similar situations. The jack-in-the-box is a toy made to reproduce mechanically the peep-bo situation, and the laughter which it evokes from children is to be accounted for largely, though not perhaps entirely, in the same way.[1] Young children are apt to be frightened by the jack-in-the-box at first, but once they have got over this fright, it becomes a great favourite among their toys, and a fruitful source

[1] An additional reason is suggested in chap. vii.

of merriment. Once a jack-in-the-box, or toy similar in its tricks, has aroused the facile, if evanescent, laughter of a child, other jacks-in-the-box and situations of like nature will tend, through mnemic causation, to provoke laughter also, and that more quickly, since the child will naturally and spontaneously relate the new fact to what is already a fact of his experience, and in default of any other direction being given to his behaviour, will react to it in the same way.[1]

The game of peep-bo and the toy jack-in-the-box are of great importance in the history of laughter, because they are the simple and rudimentary forms of many more complicated situations which amuse the adult mind in everyday life and on the comic stage.

Romping About.

I have already quoted examples of Ruth's merriment, when five and six months old, at being tossed about and at 'riding a cock-horse.'[2] She was a hardy child. When ten months old, and able to crawl vigorously about the house, she would pull herself up on her feet, holding by a chair, let go, sit down with a bump, and look up laughing.[3]

Sully, who quotes these and similar examples, gives to the interpretation of them what I can only regard as an unfortunate and misleading twist, by saying, "A part of the gleefulness of this widening experience of movement is due to its unexpected results." [4] It is only the unexpected under limiting—and very limited—conditions that contributes to mirth. The unexpected appearance of a stranger in his nursery is no more amusing to a shy child of two, than the unexpected appearance of a burglar or a wild beast in his bedroom to the man of forty. This is so obvious that it is almost incredible

[1] Through the ecphory of the engram-complex, to use the technical terms of Richard Semon.

[2] See p. 28 above.

[3] Shinn, *op. cit.*, p. 345.

[4] *An Essay on Laughter*, p. 197.

that any serious thinker should ever have maintained that the cause of laughter is to be sought in the unexpected, as such. Sully never really makes this outrageous mistake, but several of his statements, such as the one quoted above, point in the wrong direction.

In considering these instances of Ruth's fun, it is simpler and less dangerous to speak of interruption in behaviour, than to speak of the unexpected. The sources of the interruption are partly mere physical jolts, and partly fear of falling. Whether such fear of falling is innate, as Watson [1] and other writers suppose, or acquired, clearly makes no difference. If it is acquired, it takes root very early and pushes its root very deep, so that in all subsequent behaviour, if there is even a remote chance of a fall, it acts as a disturber of the peace. It gives the thrill to flying, to mountaineering, to horse-racing, to skating, to gymnastics, and even to the childish pastime—in which solemn adults have been known to indulge themselves—of walking, as if on a tight-rope, along the kerbstone of a dull modern pavement. It spiced, made emotional, and therefore noticeable to herself, Ruth's pleasure in being tossed about in the air or astride the foot of her mother.

But interruption is only half the story; it is interruption within the behaviour of love, or more accurately still, interruption within behaviour which is to some extent that of love, which gives the key to Ruth's laughter. In being tossed about by father, mother, and aunt, and in being joggled up and down on her mother's foot, it is obvious that her reactions were elicited by and towards persons whom she loved. That is enough to verify the hypothesis. Yet I suspect that her hilarity was much intensified by direct stimulation of the erotogenic zones. So again, when the energetic little Ruth bumped up and down from a chair, she was clearly *performing* for a loving and loved spectator, her aunt. I am quite prepared to admit that this element in her behaviour was not the whole of it, and that rioting in the use of new bodily powers was

[1] Watson, *op. cit.*, pp. 199–200.

what gave it character. All I am concerned to show is that such turbulent muscular activity, in itself, will not carry laughter along with it ; when it is *shot* with love, laughter may emerge.

Ruth's subsequent escapades of crawling, walking, climbing, and running, bear out this opinion. On the three hundred and seventeenth day she climbed two flights of steps, twenty in all, and her aunt records that "she was very exultant on reaching the second floor, shouting and laughing." [1] But it is to be noted that Ruth was *following* her aunt up the stairs, and being *followed* (closely, for fear of accidents) by her mother.

It is sometimes rashly stated that a child laughs triumphantly at early successes in the difficult and hazardous undertaking of walking, as though success suffused him with something like the 'sudden glory' which Hobbes thought to discover in all laughter. Closer examination of what happens will modify this opinion. The child who holds his mother's hand and laboriously toddles five steps across the room may, when it is all over, break out into a merry laugh, but it is very unlikely that the child who is left entirely alone to find his own hesitating way, without either manual or moral support, will show any disposition to laugh, whether he succeeds or fails. Rasmussen relates that when his little girl, R., began to walk, it was with funereal solemnity.[2] Very significant is Miss Shinn's story of Ruth when just over a year old: "She walked to me across the whole width of the room, smiling and proud, walking faster and faster till she was nearly running, and *threw herself into my arms with laughter and kisses.*" [3]

It is to be noted that children romping alone shout and sing and make a deal of clatter, but that they do not laugh while they are alone, until such time as they are able and accustomed to make up stories for themselves. And then, of course, they are no longer alone, but are surrounded by their own creatures.

[1] Shinn, *op. cit.*, p. 353. [2] Rasmussen, *op. cit.*
[3] Shinn, *op. cit.*, p. 360 (italics mine).

THE CHASE.

Favourite childish activities are chasing and being chased. " A boy can no more help running after another boy who runs provokingly near him than a kitten can help running after a rolling ball," says William James, in a passage now well known.[1] This is something of an exaggeration both as to the boy and as to the kitten, but the gist of the matter is there. Now we may say, if we will, that the core of the behaviour when a child chases another child, an adult, or an animal, is to be found in the hunting instinct. On the whole I think the description will pass, but it is instructive to note *when* laughter occurs. A boy, somewhat older than the children we have been considering so far, will chase another in all solemnity, especially if he has his work cut out to catch the runaway, and having caught him, he may or may not break out into laughter ; it depends on circumstances. A smaller child will run after his kitten, his father, or another child, either solemnly or with all the signs of distress or annoyance, if he thinks the fugitive is really bent on escape. Plainly, then, the chase as such, is not directly accountable for laughter. And the behaviour of the child who is being chased is similar. If he is running 'all out' to escape his pursuer, laughter will be no part of his reactions, either during the running or when at the last he is caught. It is only when he oscillates, so to speak, between the wish to get away and the wish to be captured and held, that he may laugh. Both impulses must be active and conflict with one another—interrupt one another, in short.

Let us return again to Ruth, our lively little friend. " In the fifty-eighth week," writes her aunt, " she frolicked with the dog, running at him with laughter. The sixty-fifth week she discovered the charm of 'playing catch' around tables and chairs with hilarious glee. No doubt the pleasure was partly in the dramatic element in the play (two days later, e.g. she laughed herself weak when

[1] *Principles of Psychology*, vol. ii, p. 427.

quietly playing hide-and-seek behind the furniture, and could not tire of it). . . . Through the nineteenth month she constantly wished to play 'catch,' running and laughing till she could hardly stand. . . . Once in her twenty-fifth month a boy of six so won her heart by romping and running with her that whenever he stopped for any reason, she would seize the chance *to run up and embrace him*. . . . . In the fifty-sixth week . . . she escaped supervision and got outdoors by herself, and was *captured* jubilant. . . . As before, she chased the cats (ninetieth week) ; ran away laughing to be pursued (during the whole half-year) ; and delighted, with ecstacies of laughter, in playing chase around the table (nineteenth and twentieth months esecially), and in romping of all sorts." [1] Now in all this gladsome behaviour of Ruth it is easy to trace the undercurrent of affection towards people, her dog, or the cats. For the rest, her responses are varied enough, but always, besides the undercurrent of affection, there are in her behaviour marked interruptions, obstructions, blocks, collisions, which have to be got over. Her dog was none too gentle (it had eventually to be given away) and though Ruth was a courageous little imp, it is not to be supposed that fear did not give piquancy to her feelings. In playing 'catch,' or hide-and-seek, she wanted to be caught and did not want to be caught, both at once. Probably about this time the wish to escape was the stronger of the two, because her aunt records that she was passing through a phase of seeming dislike for caresses ; she would not stay still to be hugged, but wanted eagerly to be off again. But no child, any more than an adult, can escape the influence of past experience. Ruth, little as she thought about it, and little perhaps as her aunt thought about it, was romping with the whole of her past active in the present : how could she, loved as she had been since her birth, inhibit altogether the desire to be caught and held and fondled ?

Watch carefully the familiar trick of a child with his nurse or mother, running away from her up the street,

[1] *Op. cit.*, pp. 193, 194, 196, 361, 373 (italics mine).

stopping to wait until she has almost come up with him, and then running away again, and note that the moments of greatest laughter, generally speaking, are when the mother or nurse is nearest to the child. When he is in full flight, laughter is absent: when he stops to wait, his face may be radiant with smiles, but unless the pursuer makes some manifest catching gesture, he still does not laugh; it is not until the pursuer is almost on him, and for the few moments after that, while he is beginning to draw away again, that his laughter is shrill and seemingly uncontrollable. As the 'danger' of being caught becomes more imminent, the unconscious memory of past caresses seems to become more urgent, and the struggle between the wish to be caught and caressed, and the wish to run away towards freedom, becomes more intense. Laughter is the sign vocal of this struggle and its resolution.

Teasing.

We are apt to read aggressiveness into the actions of a child before its due time, and to speak unjustly of his teasing other people or animals when in fact he is only showing his love for them, or his curiosity about them, in his own clumsy way. Thus, while at the age of six months both Ruth and Sully's boy, C., delighted in pulling other folk's hair, and in so doing may have been enjoying their first practical jokes, it is beyond doubt that this supposed teasing developed out of behaviour which was of a much simpler pattern, and in which aggressiveness, the instinct of pugnacity, or whatever we may choose to call it, had no appreciable part at all. It is important to be clear on this point, in view of the many theories of laughter which stress the hostility of the laugher towards the object of laughter. When Sully says of his boy that, at the age of six months, he delighted in pulling his sister's hair, and was thrown into a fit of laughter by her shrieks,[1] he does not profess to be relating the first occasion on which the hair-pulling took place, nor even the first time

[1] *Studies of Childhood*, p. 411.

laughter followed it. But here, as often, it is the first step which counts, and at the risk of labouring the obvious I must claim indulgence to imagine the course of the previous behaviour. In doing so I shall continue, as before, to use our small companion Ruth in illustration.

Once the knack of grasping with the hand has been acquired (involuntary grasping is, of course, innate and shows itself immediately after birth) children all begin to pull at whatever offers itself for the purpose. Early in the fifth month Ruth, for instance, began to tug at her father's and grandfather's whiskers.[1] In the sixth month she was fond of playing with strings, and would draw them through her fingers.[2] The first time C. pulled his sister's hair, then, we may reasonably suppose that the act had no more significance than seizing and pulling on any other conveniently dangling object. But it had unusual results, for it elicited a yell from the victim. Now one might safely lay a wager that if this shriek was anyway loud and shrill, it did not provoke C.'s laughter, but rather unmistakable signs of distress, and that his sister had to soothe him back into good humour. And so when the episode was repeated on a later occasion, both the hair-pulling and the shriek were in some measure different for both children. For C. the hair-pulling was not quite the simple affair it was before; unconscious memory put into it ever so slight a thrill both of love and fear; and the shriek was not simply a disturbing loud noise, but a disturbing loud noise with a slender mnemic link with caresses; and for C.'s sister the pain in her scalp was not simply pain but 'pain that is caused by little C. and that must not make me yell too loud for fear of frightening him.' Thus already an element of love has crept into C.'s behaviour (supposing it not to have been present from the first), and this element is reinforced by a hundred other occasions on which the two children come into contact with each other; and already the interruption to his behaviour caused by the shriek is

[1] Shinn, *op. cit.*, p. 190. [2] *Ibid.*, p. 141.

less violent. With every subsequent repetition of the hair-pulling it becomes less violent still, while his growing sentiment of love for his sister is enriched, until at length the disturbing power of the shriek is definitely less than the force which he matches against it, and he breaks into a laugh.

If this romancelet is credible, it shows how behaviour which has all the appearance of teasing may grow up without the co-operation of the instinct of pugnacity at all. Young children are not cruel, in the strict sense of the word; they do not inflict suffering which they know to be such, but rather torment animals and human beings accidentally. Sooner or later, of course, real teasing begins, and behaviour is then coloured by a stronger shade of aggressiveness. But, as I hope to show more clearly later in discussing the hostility of adults, one toward another, this very aggressiveness is a development out of love, a sort of twisting of love behaviour round. Proverbially, hate is very near to love, and from violent love to violent hate is but a step. Hate, in fact, grows from love frustrated. And in the less violent forms of hate, in teasing for instance, the continued activity of the love strain is still apparent. Teasing is equivocal behaviour; the child is pushed in two directions, in one by the impulse to injure his victim, in another by the impulse to show affection.

Rebelliousness.

The child's teasing of adults is not easily to be distinguished from rebellion against adult authority; from rebellion, that is to say, against the persons who are so continually hindering him in his behaviour. At the age of twenty-three months odd, his father relates, Clifford Sully "made a great noise running about and shouting in his bedroom. His mother came in and rebuked him in the usual form (Naughty! Naughty!) He thereupon replied: 'Tit mak noi' (Sister makes the noise). Mother (seriously): 'Sister is at school.' C., with a still bolder look: 'Mamma make noi.' Mother (with convulsive effort to suppress laughing, still more emphatically): 'No, mamma was in the other room.' C. (looking archly at his doll, known as May): 'May make noi.' This sally was followed by a good peal of boyish laughter."[1] When a little over three and a half Clifford was sacrilegious enough to strike his parents and follow up the blows with "a profane laugh."[2] But this was not the beginning of his rebelliousness. When, at an earlier stage in his interesting career, he was given up as hopelessly naughty and handed over to the nurse to be carried out of the room, his father reports that he would ferociously slap her on the face, presumably without laughter! [3] Ruth was boisterous too. "Once at the beginning of the twenty-second month (seventy-second week)" writes Miss Shinn, "when lifted to kiss good-night, she snatched off her grandmother's glasses, then her cap, and flung them to the floor, likewise her grandfather's glasses when the chance came, and refused to kiss any of us good-night, laughing, and romping instead." [4]

Wherein lies the effective difference between C.'s behaviour in slapping his nurse, without laughter, on the one hand, and, on the other, his behaviour in slapping his parents, and Ruth's in plaguing her grandparents, in both cases laughingly? Surely it lies just in this, that in the first case Clifford was, for the time being, an out-and-out rebel, his defiance was complete, rage possessed him; while in the other two cases, rebellion was only tentative, defiance was tempered; whatever force hate had was checked by the stirrings of love.

And so—to anticipate a little—is it always with the rebel who jests. Defiance that is whole-hearted is too urgent to be stayed by laughter; it is defiance not quite sure of itself, that allows itself to be delayed by a smile. And, in spite of all that the French philosophers have written on the complete incompatibility of laughter and sympathy, the uncertainty of the joking rebel is due, above all, to a deep-rooted, often unconscious, but

[1] Sully, *op. cit.*, p. 432.
[2] *Ibid.*, p. 451.
[3] *Ibid.*, p. 432.
[4] Shinn, *op. cit.*, p. 195.

always discoverable affection for just those persons or institutions he is rebelling against. Laughter died out of the writings of Jonathan Swift as his mind darkened against the race of man; in the last book of Gulliver it flickers only sometimes, and then feebly, in a vagabond affection for that nobler animal, the horse. Anatole France, hater of shams in politics and religion, master of the satire that bites, created that wholly lovable and ludicrous character l'Abbé Coignard. As a man ceases to love in part that which he may yet despise and hate in part, so does laughter ebb from him.

Preliminary Conclusions.

I shall stop short at this point, without at present considering 'the laughable,' that is to say, objects the mere contemplation of which tend to excite laughter. In the examples I have dealt with, laughter is only part of the whole overt behaviour, and is to be interpreted along with other movements which precede, accompany, and follow it. With the laughable, on the other hand, the laugher somehow holds himself aloof from the stimulus of his laughter. To all outward seeming his only reaction to it is to laugh at it. With only this to guide us the difficulties are greatly increased, and conclusions which may hold for the frank behaviour of young children may not hold for the subtle and concealed behaviour of adults.

Be that as it may, if we have succeeded in devising a formula for the laughter of young children it is something. It is not, I confess, the usual way of going to work in treatises on laughter. The usual way is to leave the laughter of children out of account altogether; but it is surely better to frame a hypothesis that has pragmatic value for the gay laughter of young children, even if it does not seem to square easily with the laughter, not always gay, of men and women, than to frame one which works, more or less, when applied to man in society, but leaves quite inexplicable the smile of the infant in his cradle. The first hypothesis is more likely to be right than the second, for a great deal of our solemn adult behaviour is still cradle behaviour, when we examine it fairly.

So far as the analysis has gone, therefore, I conclude that the smile begins within the behaviour of the feeding instinct. It is a kind of preparation to suck. But this instinct is too businesslike to elaborate it and put the finishing touches to it, so that we shall recognize it unmistakably for what it is. It is within the behaviour of the love instinct that this elaboration is carried out, for the love instinct is first evoked in the situation—nursing embrace—which satisfies the feeding instinct, and is moreover a vague instinct, uncertain and not very urgent in its early manifestations. The infant has leisure to work embroideries upon it, and the smile is one of the first of these embroideries. But as the impulse of love gathers energy, and as experience grows, the opportunities of interruption increase at the same time. When behaviour containing love as an element within it is interrupted, energy is mobilized against the interruption; when the interruption is suddenly removed, or weakened, some of this energy becomes surplus and escapes in the laugh. The laugh thus marks an interruption to the behaviour of love which has been overcome with a less expenditure of energy than was originally prepared for the purpose.

CHAPTER IV

SOME GENERAL OBSERVATIONS ON LAUGHTER

THE RELATION OF LAUGHTER AND PLAY.

A GREAT deal has been written on the subject of play: it tempts the psychologist and the biologist alike. "There is no subject," says Perez, "in which prolixity is easier or more tempting."[1] Fortunately, however, our present reference is limited. We are concerned with play only in its relation to laughter and comedy.

It is clear that the connection between laughter and play is very close. Were anyone anxious to deny it, his everyday speech would bewray him, since we all make use somewhat indiscriminately of words like 'amusement,' 'prank,' 'frolic,' 'fun,' 'sport,' 'joke,' and so on, leaving it to the context to determine whether they refer to play as such, or to the laughter that is supposed to accompany the play. Thus the psychological theory of laughter put forward by Professor Sully in England and M. Dugas in France merely gives scientific precision to the assumption casually made by the ordinary man. According to Sully, as we saw in a previous chapter, laughter is the means by which the child or the man announces the play mood to others; according to Dugas, all forms of laughter find their ultimate explanation in play.[2]

There are two main difficulties in the way of accepting this position, and both are serious. The first is that neither Sully nor Dugas make it at all clear what psychological meaning they give to the term 'play'; the second is that whatever psychological meaning we may eventually

[1] *L'enfant de trois à sept ans*, p. 87.
[2] *Psychologie du rire*, especially p. 116.

agree to give to this term, play appears to cover a much wider field than laughter. It may be that, when we laugh, we are always in the play attitude, though I think this would be difficult to prove in face of the examples already cited of very early laughter in infants. It is certainly not true that whenever we are in the play attitude we tend to laugh. The tragedy of *King Lear* is a 'play,' according to everyday speech, and must be brought within the scope of any definition of play that claims to be comprehensive. A hard-fought game of Rugby football is play also, and the player in this case announces his mood to the other players, not by a laugh, but by tackling low and hard, and by kicking any one or more of his opponents foolhardy enough to 'lie on the ball.' Organized games, in fact, are often quite ludicrously solemn, and the only person with an inclination to laugh is the person who is looking on without much sympathy for either side.

It is impossible in the present work to argue at length on theories of play, and I shall content myself with a dogmatic statement of conclusions, suppressing all the steps by which these conclusions have been reached. If my conclusions are unacceptable it is no great matter, since the main argument of the book does not hinge upon them.

There is no evidence for an instinct of play. Play is a nurtural form which the behaviour of almost any human instinct may take. It is not to be distinguished in any hard and fast way from earnest, but it is relatively distinguished from this by requiring the modification, more or less, of the *natural* end-result of a behaviour-cycle. The natural end-result of the behaviour of fighting is killing your adversary; the playful end-result of this behaviour is winning on points. The satisfaction of play is the satisfaction of primitive impulses which the gradual advance of civilization has circumscribed. It is a less intense satisfaction than that provided by earnest, but it makes up for this loss in intensity by a gain in security; in play, whether one wins or loses, one lives to fight another day.

Play and Art.

Play is a nurtural development out of earnest; art is a nurtural development out of play. Play modifies the end-result of natural behaviour into something comparatively harmless; art modifies this end-result still more drastically; it cuts it out altogether. The first condition of art is that we should be absolved from immediate action in respect to the stimulus that has provoked our behaviour. Art is contemplation. 'Psychical distance,' to adopt the admirable metaphor of Mr. Edward Bullough,[1] must be inserted between the artist who looks or listens and the object looked at or listened to.

The appeal which art makes can be understood only on the understanding that it arouses in us by suggestion exactly the same sentiments, built up around instincts, as are aroused in so-called practical life. The love poem excites love, martial painting the instinct of the fight. But the resulting behaviour in art is different in an important respect from the behaviour of practical life: its overt responses on, towards, or away from the stimulus, are inhibited. And if the behaviour does eventually come to *expression,* this expression is really *past* the stimulus, and leaves the situation, as represented by artist and object, substantially unchanged.

This clears the ground for the consideration of the laughable and the comic. By approaching comedy from this side we should be able to avoid some at least of the intellectualist fallacies that have so infested comic theory. The laughable is that which excites laughter *at a distance*; the laugher is to all outward seeming passive towards it; except for his laughter, his activity is limited to looking at it, or listening to it, thinking about it (perhaps), and feeling about it (certainly); he does not move towards or away from it, or seek to alter his relation to it in any way. As soon as a child has learned

[1] *Vide* "'Psychical Distance,' as a factor in art and an æsthetic principle," in *Brit. Journ. of Psychology,* June 1912.

to laugh *at* something, without attempting to meddle with it, he has fulfilled the primary condition that makes art possible. He has turned his head in the direction which leads, at the last, to the great comedies of the world. The *comic* is the laughable raised to a higher power and made fit for the uses of art.

The Problems to be Faced.

After this rapid excursion among topics even more controversial, if possible, than laughter, let us return to the main track. We saw cause to conclude that the smile and the laugh arise within the behaviour of infants as responses of the instinct of love. The laugh, which is a development of the smile, occurs when the smooth functioning of the instinct is for any reason first ruffled and then calmed again ; or, in other words, when behaviour, within which love is one strain, is first checked or interrupted, and then freed from the check or interruption. The laugh is a channel of escape for psycho-physical energy that has become momentarily surplus, through the weakening or disappearance of the obstacle to meet which this energy was mobilized in the first instance.

The remainder of this book will attempt to test these conclusions in relation, not merely to the laughter of young children, but to the laughter and play of grown men and women in their daily lives and on the comic stage.

At first glance, the simple formula we have evolved for infantile laughter does not seem promising, and to make it fit all the varieties of adult laughter would seem to require very special pleading. This would not be unprecedented in a book on laughter, as everyone acquainted with such books knows only too well. Nearly all comic theorists are comic monists. They do not agree among themselves what the formula for laughter should be, but with one accord they turn away from pluralism in this branch of æsthetics at least, being altogether persuaded that laughter must have one cause and one cause only. Unfortunately, no single formula for laughter has yet stood the test of prolonged criticism, and it seems hardly likely that a hypothesis so fantastic in appearance as the one I have offered, will fare any better. Is it conceivable that it will cover the laughter of generations of mankind at the great comic figures of European literature—Strepsiades, Panurge, Sir John Falstaff, Sancho Panza, M. Jourdain, Parson Adams, Uncle Toby, Mr. Pickwick ? Moreover, what is to be said of the comic of situation, where, often, mere puppets are manipulated, and it seems absurd to suppose that love in the spectator is stimulated at all ? How is it to be explained that men, women, children, and even, it is said, dogs, resent being laughed at ? What are we to make of derision, irony, satire ? What has wit to do with love ?

These are some of the problems that must somehow find a solution within our scheme, or break it up. Let us have at them for dangerous giants ; perhaps they will turn out to be only windmills after all.

But first of all let us get certain matters of general bearing cleared out of the way.

The Relativity of Laughter.

Nothing is laughable in itself : the laughable borrows its special quality from some person or group of persons who happen to laugh at it, and, unless you happen also to know a good deal about this person or group of persons, you cannot by any means guarantee the laugh beforehand. It is only people with the same social heritage who laugh easily at the same kind of jokes. That is why laughter so often balks at national frontiers, and dies away with the passage of time. The Greeks certainly found more to laugh at in the comedies of Aristophanes than we can ever hope to find, not merely because they did not require the scholiasts to interpret the personal allusions for them, but because they had much the same general social traditions as Aristophanes. Ours, in the twentieth century, are widely different, and it costs us both time and labour to catch the Aristophanic point of view towards Dionysus and the rest of the gods, towards the phallus and the wine skin, towards the war with Sparta, towards Æschylus, Euripides, and Agathon, and towards the constitution and statesmen of Athens. It costs us less, but still considerable, time and labour, to catch the point of view of Molière towards seventeenth-century Paris and Versailles. And yet, unless we put ourselves at approximately the points of view of Aristophanes and Molière, their comedies furnish us with few opportunities for laughter. As Mr. John Palmer has it: "Laughter is the real frontier between races and kinds of people. . . . A joke sets all nations by the ears. . . . A joke cannot be translated or interpreted. A man is born to see a particular sort of joke; or he is not. You cannot educate him into seeing it.[1] In the kingdoms of comedy there are no papers of naturalization."[2]

But Palmer exaggerates. In one of the gaps in the passage just quoted, he makes the astonishing assertion that "we are agreed, the world over, as to what precisely is grievous." One can do little with such an assertion except deny it. One race disagrees with another on this question, as on others, and we all disagree with our ancestors. If men differ about the laughable, they differ also about the grievous.

None the less, it must be admitted they do not differ so widely about the grievous. Laughter is more relative than tears. In the situation that stirs to sorrow there is a compulsive force that is absent from the laughable. For we may pass the laughable by, if our attention is directed elsewhere, whereas the grievous seizes upon us in our own despite. The grievous concerns us more vitally because it threatens us; and we detach ourselves from it in contemplation with greater difficulty. In truth, the grievous is not the true opposite of the laughable, for the latter implies always some measure of artistic

[1] You can, but it is not often thought worth while.

[2] *Comedy*, p. 5.

detachment, some degree of 'distance,' and the former does not necessarily imply this.

LAUGHTER ONLY AT THE HUMAN.

It is often said that laughter is excited only by the human. This point is forcibly made by Bergson. Several philosophers, he says, "have defined man as 'an animal which laughs.' They might equally well have defined him as an animal which is laughed at; for if any other animal, or some lifeless object, produces the same effect, it is always because of some resemblance to man, of the stamp he gives it, or the use he puts it to."[1]

This statement has been disputed, largely, I think, because Bergson uses it as a stepping-stone to a general theory of laughter which is, to say the least, controversial. Taken by itself, it is unimpeachable. When man laughs at a lower animal it is undoubtedly because he realizes some general or particular resemblance between the animal's behaviour or appearance and his own; and when he laughs at the inanimate, which he does but seldom, it is because the inanimate is for the moment invested with human values. Notice that I say 'some general or particular resemblance,' between man and lower animal. Sometimes the occasion of laughter is a gesture, trick, or habit in the animal that irresistibly recalls nearly identical behaviour in man; hence most of our laughter at monkeys. More often the resemblance is not so pointed, and the laugher is merely confessing that he and the lower animal are subject to like impulses, very general in scope, like the impulse to love a member of the opposite sex. Often again, the occasion of laughter is a failure on the part of the animal to conform to human standards of use and wont; that is to say, a general or particular resemblance is assumed or expected, and then falsified. I remember having read a poem in *Punch* about a Mesopotamian goat; the point of the poem was an 'odorous' comparison

[1] *Laughter*, p. 3.

between the goat and a Turkish prisoner. The goat, having put the greater part of an English battalion out of action by its mere presence, eventually fainted when confronted with the Turk. The Turk was, so to speak, an additional luxury, for comic purposes. The first part of the poem was amusing in itself, for the overwhelming stench of the goat was treated as a violent interruption of what the respectable English soldier had a right to expect in war. The goat broke all the rules, that is, all the *human* rules.

Of course, by far the greater part of our laughter is occasioned by, or directed at, human beings. The human touches us more closely than the non-human. Whatever is apprehended at all must, in the act of apprehension, be fitted by us into the context of our experience, and used to touch off some behaviour in us, however truncated that behaviour may be. But a mere flash of recognition, followed at once by the transfer of attention to something else, is not enough for laughter. Laughter takes a little longer than that. Before it can be aroused, attention must linger for a measurable period of time, and some degree of personal interest must be awakened. It is plain that situations in which human beings fill the stage, are more surely calculated to excite a personal interest in the spectator than those with only a very indirect human reference. Man responds swiftly to man, but only falteringly to that which is not man.

The Relative Unimportance of Laughter.

It is well to insist that whatever is laughable may well be much else besides. The links between the laugher and the object of his laughter are nearly always many and varied, even at the moment of his laughter, for human behaviour is seldom single-moulded. The observation is trite enough, but it has been forgotten by only too many writers on the comic, who, having abstracted laughter out of the whole complex reaction to a situation, the better to study it in isolation, quickly forget how unimportant it may have really been in the first place. They thus come to speak of laughter when they properly mean something else.

Bergson, for instance, entitles his book, *Le rire*, in all simplicity, and then belies his title page by writing brilliantly about other things. He discourses on the high comedy of Molière charmingly, but unfortunately often quite irrelevantly to his chosen theme. For the surprising fact about the high comedy of Molière in French, as about the high comedy of Meredith in English, is, that in whatever other ways the spectator reacts to it, he hardly laughs at it at all. When he pleased, Molière could make his audience laugh. Often he did please, to the everlasting scandal of Boileau and the fastidious.[1] But when he set out to write those comedies which the world recognizes as his greatest, he had other aims than laughter. Whether he hit these aims or not, it is certain that we do not *laugh*, appreciably, at *Tartufe, L'Avare,* and *Le Misanthrope,* any more than we laugh, appreciably, at Congreve's *Way of the World,* Meredith's *The Egoist,* or Oscar Wilde's *Importance of being Earnest.* Nor is this simply a question of nationality. It is often hastily assumed that the French find in Molière sources of laughter to which the slower wits of the English cannot pierce. That may or may not be true; for my own part, I doubt it. What we do know is that on one favourable occasion a French audience found extremely little to laugh at in *Tartufe.* The matter was tested by Stendhal. On December 4, 1822, he took a copy of the play with him to the theatre and marked in it the occasions when the audience laughed. His own words are worth quoting: "Mlle. Mars jouait; rien ne manquait à la fête. Eh bien! dans tout *Tartufe,* on n'a ri que deux fois, sans plus, et encore fort légèrement. L'on a plusieurs fois applaudi à la vigueur de la satire ou à cause des allusions; mais on n'a ri, le 4 décembre."[2]

[1] "Dans ce sac ridicule où Scapin s'enveloppe
Je ne reconnais plus l'auteur du Misanthrope."
Boileau, *L'art poétique,* chant iii, ll. 395–6.

[2] *Racine et Shakespeare,* p. 28.

It may be objected that high comedy provokes the laughter of the mind. But let us understand, if possible, what we mean by this phrase. It is not everyone who is capable of such laughter; it requires, as Meredith so constantly insisted, a high degree of social culture. The two main facts about the so-called humour of the mind are, that it is many sided, and that it is far 'distanced.' The second is the result of the first. The behaviour of the humorist is very rich and very complex, and it is largely for that reason that a great deal of 'distance' must be inserted between him and his object. The more you pack into behaviour the more you increase the opportunities in it for conflict. The comic writer of the type of Molière avoids the risk of serious conflict by straining off from the behaviour, not merely all the overt reactions, but as many of the internal emotional reactions as can be strained off without rarefying it so completely that art becomes science. The humorist of Shakespearean order does not go so far, and takes greater risks. There is more body in his behaviour, but both he and the comic writer are literally much too busy to *laugh*.

We must therefore guard against the assumption that the comic literature in which we take the greatest artistic pleasure is necessarily the best to use in illustration of a theory of laughter. The psychologist who wishes to understand laughter should arrange his material in order of complexity, beginning at the point where laughter is simple, loud, and unmistakable, and working up, rather than down, the scale of culture. For this attempt to be successful, he must be ready, for a time at least, to inhibit his literary and moral judgment towards what comes under his notice. He must learn to take the hypergelast to his bosom without flinching, and must accustom his ears to the loud horse-laugh at the indecent and the obscene.

Laughter and Surprise.

The relation of laughter to surprise may profitably be considered before we go further. In popular psychology laughter is ascribed to surprise; we laugh, it is said, at the new and unexpected. Many eminent writers, beginning with Cicero, have held much the same view.[1]

Clearly, it is no explanation of laughter to say that it is the expression of surprise. Almost anything may be the expression of surprise. Surprise is negative—a state of doing nothing; or, since no organism can be strictly said to do nothing until it is dead, we may more accurately call surprise the state of doing just as little as possible at the moment, in order that the organism may be able to do whatever is necessary the next moment. Whatever positive character surprise may have, it borrows from the behaviour immediately preceding and immediately succeeding it. In itself it is a mere interval. It therefore depends on what we are doing when we are surprised, and on the meaning we find in the object surprising us whether, after the interval of no response, we laugh, or cry, or run away, or make a wry face, or clap our hands, or fall down in a fainting fit. All these are possible reactions after a state of surprise, and there is nothing in the state itself to lead us to one rather than to another.

Yet there is reason in the popular emphasis on the relationship of laughter to surprise. While surprise does not of necessity lead to laughter, laughter is of necessity preceded by a moment of surprise, or a moment of no response, however induced. 'Chestnuts' have no power over our laughter; the funniest story in the world ceases to provoke a smile in us as soon as we know it by heart.

This is universally recognized, but its full effect is disguised in various ways. In the first place, we quickly forget. Especially do we forget what has only made us laugh, because we seldom pause over it long enough to let it hook on firmly, so to speak, to the systems of ideas we are constantly using. So we may happen upon the same incident or the same story again and again, and barely recognize it. In the second place, we easily confuse the total pleasure we get out of any given situation,

[1] See Appendix, *passim*.

with the pleasure we get out of laughing at it, though the latter pleasure may be only a part, and sometimes a very minor part, of the former. I have already touched on this point in the preceding section of this chapter, but I cannot resist returning to it here, because it is of great importance, if we wish to hold the issue clear. The first time we read *Henry IV* we laugh at the Falstaff scenes; they are new to us. On many occasions of rereading we still laugh, either because we have forgotten a great deal of what we read before, or, more probably, partly for that reason, and partly because we failed on previous occasions to perceive all the laughable aspects of Falstaff and his crew. But sooner or later there comes a time when we can go straight through the play with hardly a smile on our lips; we now know it too well to be provoked to laughter. Yet our enjoyment of Falstaff has not disappeared with our laughter at him. It may be true, as he said of himself, that "the brain of this foolish-compounded clay, man, is not able to invent anything that tends to laughter, more than I invent or is invented on me"[1]; but long after we have ceased to laugh at Falstaff we continue to take pleasure in his perennial youth, his inexhaustible resource, and his sanity; and we still relish his parody of *Euphues*, his catechism on honour, and his outwitting of Justice Shallow. The sources of pleasure which the comic holds for us are wider and deeper than the sources of our laughter.

The deadening effect of familiarity on laughter is disguised also by our suggestiblity, by our inveterate habit of 'showing off,' and by various social conventions. If we tell a good story, deliberately, there is nothing in it directly to excite our own laughter; for we know the 'point' beforehand, even though we hold it back until the end for effect. For us there is nothing new and unexpected in the story. But the moment our audience laughs, our instinctive tendency to do whatever they are doing, simply because they are doing it, is excited, and we may have much ado to inhibit it. The professional story-teller prepares himself to resist this tendency, and

[1] *Henry IV*, Part II, Act I, Scene 2.

generally succeeds. At the most he greets the laughter of his audience with nothing but a friendly smile. Yet even he breaks out sometimes, in sympathy; and when this happens, both he and his audience are apt to assume that he is laughing at his own jokes, whereas in truth he is laughing at laughter. Again, we all know the man who spoils his own jokes by laughing at them before he has succeeded in getting them told. Generally, I suspect this is of the laughter called 'nervous.' When such a man begins to tell a funny story his attitude of mind is curiously mixed. He wants to acquit himself well, and to attract attention to his own prowess; he caresses himself for being rather a fine fellow. At the same time there is in him a strain of uncertainty about his being really such a fine fellow after all; he is a little shy, and to find his audience 'all ears' embarrasses him. To put it technically, his behaviour is ambivalently auto-erotic. His shyness is continually getting in the road of his story-telling, and being as continually pushed out of the road again. He gets his story told, but only at the cost of spoiling it by laughter of his own, that expresses, not so much his anticipatory enjoyment of the 'point,' as his oscillation of mind in respect to his own behaviour. We are all like him in some degree. But those of us who are good story-tellers keep our doubts about our own ability more deeply repressed, and those of us in whom our doubts are stronger than our self-esteem, refrain altogether from telling funny stories in public.

Transposing what has been said about the relationship of laughter to surprise into still more general terms, brings us round again within measurable distance of our previous formula. Surprise is just the emotional state of being interrupted. Surprised, we abruptly break off whatever we were doing, and then, having discovered what the interruption means—for us—we either resume our former behaviour or begin doing something else more appropriate to the new situation. Laughter never occurs except as the sequel to some interruption of behaviour.

CHAPTER V

THE SEXUAL, THE OBSCENE, AND THE INDECENT

THE SEXUAL AND RESISTANCE.

THE two terms *obscene* and *indecent* are generally used synonymously, but I wish to make a distinction between them which is, I think, in accord with modern scientific usage. By the obscene should be understood the directly sexual exposed against resistance, and by the indecent, the indirectly sexual exposed against resistance. According to this distinction a joke is obscene which calls attention to any part of the directly sexual process which is not usually spoken of, and a joke is indecent which calls attention to an excretory process which is not usually spoken of. The distinction must not be made too rigorous.

The sexual and resistance—these are what give character to the obscene and the indecent. Without the resistance imposed by modesty, disgust, social convention, or what not, both the obscene and the indecent disappear as such, leaving only the unqualified, unmoral, animal functions of sex, excretion, nutrition, digestion, and so on.

There is no pretending that we do not enjoy the obscene and the indecent. And we laugh at them. But it is not to be hastily concluded that our enjoyment follows from our laughter: rather does it precede our laughter. Our original pleasure in the obscene and the indecent is just our perennial pleasure in the sexual. If the race is not to die out, we must needs take pleasure in the sexual, by the functioning of which the race is kept in being; and it is not enough that we should take pleasure in sex only when we participate in it on our own account, performing the sexual act in whole or in part; we enjoy the sexual when it is removed to a greater or less 'distance' from ourselves, when we only dream about it, tell or hear stories about it, investigate it scientifically, or contemplate it in the mood of the artist. A hint of the sexual, addressed to any of our senses, starts off in us behaviour which must be called sexual also, however fragmentary or 'distanced' it may be, and from the functioning of this behaviour comes our pleasure.

Yet very deep in the sexual lies a resistance which interferes with it in some measure, and a wholly frank and unfettered display of it is inconceivable at any stage of human evolution. It is inconceivable even for the higher animals other than man. Modesty, the resistance opposed to the simple functioning of sex, grows out of fear, the male fearing interruption by a rival, the female fearing sexual aggression at the wrong moment,[1] and this rudimentary form of modesty is already developed in all mammals. The later developments of modesty, the complications introduced into it at higher levels by disgust, by social tradition, by religion, its progress down the ages—mostly by sudden leaps varied by long pauses and fantastic twistings upon itself—and the strange inconsistencies of conduct to which it leads, must not be allowed to disguise from us the fact that it is inherent in sexual behaviour almost from the beginning.

Laughter at the Sexual.

The easiest way to evoke laughter at the sexual is to call into activity this inherent resistance of modesty. But this is not always necessary in any marked degree, and we enjoy many a laugh at the sexual on occasions when modesty is left asleep. Such laughter is not strictly directed at the obscene. The Greeks of the time immediately preceding that of Aristophanes were so accustomed to the public exhibition of the phallus—at least at certain times of the year, and with the proper cere-

[1] Cf. Havelock Ellis, *The Evolution of Modesty*, p. 39.

monies—that its mere appearance on the comic stage hardly stimulated the resistance of modesty at all. When the comic poets, therefore, wished to raise a laugh at the phallus, they were unable to count upon a sufficiently strong automatic or intrinsic resistance within the behaviour of their spectators, and had to invent special devices for provoking an accidental or adventitious resistance on which the laugh could turn. According to the account given by Aristophanes in the parabasis of *The Clouds*, these special devices were chiefly mechanical. The comedians exaggerated the colour and the size of the phallus, and thereby "set the boys a-laughing." The result of this double exaggeration was a momentary disturbance of behaviour in the spectators, quickly surmounted. 'The boys' were accustomed to the appearance of the phallus, and their first glance at it started off habitual behaviour into which modesty introduced little or no friction. This behaviour was manifestly sexual, though distanced by tradition. Their second glance, however, checked or interrupted the even flow of this habitual behaviour, for something new and unusual about the phallus was now perceived. The third glance dissipated the interruption—it was only a phallus after all.

Very similar—strange as this may sound—is much of the laughter which mankind has enjoyed, and still enjoys, in jibes at women and marriage. Some of it is obscene, a great deal of it is not. Aristophanes does not tire of poking fun at the Athenian women, accusing them of being lecherous, deceitful, petty thiefs, and debauched with wine. The accusation of lechery may be left on one side for the moment, as all jokes in this regard clearly partake of the obscene. Their alleged deceitfulness also may be passed over for the moment, since the usual accusation which Aristophanes makes is that wives deceive their husbands by passing off 'bought' children as their own, and this also may be said to border on the obscene. But their fondness for wine is a never-ending source of mirth; the comedies are filled with amusing instances.

Perhaps the wittiest example occurs in the *Thesmophoriazusæ,* after Cleisthenes has caused the women in the Thesmophorium to be suspicious of the sex of the disguised Mnesilochus; the scene continues:[1]

MICA. (*To* CLEIS.) Step back, sir, please, and let me question her
On last year's rites; a little further, please;
No *man* must listen now. (*To* MNES.) Now, stranger, tell me
What first we practised on that holy day.
MNES. Bless me, what was it? first? why, first we—drank.
MICA. Right; what was second?
MNES. Second? Drank again.
MICA. Somebody's told you this. But what was third?
MNES. Well, third, Xenylla had a drop too much.
MICA. Ah, that won't do. Here, Cleisthenes, approach.
This is the *man* for certain.

A little later in the same comedy Mnesilochus, put to his shifts to escape the wrath of the women, seizes Mica's baby and proceeds to undress it. Undressed, it turns out to be

a flask, and not a baby!
A flask of wine, for all its Persian slippers.

Mnesilochus moralizes on the incident—

O ever thirsty, ever tippling women,
O ever ready with fresh schemes for drink,
To vintners what a blessing: but to us
And all our goods and chattels, what a curse!

Throughout the Middle Ages, also, women and the lesser clergy were the most frequent objects of popular wit. Apart altogether from the inexhaustible subject of cuckoldry, there runs through the fabliaux, according to M. Bédier, what may almost be called a spirit of hatred against women, arising from "ce fond de rancune que l'homme a toujours eu contre sa femme."[2] One of the

[1] This and the two following quotations are from Rogers' translation.
[2] Joseph Bédier, *Les Fabliaux*, p. 321. The actual quotation is ascribed by Bédier to Maspéro.

standard 'morals' of the fabliaux is summed up in the following quotation[1] from one of them:

> Enseignier voil par ceste fable,
> Que fame est plus que deiable;
> De ma fable faz tel defin
> Que chascuns se gart de la soe,
> Qu'ele ne li face la coe . . .

In the third part of *The Towneley Plays* it is Noah's wife who provides the fun. Poor Noah has much ado to persuade her into the ark. She objects to it first because she cannot tell fore from aft.[2] She then protests that she has some spinning to do, which cannot wait.[3] Finally she appeals to the wives in the audience,[4] an appeal which Noah echoes on his own account to the husbands, with better effect:[5]

> NOE. Yee men that has wifis whyls they ar yong,
> If ye luf youre lifis chastice thare tong:
> Me thynk my hert ryfis both levyr and long,
> To se sich stryfis wed men emong;
> Bot I
> As haue I blys,
> Shall chastyse this.

Which he proceeds to do. I made a rough and ready analysis once of the first fifty of *The Hundred Merry Tales*,[6] with a view to discovering the relative frequency of stock *points*. I had no theory of laughter to illustrate at the time, and I give the table exactly as it is set out in my notes: Ridicule of women, 16; ridicule of priests and priestctaft, 14; sexual jokes, 10; ignorance and gaucherie, 8; cuckoldry, 6; covetousness, 5; ridicule of Welshmen, 4; cowardice, 4; killing and stealing, 3; ridicule of religion, 3; obscenity, 3; snowball effect, 2; puns, 2; beating, gluttony, pedantry, lawyers, mistaken identity, medicine, practical jokes, riotous living, 1 each. The total of the numbers is more than fifty, because

[1] Bédier, *op. cit.*, p. 324. [2] *The Towneley Plays*, Part III, ll. 330–1. [3] *Ibid.*, ll. 337–42. [4] *Ibid.*, ll. 386–96. [5] *Ibid.*, ll. 397–403. [6] Reprinted in *Shakespeare's Jest Books.*

some of the tales contain more than one *point*; by 'ridicule of women' I plainly meant 'ridicule without actual obscenity,' by 'sexual jokes' I meant what I have now called the obscene, and by 'obscenity' I meant what I have now called the indecent. The analysis is admittedly of the roughest, but, such as it is, it emphasizes the constancy with which jests at or about women found favour with the casual reader at the time of the Renaissance. The nineteenth tale is a good example. It is entitled, "Of the wedded men that came to heuen to clayme theyr herytage."

> A certayn wedded man there was whyche, whan he was dede, cam to heuen gates to seynt Peter, and sayd he cam to clayme hys bad heretage whyche he had deseruyed. Saynt Peter askyd hym what he was, and he sayd a weddyd man. Anon Saynt Peter openyd the gatys, and bad hym to com in, and sayde he was worthye to have hys herytage, bycause he had had much troble and was worthye to haue a crowne of glory. Anon after there cam a nother man that claymyd heuen, and sayd to Seynt Peter he had hade ii wyues, to whom Saynt Peter answered and said: Come in, for thou art worthy to have a doble crown of glory; for thou hast had doble trouble. At the last there cam the thyrd, claymynge hys herytage and sayde to Saynt Peter that he had had iii wyues, and desyred to come in. What! quod Saynt Peter, thou hast ben ones in troble and thereof delyueryd, and than wyllingly woldyst be troblyd again, and yet agayne therof delyueryd; and for all that coulde not beware the thyrde tyme, but enterest wyllingly in troble agayn: therefore go thy waye to Hell: for thou shalt neuer come in heuen; for thou art not worthy.
>
> Thys tale is a warnyng to them that haue bene twyse in paryll to beware how they come therin the thyrd tyme.

When the writers of the twentieth century invent new jokes against women they alter the details, here and there, and perhaps wrap them up in a covering of pseudo-biology. But when all the wrappings and trimmings are plucked away the new jokes are just the old jokes over again, and Mr. Bernard Shaw's attitude towards Ann Whitefield in *Man and Superman* is much the same in essence as the attitude of Aristophanes, the jongleurs, and Richard Tarlton towards the women of their times.

The jongleur called woman 'more than devil,' Mr. Shaw calls her the incarnation of the Life Force. *Plus ça change, plus c'est la même chose.*

How are we to explain this immortal laughter of men? It would seem that the general attitude of man towards woman is what the psycho-analysts would call ambivalent. Woman is for man the natural object of both love and hate, and his attitude towards her is now predominantly the one, now predominantly the other, and generally both together in some measure. The ambivalence of emotion may be, and constantly is, disguised. In this our well-mannered century we take greater pains than did the peasants and merchants of the Middle Ages to varnish over the antagonism which man has for woman, nor do we require to hedge ourselves round with so many sexual restrictions in the definitely ambivalent form of taboos as men of still more primitive races. But as soon as we scratch below the varnish—in laughter, in dreams, in mental diseases—we come upon the same "fond de rancune" on which rest, for example, both the mother-in-law taboo of the savage and the mother-in-law joke of modern man.

Hate being a development of love, a turning of it inside out, it is not difficult to understand how laughter should pass over from the behaviour of love to the behaviour of its derivative, hate. The laugh is a non-contributory response, marking interruption, developed within the behaviour of love, and as such there is no reason at all why it should not serve equally well as a non-contributory response, marking interruption, within the behaviour of hate, which is so inextricably bound up with love. Ambivalence of emotion is paralleled by ambivalence of gesture. Those writers, therefore, who have thought to discover the secret of laughter in malice or the desire to degrade have not been altogether wrong. To laugh at a person may be to vilify or degrade him in a way, as Aristotle was among the first to maintain,[1] nor is it without good reason that we all, on occasion, resent being laughed at.

[1] *Nicomachean Ethics*, iv, 8, 9.

The derision theory of laughter is at fault only when it pretends to cover the whole of laughter, and when it fails to point out that an *unqualified* attempt to degrade does not eventuate in laughter. Hate is built up from love, and not vice versa; love is primary and positive, hate is secondary and negative. And laughter is more at home in love behaviour than in hate behaviour. We may, indeed, find the laugh occurring again and again in a love situation in which we can discover no effective trace whatever of ambivalence, into which no element of hate seems to have insinuated itself; but the converse is not true. Derision is degradation tempered, qualified, toned down, by an opposing force of love, and unless this opposing force retains some at least of its effectiveness as against the force of hate, laughter disappears. Othello, when his love was poisoned, called Desdemona whore, simply, bitterly, thinking to degrade her. This was no attempt at derision; Othello had no laughter left, for his love was powerless in the grip of a destroying hate. Yet a man may call a woman a little whore and laugh. The qualifying adjective represents a qualified intention. Hatred is not wholehearted, but is modified and restrained by a counter-force of love.

And it is plain that in the undying struggle between love and hate in the relationship of the sexes to one another, love is the stronger and must prevail—or at least always has prevailed, since the race goes on. Aristophanes—to keep to the subject of laughter—does not suggest that the foibles of the Grecian women, on which he hangs his jests, act as any real hindrances to the irresistible desires of men. On the contrary, it is the women who, sorely persuaded by Lysistrata, withdraw themselves for a season from the pleasures of love, and it is the men of Athens and Sparta who are brought by the pains of continence to put a speedy end to the Peloponnesian War. For all his jibing at Doll Tear-sheet and Mistress Quickly, Falstaff came no less frequently, "saving your manhoods," to Pie-Corner. And though she has to chase him half across Europe, Ann Whitefield is permitted, not to say encouraged, to secure Jack Tanner at the last.

The prevailing attitude of man towards woman, then, on which every comic writer can count from his setting out, is a mixed or ambivalent attitude of love and hate, with a greater preparedness for the former than for the latter. On this foundation he works. He may assume the disposition to love to be sufficiently explosive at all normal times and in all normal men not to need prolonged or forced coaxing. A stimulus word in the title—as 'Of the *wedded* men that came to heaven'—or a series of stimulus words or phrases at the beginning of the story may be enough to set the reader's behaviour off on the proper road. Once this love behaviour, or love-hate behaviour, is well started, all the comic writer has to do is to introduce a momentary crinkle or ripple into his narrative to provoke a corresponding crinkle or ripple in his reader's behaviour. So long as this is slight, easily overcome, and not of such a kind as to deflect standardized sentiments or provoke thought, it will be carried off with a laugh.

But the comic writer who aims at arousing our laughter at women, does not always trust so lightheartedly to our readiness to respond with the appropriate behaviour. Rather does he studiously, though unobtrusively, work up to his comic situations, leaving little to chance. He crowds one stimulus upon the heels of another, holding our attention to the love issue. When, like Aristophanes, he is sure of himself and his art, and when, like all the great comic writers, he has other purposes besides laughter, he may allow his imagination, and therefore that of his readers, to wander more freely over the field of human endeavour. But before making a hit at women or throwing out a jest that draws its force from the sexual, he often prefers to lead the imagination back by a few subtly chosen and effective words into sexual channels, so that laughter shall be unwittingly prepared for.

Aristophanes opens the *Lysistrata* by striking the key-note four times in the first two lines:

Now were they summoned to some shrine of Bacchus,
Pan, Colias, Genetyllis, there had been
No room to stir, so thick the crowd of timbrels.
And *now!*—there's not one woman to be seen.

Bacchus and Pan were notoriously libidinous, Colias and Genetyllis were nick-names of Aphrodite. Shakespeare too, quite early in his dramatic career, showed himself a master in this poetic sleight-of-hand. Think of the opening of *A Midsummer-Night's Dream*, a faëry comedy of love.

THE. Now, fair Hippolyta, our nuptial hour
Draws on apace; four happy days bring in
Another moon; but O, methinks, how slow
This old moon wanes! she lingers my desires,
Like to a step-dame, or a dowager
Long withering out a young man's revenue.
HIP. Four days will quickly steep themselves in nights;
And then the moon, like to a silver bow
New bent in heaven, shall behold the night
Of our solemnities.
THE. Go, Philostrate,
Stir up the Athenian youth to merriments;
Awake the pert and nimble spirit of mirth;
Turn melancholy forth to funerals,—
The pale companion is not for our pomp.—
[*Exit* PHILOSTRATE.
Hippolyta, I woo'd thee with my sword,
And won thy love, doing thee injuries;
But I will wed thee in another key,
With pomp, with triumph, and with revelling.

There is no resisting it. All unwitting, the audience have adjusted themselves within a few moments of the beginning to the mood that the rest of the play requires.[1]

A vague preparedness for love: that is the first care of every comic poet who is about to raise a laugh at the sexual and who has learned the tricks of the art. But often immediately before cracking a jest, he may find it wise to bring his spectators' behaviour to still greater precision. The conversation between Lysistrata and Calonice that follows the opening of the play con-

[1] Cf. also the opening speech of the Duke in *Twelfth Night.*

tinues for some lines without any direct sexual references. Then it narrows down again when Calonice says:

> 'Tis hard, you know, for women to get out.
> One has to mind[1] her husband: one, to rouse
> Her servant: one, to put the child to sleep:
> One has to wash him: one, to give him pap.

A series of homely images keeps the spectators' attention revolving round women and their ways. And with this preparation, the obscene jokes begin. It is instructive also to watch how Sterne works up to his first sexual joke in *Tristram Shandy*. The book opens: "I wish either my father or my mother, or indeed both of them, as they were in duty both equally bound to it, had minded what they were about when they begot me." This is definite enough; the reader's attention is caught and held, and Sterne can afford to dally with it, pretending to wander away to other matters, but always twisting back to throw in another word or phrase that keeps his readers' behaviour on the main track. "What they were then doing," is followed by "the humours and dispositions that were then uppermost," and by "proceeded accordingly," and then, the particular situation having been fixed down, the nimble Sterne skips away into a digression on "the animal spirits"—itself a useful stimulus phrase for his purposes—"and how they are transfused from father to son, etc., etc." The digression is almost too long, in spite of the careful preparation he has made: it is touch and go, by the beginning of the next paragraph when the point of the joke comes off, whether the previous subtly achieved concentration of the reader's behaviour into a sexual channel has not been dissipated. For a reason that will appear in the sequel, I think the introduction of the devil into the last lines of the digression does much to save the situation. Be that as it may, the point of the story is all held over till the last paragraph.

[1] *Mind* is rather colourless; Hickie translates "poking about her husband."

"Pray, my dear," quoth my mother, "have you not forgot to wind up the clock? . . ." "Good G—!" cried my father, making an exclamation, but taking care to moderate his voice at the same time, "Did ever woman, since the creation of the world, interrupt a man with such a silly question?" "Pray, what was your father saying?"—"Nothing."

The Mother-in-law.

It is not difficult to understand why men should crack jests at the expense of their wives, and at the expense of women who might be their wives, since the ambivalence of their emotional attitude is easily demonstrated. The reasons why the mother-in-law should be chosen so often as a butt are more obscure. It may be said that under modern conditions of marriage, with each newly wedded couple setting up a separate household, the wife's mother only too frequently becomes a nuisance in the new home because she attempts to retain her former ascendancy over her daughter, in this way gaining the dislike of her son-in-law, who will not acknowledge her authority and who vents his annoyance by laughing at her. This is true, but it is not the whole truth of the matter. To account fully for the persistence and ubiquity of jokes at the mother-in-law among modern nations we must probe deeper into human behaviour, and not be content only with its conscious layers. This has already been done for us in outline by Professor Freud in the first chapter of his *Totem and Taboo,* and I cannot do better than summarize his account. After quoting several typical examples of the well-known and very wide-spread mother-in-law taboo among primitive peoples,[1] and after noting the difficulties of the relationship between son-in-law and mother-in-law among civilized races, he proceeds to show that this relationship is really ambivalent to an unexpected degree, that is to say, not merely does a son-in-law feel dislike for his mother-in-law, partly for the obvious reasons given above, and partly for others

[1] The fullest record of these known to me is contained in Crawley's *The Mystic Rose.*

deeper rooted, but he is also attracted by her to an extent of which he is usually quite unconscious. "The path of object selection has normally led him to his love object through the image of his mother and perhaps of his sister; in consequence of the incest barriers his preference for these two beloved persons of his childhood has been deflected and he is then able to find their image in strange objects. He now sees the mother-in-law taking the place of his own mother and of his sister's mother, and there develops a tendency to return to the primitive selection against which everything in him resists. . . . An added mixture of irritability and animosity in his feelings leads us to suspect that the mother-in-law actually represents an incest temptation for the son-in-law, just as it not infrequently happens that a man falls in love with his subsequent mother-in-law before his inclination is transferred to her daughter."[1]

If this account is substantially correct, and the attitude of the average man to his mother-in-law is as markedly ambivalent as Freud suggests, it is evident that this is precisely the condition most favourable to laughter. Hate, in the mild form of irritability or annoyance, may be the most noticeable factor in his behaviour towards his wife's mother, and the only factor of which he is fully conscious. But this hate is itself very largely the outcome, the reverse side, of love that is repressed but remains unconsciously active. His total behaviour, unconscious as well as conscious, is by no means all of a piece, and it does not greatly matter whether we describe it as love behaviour checked by hate or hate behaviour checked by love. In such contradictory or ambivalent behaviour laughter is ready made.

Laughter at women, then, especially wives, potential wives, and the mothers of wives, and at institutions based on sex, like marriage, may be excited without actual obscenity, that is to say, without uncovering the sexual in a manner unusual in public, and the process by which this innocuous laughter is excited may be reduced

[1] Freud, *op. cit.*, pp. 26–7.

to a formula. Love behaviour, or its derivative, hate behaviour, is first stimulated more or less faintly in the person who is to be made to laugh, and this behaviour is then ruffled for a moment and smoothed out again. The comic writer carries out the ruffling deliberately, either by momentarily accentuating one side or the other of behaviour inherently ambivalent, or by introducing an interruption from some extrinsic source. But he does not always complete the smoothing-out process. He may merely hint at it and leave it to the laugher to finish off: a joke is broken off short at the *point*. And it is just here that so many jokes go wrong. So long as the author keeps hold of the situation he can control it—so far as one human being can ever control the behaviour of another—but immediately he relaxes his hold all sorts of mischances may occur, inhibiting laughter. The ruffling of behaviour—the interruption—must not be so powerful as to prevent the intended laugher from easily and rapidly smoothing it out on his own account, and its power over him depends very largely on his circumstances and general cast of mind. One should not try, for instance, to raise a laugh out of the story of the three wedded men in a circle of austere Calvinists. To folk of this way of belief 'heaven' and 'hell' are much too heavily loaded terms, and the balance of the different parts of the story is altogether disturbed. Nor is it altogether wise to tell a story, the point of which turns on a jibe against women, to a man still smarting under an injury inflicted on him recently by a woman. The story will catch him on the raw, for the normal ambivalence of his behaviour at the mention of women has been upset, and his mind will go furiously to work along lines of association peculiar to himself that will leave no loophole for the escape of the laugh.

Laughter at the Obscene.

The jester who is ready to make use of the obscene, has an easier task than one who is more scrupulous in the choice of his materials, for the obscene contains an even stronger contradiction ready made within itself than the merely sexual. Our attitude to the obscene is so openly ambivalent that we are generally conscious both of our liking for it and our dislike of it. It simultaneously stimulates in us sexual behaviour and modesty, and we are fully aware of both. The comic writer does not need to exercise his wits to discover supplementary interruptions to behaviour; he need only mention that which modesty frowns upon, and the thing is done.

This is the first reason why obscene jokes are so common and so popular among savages and the less educated of all races. They are so easy. A single suggestive word, casually dropped, will set all the ploughboys and dairymaids giggling; a single obscene gesture will set the music-hall in a roar.

The second and more important reason why obscene jokes are popular, is that they are a more powerful stimulant of sexual behaviour than jokes of any other kind. It is obvious that the obscene becomes the obscene simply because it is too exciting. Man in society has a large variety of things to do; sex is only one interest among many. But the instinct, being very old and very powerful, has a way of taking charge of behaviour at awkward moments, unless it is kept down and pushed out of sight. Each age arrives somehow at a *modus vivendi* in the matter, so much of the sexual is publicly tolerated, so much is labelled 'the obscene' and put under cover. The Greeks were able to tolerate more of the sexual in public exhibition than the Elizabethan English, the Elizabethan English more than the English of to-day, the English of to-day more (probably) than will the English—if there are any left—of a thousand years hence; but in every age there is a line drawn across the sexual at some point, and everything below that line is counted the obscene if it is uncovered at the wrong moment. But, just because sex is so powerful and the pleasure to be had from its functioning so intense, man is always eager to break through his own rules of prudence and to uncover that which he agrees on the whole should be concealed. The obscene is no sooner put decently out of the way than it acquires a new attraction, the attraction of forbidden fruit. Pleasure, as we saw in the first chapter, is never more intense than when it just overbalances displeasure, and the sexually forbidden, if the prohibition is just overcome and no more, will bring greater pleasure than the sexually permitted.[1]

But the prohibition must be overcome somehow. Modesty must not carry the day. Ordinary men and women of the middle class to-day will hardly tolerate mere obscenity, and a story that is only smutty revolts them. To bring them pleasure an obscene joke must be neatly turned or provocative of thought, or both. It must, they say, be witty. In other words, resort must be had to various devices to weaken or circumvent our vigilant modesty. Freud has dealt with this point at considerable length and very thoroughly, in his book on wit, and I shall return to it in a later chapter on the same subject. For the present it is enough to notice that in proportion as obscene jokes are made witty, so do they provoke less and less laughter of an audible kind. This is exactly what we should expect to find. The best wit is very rich in content; it makes the hearer pause, and think; and thought uses up the energy that might otherwise go to the laugh. This may be illustrated by an obscene witticism borrowed from Freud. It was made by some anonymous artist at a banquet in Vienna, and runs: "A wife is like an umbrella, at worst one may also take a cab." I think it probable that this witticism is less obscure at first sound to men of Continental nations than to the English, because it is less obscene to the former. They are franker about premarital relations with prostitutes, and indeed about post-marital relations also, which give point to the witticism. But at the best it is obscure. To understand it one has to turn it over

[1] Women who are sexually anæsthetic with their own husbands may be the reverse with other men; see Ernest Jones, *Papers on Psycho-Analysis*, ch. xxxii.

and over in one's mind, follow up various lines of suggestion, puzzle it out, in fact; and then, when at last one has caught its meaning, one may turn back and admire the art that compressed so much into so few words, or one may continue to think along lines that the witticism has hinted at—on the limitations of wedlock, the polygamous tendencies of man, the unsolved problem of prostitution, and so on almost indefinitely. Whatever one's behaviour may be, there is no leisure for laughter in it.

In this way do we circumvent our modesty and snatch a momentary and highly distanced satisfaction from the obscene. We allow the obscene to pass because of other qualities that it brings in solution with it.

But instead of circumventing our modesty we may compromise with it, and this is a more effective method if our only aim is to enjoy the sexual. It is also the method that results in the greatest laughter. We may agree to take certain recognized holidays, striking a bargain with ourselves. On condition that we live decently and respectably most hours of the day, or most weeks of the year, we may claim the right to relax our prudence in the smoke-room among men of like temper with ourselves, or at certain acknowledged festivals like the Dionysia, Harvest-Home, Mi-carême, or the Feast of Fools. When certain dignitaries of the Mediæval Church took offence at the licence shown at the Feast of Fools, and endeavoured to suppress it, the theological faculty of Paris presented the case for its retention in admirable terms. "We do this according to the ancient custom," they wrote in their petition, "in order that folly, which is second nature to man and seems to be inborn, may at least once a year have free outlet. Wine casks would burst if we failed sometimes to remove the bung and let in air. Now we are all ill-bound casks and barrels which would let out the wine of wisdom if by constant devotion and fear of God we allowed it to ferment. We must let in air so that it may not be spoilt. Thus on some days we give ourselves up to sport, so that with the greater zeal we may afterwards return to the worship of God."[1] No nation recognized the need for intercalary days of riot better than the Greeks. If the instruments that we use in the art of music, they said in effect, require that their strings should be loosened and unbent from time to time, how much the more should we unbend and loosen for a season the body, that is the instrument of the art of arts, life.[2]

It is not until we realize that the Greek comedies were performed at a time of Dionysiac revelry that we can understand Aristophanic obscenity aright. We are apt to assume that the Greeks must have been utterly shameless always. They were not. They were only relatively shameless at certain times of the year. "Le vin et l'amour vont ensemble," writes M. Couat, in an eloquent passage of his book on Aristophanes, "l'un prépare à l'autre ; sous leur influence les hommes redeviennent de simples animaux, innocents et immondes. Au temps de la vendange, hommes et femmes, grisés par la liqueur divine qui fermente dans leurs veines, se livrent à l'amour. C'est pour cela que les comédies anciennes, conformément à la tradition antique, se termine par une orgie ; l'ivresse explique et excuse la lubricité. . . . Les Athéniens ont l'imagination plus licencieuse que les mœurs. Ils aiment, le jour de la réprésentation, à se croire ramenés par la puissance de la poésie, à l'état de nature ; à sentir brûler en eux la vie grossière et ardente des faunes et des satyres qui hantent les gorges du Parnès et du Cithéron. Ils n'y mettent aucune pudeur ni aucune mauvaise pensée ; ils rient en enfants de ces choses naturelles dont ils n'ont pas appris à rougir. Animés par la route faite pour arriver à temps au théâtre, échauffés par le spectacle qui les tient attentifs pendant des heures, sous le soleil ardent, perdus dans la foule qui les environne et sur laquelle passe un souffle de désir et de folie, au milieu des cris, des rires, des sueurs, des odeurs chaudes qui se dégagent de l'immense amphithéâtre, ils redeviennent

[1] Quoted by Havelock Ellis in *Sex in Relation to Society*, p. 219.
[2] Plutarch somewhere makes this actual comparison.

7

l'homme primitif qu'il y a en chacun de nous et dont la nature fait servir à ses fins les instincts brutaux. Ils retrouveront chez eux, avec plaisir, au sortir de cette orgie imaginaire, les oignons, la bouillie dont se compose leur repas, et l'honnête lit conjugal. Demain ils reprendront leur existence de tous les jours ; Dicéopolis cultivera son enclos, Trygée labourera son champ, Philocléon reprendra sa place au tribunal, Lysistrata et Praxagora racommoderont la tunique et prépareront la soupe de leurs maris."[1]

The Greeks were having a moral holiday when they witnessed the comedies of Aristophanes and his contemporary poets. It was the sort of moral holiday on a grand scale that Charles Lamb pleaded for on a smaller scale in his essay *On the Artificial Comedy of the Last Century.* Lamb was entirely right in his plea for the cultivation of 'middle emotions,' in his claim to be entitled "to take an airing beyond the diocese of the strict conscience—not to live always in the precincts of the law courts—but now and then, for a dream-while or so, to imagine a world with no meddling restrictions—to get into recesses, whither the hunter cannot follow me:

Secret shades
Of woody Ida's inmost grove,
While yet there was no fear of Jove."

He was wrong only in his suggestion that the world in which the characters of the Restoration comedy disported themselves was as unreal to the authors and spectators of the time as it is to us. Had the comic writers ever thought of it, this was the real defence they should have put up against the attacks of Jeremy Collier. But not for a moment did they ever pretend that the world they portrayed on the stage was an Atlantis, a fiction, a dream to be contrasted with the real world outside the theatre doors ; and as long as they protested that they were holding the mirror up to Nature, Collier's criticisms were unanswerable. The world of Aristophanes' comedies,

[1] A. Couat, *Aristophane et l'ancienne comédie attique*, p. 379.

however, was in truth an Atlantis, a dream, a play-world to his spectators. And that for three reasons. First, because the Greeks were a highly artistic people, and able to maintain the artistic attitude towards an object with only the slightest degree of 'distance' between themselves and it. Secondly, because social and religious tradition separated off what took place at the Dionysiac festivals from what took place during the rest of the year. And thirdly, because Aristophanes turned his world so completely topsy-turvy that no one could ever be fool enough to confuse it with the real world of everyday.

But Couat exaggerates the dissociation between earnest life outside, and playful life inside, the amphitheatre at Athens, when he says that the spectators brought in no shame with them. If that were strictly true most of the obscene jests would have fallen altogether flat. What in effect happened was that the spectators came in a holiday mood, prepared to give their 'coxcombical moral sense' a rest so far as that can be done. It can never be done entirely—unless in cases of truly pathological dissociation. The dissociation that is effective for play does not consist of a fine and intricate dissection ; it is rough and ready, following for the most part the lines of demarcation between the instincts and the various systems of sentiments built up around the instincts. Modesty is too intimately linked to sex to be broken off from it for play. You may weaken it, but you cannot inhibit it altogether. The Greeks may have weakened it by wine, by congregating in vast crowds, by heat, by fatigue, by any and every means of interfering with the control normally exercised by the higher controlling centres, on the continued functioning of which modesty to some extent depends. But they did not abolish it so long as they continued to laugh at obscenity. Couat is misleading when he speaks of them laughing, as children, at natural affairs about which they had never learned to blush. That is precisely what children do not do. They enjoy natural functions, they delight in nakedness, but it is not until they have begun to feel shame, or modesty, or disgust, in some slight measure, that they begin to laugh when nakedness is displayed or natural functions are referred to. If we suppose Virginie arriving in Paris for the first time, says Baudelaire, we must also suppose her at that time incapable of laughter. Laughter comes to her as her early innocence is sullied by the evil of the city.[1]

CUCKOLDRY.

Why should a man whose wife has been unfaithful to him be an object of laughter? Because, say some, we all find some malicious satisfaction in the misfortunes of others, either immediately, through an inborn tendency to relish pain in other people, or mediately, through our preening of ourselves on our own happier lot. On this view, laughter is just the expression of our own complacent triumph.

Let us examine the matter more closely.

There is no evidence whatever to justify us in assuming an inborn or instinctive tendency to take pleasure in the displeasure of others, simply as such. Indeed, there is strong evidence of the precisely opposite tendency, suggestibility, in accordance with which observed behaviour in one person tends to provoke similar behaviour in the observer. The impulse to inflict pain or displeasure on others, or to enjoy it when it is inflicted by some other agency, is real enough in human life, but it is not the simple affair that the theory I am criticizing would lead us to suspect. It is an impulse subordinate to certain instincts: anger, fighting, and—strange though it may sound—love, and in love at least it seems to be always the outcome of our inveterate tendency to off-set our own pleasure by the greatest amount of displeasure that it will stand. The pain of others is felt as pain by us, if it is felt at all; but at certain times we covet this

[1] "Il est certain . . . que le rire est intimement lié à l'accident d'une chute ancienne, d'une dégradation physique et morale."—Ch. Baudelaire, *Curiosités esthétiques*, p. 363.

pain that it may introduce into our total feeling the negative quality without which the positive quality of pleasure would not be intense enough.

From this point of view, the remark made so long ago by Plato,[1] that we find both pleasure and pain in the misfortunes of our friends, takes on a new meaning. Their misfortunes are strictly subordinate to our continued friendship, and the displeasure they bring is strictly subordinate to the pleasure it gives. We use their misfortunes to give piquancy to our friendship.

Returning now to our immediate subject, we should note in the first place that there is nothing necessarily laughable in the husband who is deceived by his wife. On the contrary, if we are bound by close ties of affection to him, and he takes the event deeply to heart, or if we are of a severe moral cast of mind, or if we pass on in thought beyond the mere event to more serious consequences, actual or possible, following from it, then indeed the plight of the husband is no laughing matter.

In the next place, we should note that it is the unfaithfulness of a wife to her husband and not that of a husband to his wife that has been for centuries one of the stock jokes of the human race. I do not suggest that it is impossible to reverse the situation and get fun out of it; and, of comparatively recent times, this has been done not infrequently. But there is no popular name corresponding to *cuckold* for the wife whose husband has strayed from the narrow paths of chastity; no name has been needed, for so few jokes have been made about it. The fact that jokes are now being made about it is the result of a slow change in the standard beliefs about marriage. There is not now among women, never has been, and I suspect never will be, so imperious a demand for faithfulness from men as the demand that men have nearly always made for faithfulness from women. And for good reason: sexual behaviour is of much less relative importance in men than in women, it is more easily dissociated from the rest of experience. None

[1] In the *Philebus*.

the less, within quite modern times, the belief has gained ground that if a wife must remain faithful to her husband, so must a husband to his wife, and widespread acceptance of this belief is followed at once by an increase in the number of jokes which depend on a temporary rejection of it. Jokes are made about the infringement of rules, not about the keeping of him.

When we speak of laughter at a cuckold, also, we are often misled by an elliptical use of words, and fail to follow the actual steps of our behaviour in the order in which they are taken. The cuckold may well present a ridiculous figure, and we may feel a certain degree of contempt for him, if we pay much attention to him at all. But this is generally *after* the story, and *after* the laugh. During the first hearing of the story our interest in the husband is quite secondary. He is merely the obstacle that the wife and her lover have to get past. Our first laughter is *with* the wife, and any subsequent laughter *at* the husband is really another affair.

Let us test this by two examples.

Bédier tells a good story, from the fabliau entitled *Le Dit de Pliçon.*[1]

A husband enters suddenly, and the gallant has just time to hide behind the bed.

" Sir," demands the lady of her husband, " if you had found a man in here, what would you have done ? "

" With this sword I should have chopped his head off."

" Bah ! " she replies, making shift to laugh loudly, " I should have lightly prevented you from doing that : for I'd have thrown this cloak round your head, as if in jest, and he'd have escaped."

She suits the action to the word, while the lover does, in fact, slip out, and she shouts to her laughing husband, all entangled in the cloak :

" He's escaped ! Run after him, for he's gone."

Now, in this story as it stands, it is evident that the husband interests us only in so far as he puts the wife

[1] Bédier, *op. cit.*, p. 320.

on her mettle. He is the obstruction she has to get past, and we, identifying ourselves with her and caring nothing at all about him, laugh as soon as she has circumvented him. Neither during nor after the story do we think seriously about him at all. He is a lay figure, endowed for the time being with a capacity for getting in the way. At no stage do we set him up and laugh *at* him. We are too busy sympathizing with, and admiring, the coolness and the ingenuity of the wife. As the poet himself says, in his comment on the tale, the trick she played was " biaus et grascieus."

Another useful exercise, if we wish to trace the stages of our laughter at cuckoldry—and at the obscene in general—is to go carefully through Chaucer's *Miller's Tale,* preferably for the first time of reading. In the *Miller's Prologue* Chaucer makes due preparation for the tale that is to follow by telling us that it treats of harlotry (i.e. ribaldry), and by suggesting that if we are too moral to relish such a topic, we may turn the page and look for another tale more edifying ; he well knew that there was no more effective way of arousing our curiosity. For himself he had no scruples : " Men should not make earnest of game," he says—a motto Lamb might well have set at the head of the essay *On the Artificial Comedy.*

Now it is curious to note that of the four characters in the story who can be said to count at all, the husband, John the carpenter, is the only one who is not fully described. The first three lines tell us :

> Whylom ther was dwellinge at Oxenford
> A riche gnof, that gestes heeld to bord,
> And of his craft he was a Carpenter.

Later, we learn that he was jealous of his wife and kept her 'narrow in cage,' being much older than she and 'simple.' That is about all we learn of him, through description, and his actions tell us little more. Clearly, it was not the author's intention that our interest should fix on him. To be contrasted with this is the significant description of 'hendy Nicholas,' the lover, fair Alison, the wife, and lusty Absolon, the parish clerk. Of the first we are at once told, appropriately enough, that

> Of derne love he coude and of solas;
> And ther-to he was sleigh and ful privee,
> And lyk a mayden meke for to see.

Alison is eighteen years of age, and has a 'likerous yë.'

> As any wesele hir body gent and smal . . .
> There nis no man so wys, that coude thenche
> So gay a popelote, or swich a wenche.

Absolon, again, is a 'merry child' and an amorous, a serenader of women, and a tavern haunter, the companion of galliard tapsters.

By the end of the story, John has been made cuckold, Absolon has been turned off with an indecent 'jape,' and Nicholas has had to pay for his success in love with a handbreadth of skin from his rump. Alison is the only person who escapes scot-free. Yet at no point in the story does Chaucer stress the ridiculing of the husband, and that in spite of the fact that it is supposed to be told to offend the Reeve; and when it is told, it is only the Reeve among all the pilgrims who suggests that the carpenter has been derided. He, of course, was unable to listen to the story with the proper 'distance' between himself and it. What the other pilgrims are said to have laughed at was,

> this nyce cas
> Of Absolon and hendy Nicholas.

For the rest,

> Diverse folk diversely they seyde;
> But for the more part they loughe and pleyed;
> Ne at this tale I saugh no man him greve,
> But it were only Osewald the Reve.

I do not wish to labour the point unduly. I would not be thought to imply that a story of cuckoldry might be contrived without a husband in it to be cuckolded—a kind of ribald Hamlet with the Prince of Denmark left out. My object is merely to cast doubt on the accepted opinion, that the essentially comic fact in such a story is the ridiculing of the husband. The essentially comic fact is really the success of the wife. The husband, in the first instance, merely represents the obstruction that has to be got past. If, in the second instance, we turn back on our traces, and concentrate our attention on him, he may, or may not, be a comic figure on his own account. But this is a second step in the behaviour, a duplication of laughter, and it is not strictly necessary that we should take it.

Laughter at the Indecent.

The important fact about the indecent is that it is just the sexual at one or two removes, and that it borrows its force from the sexual. Although for my own part I am prepared to accept in the main the 'cloacal theory' developed by Freud and his followers, according to which, for the young child, sexual functions, urination, and defecation are all inextricably jumbled in the notion of a common cloaca, it is not necessary for our present purposes to commit ourselves to this view. We do not need to decide whether sexual and excretory functions are first identified and then distinguished or first distinguished and then intimately associated. What is indisputable is that they are intimately associated for all normal persons, and that in certain cases of sexual perversion—in the case of certain 'voyeurs' for instance—excretory processes come to be more important, sexually, than the specifically sexual act itself. In default of analysing the matter any more deeply, it is enough to treat it as a case of 'association by contiguity.' As Havelock Ellis remarks: "That fantastic fate which placed so near together the supreme foci of physical attraction and physical repugnance, has immensely contributed to build up all the subtlest coquetries of courtship." [1] And, it may be added, has immensely contributed to the amusement of mankind.

Laughter at the indecent, then, is parallel to laughter at the obscene. In both cases the behaviour within which the laugh occurs is essentially sexual, though the obscene, being a more direct stimulus, is more likely to start behaviour that everyone can recognize at once as sexual. In both cases also, before laughter can occur, a resistance must be overcome. The resistance against the indecent—disgust for the most part—is so strong in most grades of modern society that it is difficult to get past it. An indecent joke has to be more than usually clever to raise a laugh.

The Lowering of Tension.

I foresee that a strong objection may be raised to the above description of laughter at the obscene and the indecent. It may be objected that the behaviour into which the obscene or the indecent suddenly pushes itself is not necessarily sexual at all, and that it is the mere intrusion of the sexual fact into a context where it is incongruous that provokes the laugh. On this showing, laughter may occur either because the incongruous is perceived, or because the perception of the incongruity abruptly relaxes the tension of the former behaviour.

Neither now nor later need we waste any time in criticizing the incongruity theory of laughter in its extreme form. It is obvious that incongruity in itself is no more comic than tragic. The behaviour of murdering one's father and marrying one's mother is utterly incongruous with our accepted notions of what men do and should do; yet no one, so far as I know, has attempted to treat the story of Œdipus in a comic vein. Incongruity is as we take it—tragic, comic, or indifferent, according to circumstances.

There is much more to be said for the view that it is a 'descending incongruity' which is provocative of

[1] *The Evolution of Modesty*, p. 51.

laughter. This view was first put forward in these words by Herbert Spencer, and I have already accepted a modified form of it.[1] A descending incongruity lowers the tension of behaviour, bringing it down from a relatively high to a relatively low level. Behaviour on the lower levels involves less strain, uses up less energy, and if the drop is made suddenly enough, there will be a temporary balance of energy mobilized and ready in the organism over and above what is now actually required. This may well add vigour to the laugh at the obscene or the indecent ; but it is by no means the whole explanation of such laughter, as may be seen from careful examination of the different stages in behaviour, up to and including the laugh. If we suppose an orator, in the middle of an eloquent speech designed to arouse indignation in his hearers against some oppressive Government, suddenly and inadvertently committing a 'Spoonerism,' and, by transposing the initial letters of two words, directing attention to the obscene or the indecent, what undoubtedly happens is that the thread of the discourse is broken, and that the audience come down with a bump from the high level behaviour to which the orator intended to keep them. For a moment they are at a loss. The obscene or indecent words have acted as an interruption. But the interruption contains another interruption within itself, like a box within a box. The Spoonerism automatically starts off sexual behaviour which is promptly hindered or checked by modesty or disgust. For a fraction of time the behaviour of the audience oscillates. Then the sexual behaviour joins forces, so to speak, with the previous, dammed-up, supposedly non-sexual behaviour, and together they sweep the obstruction aside with such ease that plenty of surplus energy can be released in the laugh. It is to be noted that after such an incident quite a measurable period of time must elapse before the attention of the audience can be brought back again to the main issue. This is why, also, people who at ordinary times would not laugh at an obscene or an

[1] See chap. III. above.

indecent remark, even if it were unintentional—people in whom the resistances of modesty or disgust are too strong to be lightly overcome—may astonish themselves and their friends by bursting into a giggle when the obscene or the indecent breaks into an occasion of solemnity; the sexuality of such people may not be strong enough alone to break through, but fused with other behaviour of one sort or another it becomes irresistible.

Laughter at the Naïvely Sexual.

The behaviour of the laugher is the same in outline, whether the sexual stimulus of laughter is intentionally or unintentionally applied. The first effects of the stimulus are quite unconscious, the habit-patterns in the laugher being so firmly established that sexual behaviour in him is *started* instantaneously. Later, however, this behaviour may be considerably modified by the knowledge that the person who applied the stimulus did so either deliberately or inadvertently. As a general rule, knowledge that it was deliberate will strengthen both the positive and negative elements in the laugher's behaviour; it will add force to his sexuality and to the resistance of modesty at the same time. Conversely, knowledge that the joke was accidental will dilute the whole behaviour of the laugher.

Freud tells a pretty story of the naïvely sexual:[1]

A brother and a sister, the former ten and the latter twelve years old, produce a play of their own composition before an audience of uncles and aunts. The scene represents a hut on the seashore. In the first act the two dramatist-actors, a poor fisherman and his devoted wife, complain about the hard times and the difficulty of getting a livelihood. The man decides to sail over the wide ocean in his boat in order to seek wealth elsewhere, and after a touching farewell the curtain is drawn. The second act takes place several years later. The fisherman has come home rich, with a big bag of money, and tells his wife, whom he finds waiting in front of the hut, what good luck he has had in the far countries. His wife interrupts him proudly,

[1] *Wit and its Relation to the Unconscious*, p. 294.

saying: "Nor have I been idle in the meanwhile," and opens the hut, on whose floor the fisherman sees twelve large dolls representing children asleep.

My own small boy furnished another instance on being shown a picture of a milkmaid with her pail. "Is she going to milk or unmilk the cow?" he asked. This being an obvious poser for his mother, he was good enough to explain. "I mean," said he, "is she going to put the milk in or take it out?"

Laughter at such stories is easy, but it is neither loud nor prolonged. The whole behaviour of the laugher is relatively placid. It begins by being love behaviour of a gentle kind, since, in default of any other specific direction being indicated, we all react with a readiness for love at the mention of children. The naïve references to the sexual, though they bring the laugher's behaviour to greater precision, do not act as vigorous stimuli. And since these references do not mean anything more than they say, and are not taken to indicate sexual aggressiveness in the child, the resistance offered to them by modesty is of the slightest also. The initial force behind behaviour is weak, and the interruption is weak. The laugh is therefore weak too.

CHAPTER VI

THE PHYSICAL

WE have seen how laughter at the obscene and the indecent is aroused. Attention is suddenly directed to parts of the body or to bodily functions which it is not usual to expose in public, the exposure simultaneously excites sexual behaviour and a resistance to it in the form of modesty or disgust, and the overcoming of the resistance may set free energy to escape in the laugh. Such laughter agrees with the previous formula—'love behaviour, interruption, overcoming of the interruption.'

But laughter may be aroused by the laugher's attention being suddenly directed to parts of the body or bodily activities which do not seem to have any reference to sex, and the exposure of which does not immediately excite either modesty or disgust. Falstaff has a huge belly, and "lards the lean earth as he walks along," his henchman Bardolph has a beacon nose, A B has false teeth that do not fit, C D has a hump on his back, E F has a persecuting squint in his eye, Charlie Chaplin makes himself up to show enormous feet, the circus clown trips over anything or nothing, bumps into obstacles that everyone can see but himself, and gives himself up willingly to be buffeted and kicked by the master of the ring.

No previous theorist, so far as I am aware, has ever suggested that bodily deformity, awkwardness of movement, and personal assaults, in so far as they provoke laughter, have anything to do with love behaviour. They are regarded by Alfred Michiels, for example, as deviations from the human ideals of personal beauty, grace of movement, and gentleness of manners, and they are comic, in his opinion, because all deviations from the absolute ideal of human perfection are comic so long as they are not so pronounced as to cause pain.[1] Bergson has another explanation. Distortions of feature and clumsinesses in gesture, he says, are mechanical or *tend* in that direction; mechanism is precisely what life and society dare not tolerate, and laughter is a punitive device to counteract it.[2] Other writers, as we might expect, see in the laughter we are now considering, an unmistakable expression of joy in the degradation of others. Even Sully, who does not accept this as a complete explanation, admits that something like malice may be one element in the attitude of the laugher.[3] For the most part, however, he—and others of his way of thinking—would see in deformity, clumsiness, and aggressiveness, just breaches of rule, contradictions not so much of what ought to be, æsthetically, morally, or socially, as of what usually *is*. Before they can become laughable, a face must be unusually ugly, a gesture unusually gauche, feet unusually large, and a kick or a slap an unusual incident in the circumstances in which it occurs.

It is quite obvious that deformity, clumsiness, and personal assaults, in so far as they occasion laughter, are not what we are accustomed to, and that they therefore break in upon our behaviour with some slight shock of surprise, interrupting it. So long as parts of the body keep near to the average in size, shape, and colour, and gestures near to the average in rhythm and vigour, they pass unregarded; it is the nose that is outside the average limits in size, colour, or shape, and movements of head, trunk, or limbs, that are more than usually violent, jerky, or stiff, which catch attention, and may occasion a laugh. And in this respect addition is more effective than subtraction. A big nose, like Cyrano's, is more likely to be laughed at than a small one; it is so much more easily seen.

There is no doubt, therefore, about the interruption to behaviour. But again, if this interruption is not easily

[1] *Le monde du comique et du rire*, passim. [2] *Le rire*, passim.
[3] *An Essay on Laughter*, p. 89.

overpassed, no laughter follows. We commonly say that it is *thoughtless* to laugh at deformity, and the statement is psychologically accurate. For we must not *think* about deformity, about gaucherie, or about personal aggressiveness, if we wish to get fun out of them. We must take them, so to speak, as they are or as they appear, without consciously following out their associations. If once we begin to think, away goes behaviour in other directions, using up the surplus energy that should have escaped in the laugh. Our pity is aroused, or fear, or anger, or some other kind of behaviour that is similarly consumptive of energy.

So much is simple enough. What is much more difficult is to determine the nature of the behaviour within which the interruption takes place.

The first difficulty is to find simple enough examples. It is but seldom that the mere appearance of an object, or a mere sequence of events, abstracted from *all* conscious associations, excites our laughter. Falstaff's enormous paunch has *meaning* for us, as it had for his associates; it *means* an intolerable deal of sack and sugar, and much unbuttoning upon benches after noon. The squabbling of the dancing, fencing, music, and philosophy masters in *Le bourgeois gentilhomme* has meaning for us too, and it is not the mere appearance of a rough-and-tumble on the stage that provokes our merriment. It is true that nothing to which we attend is ever entirely devoid of meaning, since we should not attend to it if it were, but the meaning lent to some objects and some events appears to be of the slightest, and we may begin with them.

Punch and Judy.

The figure of Punch, who still finds great favour with children, according to the returns of Dr. Kimmins,[1] is laughable on account both of his personal appearance and his actions. The characteristic features of his

[1] "Visual Humour," in *Strand Magazine*, April 1922.

personal appearance are: that he is a dwarf—'a little man,' children would call him—that he has a long hooked nose, that his chin, also long and hooked, nearly meets his nose, and that he has a hump on his back, surprisingly like his nose and chin. He wears, besides, a pointed hat, and rejoices, I believe, in a good round belly, though I do not think children pay much attention to the last. The two actions which stick in the memory of children as characteristic of Punch, and which cause loud glee at every entertainment, are his beating all the other puppets with his staff, and his throwing the baby out among the audience.

There is not much difficulty in accounting for children's laughter at the tossing of the baby. It fits our previous formula exactly, and we need not spend much time over it. Every child who is following the course of the drama closely is in some measure in love with Judy's baby. When Punch ruthlessly tosses it away, each child has a momentary gasp of apprehension, from which he recovers at once on recollecting that the poor baby is only a doll after all.

Laughter at Punch's nose, chin, and hump is not so self-evident. In this connection we should note first of all the general attitude of the child on Punch's first appearance. If the child is already familiar with dolls in his own nursery, the first sight of the puppets acts as a stimulus to those sentiments or systems of sentiments which have been built up around dolls. And these sentiments have been organized chiefly round the core of the love instinct; however children may vary their behaviour towards their dolls, it never gets very far away from, and is always coming abruptly back to, love behaviour of one kind or another. Such a child, already experienced with dolls, reacts instantaneously to the sight of Punch and Judy with incipient love behaviour. And even if the child is a slum child, with no nursery but the streets, his behaviour will not be essentially different. He may never have handled a real doll, but he has handled substitutes of one kind and another, for the tendency to play with dolls or their equivalents is universal, and class and education make little difference to it. It is, in fact, simply one of the ways in which the instinct of love finds an early outlet.

The first way in which the child responds to Punch, then, is to love him as a doll, no matter at what 'distance.' But the puppet is no ordinary doll. There is something new and unusual about his appearance. This fact alone is enough to make the child pause a moment, for the new is always a check to behaviour, and in it is always the germ of fear. As the check or interruption is overcome—the child realizing that there is nothing really frightening in the nose and chin and hump—laughter breaks forth.

On this showing, any peculiarity in the appearance of Punch, provided it was sufficiently marked to catch the eye of the child, would do well enough to raise a laugh, and I think this must be admitted to be true. But it may well be asked why the deformities which Punch has are precisely what they are. Punch was not invented by some anonymous artist of antiquity; like the genuine ballad, he has been slowly fashioned by countless generations of men; he is the product of a tradition reaching back an immense distance into the past of the human race. Why, in the passage of centuries, should he have come to possess a hooked nose, a hooked chin, a hooked hump, and a pointed hat—just these characteristics and not others? It may be accidental, but if so, it is surely a remarkable coincidence that in popular conceptions of devils, witches, elves, and gnomes, pointed or hooked noses, pointed or hooked chins, pointed ears, high pointed hats, pointed shoes, and horns of various kinds, are constantly recurring. The conclusion is irresistible that the special features of Punch have been acquired for a reason.

In a paper on "The Theory of Symbolism," Dr. Ernest Jones has traced at some length the linguistic connections of the name Punch, and its Italian equivalent.[1] The

[1] *Papers on Psycho-Analysis*, pp. 141–2.

results are sufficiently startling. Whether we take the Italian original or the English contamination, we come almost at once on the directly or indirectly sexual, and, on the linguistic evidence at any rate, we are forced to the conclusion that the figure of Punch is a symbol for the phallus.

Similarly, it does not need any extensive experience in the analysis of dreams to discover that the nose, the chin, a horn (hump), a stick, and a hat, are regular sexual symbols, standing for the phallus also. We have to admit, therefore, that from one point of view Punch appears as a phallic symbol, with other subsidiary phallic symbols attached to him.

It may be objected that even if this is true it is irrelevant, because children cannot be expected to know it. I admit at once that children are unaware of the phallic significance of Punch when they laugh at a Punch and Judy show, and I am prepared to admit also that without such phallic significance he would still be an amusing figure, for the reason already given, namely, that he is not merely a doll, but an unusual doll. In other words, I should hesitate to base an explanation of the laughter at Punch exclusively on his being a phallic symbol. But it is not so certain as it might seem that children are not unconsciously influenced very considerably by the symbolism of Punch, and it is quite certain that adults are so influenced, however they may protest to the contrary. To show how this comes about will, I fear, require a somewhat long digression on the nature of symbolism, but this digression will be useful for future reference also.

Symbolism.

There is nothing really mysterious about the making of symbols, though many popular writers on psychoanalysis would lead us to think there is. It is by the making of symbols that a child learns, and unless he were continually making them he would learn nothing. Learning proceeds by the relating of the unknown to the previously known. The unknown is an uncomfortable companion, and unless the child runs away from it—which he very often does—he must fit it somehow into the experience he already has. The simplest way of relating it to the already known is to pick up resemblances, to discover in the new something that is *like* something else in the old. The resemblance that the child happens to see may appear fantastic enough to the adult; Clifford Sully, when confronted with a pocket compass, called the fluttering needle a bird.[1] A still more amusing instance is given by Mr. Arthur Allin, who tells of a little German girl who compared the taste of champagne to feet that have gone to sleep.[2] Resemblances are not, however, picked up indiscriminately. The resemblance that will be attended to, and the possible resemblance that will be overlooked, depend on two factors closely related—the impulse dominant at the moment in the person who attends, and the richness or poverty of the systems of experience that he brings to focus on the situation. We attend to resemblances that interest us, and we fail to attend to those that do not. Interest flows from the known to the unknown, and not vice versa. The new borrows meaning from the old; it becomes what the Behaviorists call a substituted stimulus, acquiring some of the same power over our behaviour as belonged to the old object or event to which it is now found to bear a resemblance; and the older, stronger, and more constant the impulse is, in the service of which resemblances are picked out and substituted stimuli established, the more numerous and the more effective are these in turn likely to be.

The instinct of love is very old, and in the child extensive rather than intensive. It is diffuse, and becomes attached to an enormous number of different objects, to some of which it may remain permanently attached, from others of which it must sooner or later be detached again.

[1] Sully, *Studies of Childhood*, p. 29.
[2] "Ebenso wie eingeschlafene Füsse." Allin, "On Laughter," in *Psychological Review*, May 1903.

It is this detaching of the instinct of love, permanently or temporarily, from objects and events to which it has become linked, that creates half the difficulties in the early education of the child. Central in the instinct are sexual processes, and the child is interested in these and in objects connected therewith, just as he is interested in all other love processes and love objects. But as soon as he begins innocently to show this interest in sex, society descends upon him, not without violence, and forces him to realize that it is an interest not to be openly indulged. The consequences are many and varied. We are not concerned with them all, but only with those affecting the process by which substituted sexual stimuli are set up. On being forbidden by his elders to show his interest in sex, the child formally acquiesces on the whole, represses the interest to some extent, and ceases to attend as closely and as frequently as he formerly did, to sexual objects and events. But he does not, because he cannot, repress the interest altogether. Nor can he cease to attend to all the many and various objects and events in the environment within which he has already discovered sexual resemblances, that is, resemblances, fancied or real, to what he knows or imagines sexual objects and events to be. For these secondary objects and events, these substituted stimuli of sexual behaviour, are generally common objects and events, not to be avoided by any ordinary means in daily life. To get over the difficulty he compromises. In order to live more comfortably in their constant presence he proceeds to forget that they ever had any sexual meaning for him; he represses their sexual associations.

But an association once made is not so easily disposed of. It may be forced out of consciousness and forgotten, but there is no getting rid of it altogether. So far as we can tell in the present imperfect state of psychology nothing is ever completely lost, however difficult it may be to find, and however eager we may be to lose it. Some of the forgotten sexual resemblances are preserved in vulgar words that everybody knows but nobody uses in polite society, some are preserved in the technical terms or the slang of special trades or professions—in the slang of criminals best of all—some are preserved in everyday speech without our being aware of it, and all are recoverable in dreams, through hypnosis, or by other psychological devices. And the experience of psycho-pathologists everywhere shows that these forgotten associations remain almost incredibly powerful in determining behaviour that is supposed to be consciously controlled.

It is in this way that sexual and other symbols are made. There is noted in some common object or event a resemblance to some other object or event more directly connected with the instinct in question; the resemblance is then repressed, and the common object or event becomes a true symbol for the other, its meaning being unconscious but effective.

From what has been said it might be supposed that a child had only to follow his own wayward fancy in the making of symbols. He does follow his own fancy, but it is not so wayward after all. Being essentially of the same psycho-physical make-up as all other children, of Polynesia, of Babylon, of Rome, and of London, he hits upon much the same resemblances as they, and adopts much the same symbols. Individual differences there must be, undoubtedly, yet these are of the slightest when compared with the unanimity shown by the childish and primitive mind in all races and stages of civilization in the choice of symbols. So, though it may be difficult to prove that any particular child has made any given symbol for himself, the probability nearly amounts to certainty that at some period of his childhood he has adopted—and forgotten—most of the regular symbols which we come across in dreams, in religion, in poetry, in folk-lore, and in insanity.

Returning to the Punch and Judy show from which we started, we are now in a better position to understand why Punch's nose, chin, hat, hump, and staff, have the effect they do. Not merely is Punch a doll, with peculiarities of features which check for a moment the childish audience's usual behaviour towards dolls, but these very peculiarities have an unconscious sexual significance for at least the majority of that audience, and thus reinforce in another way the love behaviour already induced. Love behaviour is doubly conditioned, and the pleasure it brings is the stronger in consequence.

Personal Violence.

I referred also to Punch's reprehensible habit of setting about his fellow puppets with his stick, as one of the constant causes of merriment in the audience. Here again I think the laughter of children, and still more that of adults, may be traced to more than one source.

Spectators take sides in any quarrel they observe. They take both sides, because they cannot help it, the suggestive effect of all observed behaviour being irresistible. Consciously, of course, they may identify themselves more strongly with one side or the other, and may be inclined to deny any sympathy at all with the side to which they believe themselves opposed, but unconsciously they have always the dual sympathy. In the present case, Punch may be the dearest love of the childish audience, but the other puppets are dolls also, and loved in their degree, and it is a more or less shocking interruption to such love to see them belaboured by the rascally Punch. Judy especially is an object of not merely unconscious affection, and for some of the more tender-hearted spectators who are openly fond of Judy it is too shocking an interruption to be laughed at, to watch her being maltreated by the wicked Punch. Yet for the most part the audience is prepared to take the interruptions cavalierly, as is intended, and laugh them off. That is because they are more continuously and more strongly on Punch's side. They back him. That is to say, the behaviour of Punch sets off equivalent though distanced behaviour in the audience, the one following the other step by step. Punch's behaviour is that of hate, in varying degrees of intensity, and with various other complications which may be neglected. Hate, as we saw in the previous chapter, is a derivative of love, on the principle of ambivalence, and the attitude of the spectators who follow Punch's doings is unmistakably ambivalent so long as they continue to laugh. On the whole they are in agreement with him, applauding his forcible methods of showing dislike for his wife, the policeman, and the other puppets. But the agreement is not whole-hearted, for the spectators see with other eyes besides those of Punch, and their sympathetic hate has to get past the obstructions of sympathetic love. If I set out to horse-whip another man, I go through with it without any temptation to laugh, for hatred is in undisputed possession of my mind. A close friend of my own, watching the episode, and persuaded that I have good cause for what I do, will not laugh either; he sees only with my eyes. A close friend of the other man, eager but powerless to interfere, will not find the episode amusing; he sees only with the eyes of the other man. It is the more impartial spectator, who can and does see with the eyes of both parties to the dispute, that gets laughter out of it. His sympathies are divided.

On this basis, personal violence is effective for laughter because it provokes ambivalent love-hate behaviour. Approaching the problem from another angle we come unexpectedly to the same conclusion. Thrashing has undoubtedly sexual associations, which we come upon in dreams, in sexual perverts, and in religious cults. In dreams, beating, especially beating a child, regularly symbolizes masturbation; flaggelation is a recognized means of stimulating sexual excitement, and may be actually substituted for the performance of the sexual act, thus becoming a perversion; in many religious sects the connection between self-scourging and sexual orgies is much too close to be accidental. Personal violence, in fact, is always sexually stimulating in some degree, not only to the person who uses it, but also to the person against whom it is used. This effect may be obscured by the pain that is simultaneously caused, but if pain is for any reason repressed or dulled, as it is in conditions of ecstacy or by the action of anæsthetics, the sex-stimulating effect of physical violence becomes evident. Sadism and Masochism are only exaggerations of tendencies present in all normal individuals.

Now if, instead of having to suffer buffeting in their own persons, children and adults can watch others being buffeted, it is clear that the direct stimulus of pain is removed and only a sympathetic stimulus remains. The pain they now suffer is pain by suggestion, which is certainly feebler than pain immediately felt. It may be supposed that the sexual element in behaviour, now also induced only suggestively, is correspondingly weakened, and that the loss on one side will be balanced by a loss on the other. But this supposition fails to take into account the difference between behaviour that brings pleasure and behaviour that brings displeasure. The dice are always loaded in favour of the former. It is invariably cherished, nursed, coaxed, and prolonged, whereas from displeasure we tend always to escape by all possible means and with all possible speed.

It is largely because of its effectiveness in stimulating sexual behaviour in this way—however unconsciously—that physical violence is so often used by the circus clown or the pantomime comedian to raise a laugh. Depending so much upon unconscious associations, mere knock-about, which so greatly delights a child, stirs the laughter of the adult only when by one device or another he has been temporarily thrown back into childish modes of thought and feeling, getting nearer, so to speak, to his own unconscious. The circus managers, and the producers of pantomime and funny film, rely upon this happening, and their livelihood would be precarious indeed if they could not count on the majority of their audience, adults as well as children, being in a mood to play, to unmake and dissociate most of the standard beliefs of working life, and to behave for the nonce as a small child. This regression of the grown-ups to the childish is partly deliberate and partly induced. Good intentions are helped by circumstances, by crowding, by popular music, by the manipulation of lighting, and by a thousand devices which experiment has shown to have the desired effect.

Gaucherie.

We have next to consider laughter at awkward mishaps, in which is disclosed some failure to control movements of the body in accordance with the demands of the situation.

On turning to the section dealing with this subject in Alfred Michiels' *Le monde du comique et du rire,* I was sufficiently surprised to find that the best example that occurred to the mind of the author, and that he has quoted at length, is one confirming, in a curious way, the main thesis so far maintained in the present work, that laughter is essentially a love response. Michiels chose it, of course, with no such intention. His aim, as I have already pointed out, was to demonstrate that laughter is caused by failure to keep up to ideal standards of conduct. With this aim in view, he summarizes an incident from *Le roman bourgeois,* of Furetière. The following is a free translation, with abridgments, of his account.

Nicodème, who is sincerely in love with Javotte, dresses himself up in his best to pay her a visit. He finds her with her mother, and sorely ill-disposed towards him. The interview is most unsatisfactory, and he makes an excuse to leave. Getting up to make him a silent bow, Javotte lets fall a reel of cotton and her scissors, which were on her lap. Nicodème dives to pick them up; Javotte, on her part, bends down to forestall him: in this double movement their foreheads bump together so violently that a lump is raised on each. In despair at his clumsiness Nicodème tries to make a hasty retreat, but he fails to notice a rickety buffet behind him, and knocks against it so roughly that he overturns a highly prized piece of porcelain. The mother breaks out into invectives against him. The poor swain, covered with confusion, tries to pick up the bits, so that he can have a similar piece sent along; but, stepping hurriedly, with new shoes, on to a part of the floor that has been newly waxed in preparation for the wedding, he loses his footing, and, as on such occasions one habitually clutches at whatever comes to hand, he hooks on to loops of cord holding up a mirror on the wall; his weight breaking them, Nicodème and the mirror come down together. The mirror was the worse hurt, and broke into a thousand pieces; the ill-starred gallant got off with two slight bruises. The mistress of the house shouts louder than ever. "Who has brought along this bull calf, this breaker up of homes?" and makes as if to drive him out with the broom. The shamefaced Nicodème reaches the door of the room; but in his embarrassment and hurry he opens it so violently that it strikes against a guitar hung on the wall, and sends it flying.

Never, i' faith, adds Michiels, did unfortunate lover beat a more comic retreat.

I am prepared to take his word for it. Certainly the incidents would provoke peals of laughter from an audience that saw them acted on the stage. And the general cause of such laughter seems obvious. At no point are we allowed to forget that the clumsy fellow is a lover; when we are in danger of forgetting it, the author—or Michiels, improving on the author, I know not which—neatly recalls our minds to the fact by the remark that the floor has been newly waxed for the wedding. The undercurrent in all the behaviour of the reader is love behaviour, sympathetically induced. This is perhaps the easiest of all behaviour to induce by suggestion: 'All the world loves a lover,' or more accurately: 'All the world *loves with* a lover.' Each new clumsiness breaks the current, like a rock in the bed of a shallow stream. But the current is not dammed back; it merely foams over the obstruction. Laughter is the foam.

But this is not all there is to be said about the story. Each instance of clumsiness must be taken on its merits, and can be considered in isolation from the others.

The first is the mutual bumping of foreheads. In this connection it is worth noting that it would have been less amusing, on the whole, if Nicodème had bumped his head against that of the old lady, instead of against that of his betrothed, though even the old lady would have sufficed, being a prospective mother-in-law. It is difficult to describe in words what the spectators feel when the two foreheads bump, because words are bound to indicate far more precision in their behaviour than there really is. But the twists and turns, each as rapid and fleeting as a lightning flash, seem to be: love in a huff (the lovers, remember, have just been quarrelling decorously)—love slightly warmer (the lovers approach one another)—love quite warm (the lovers *touch*)—instantaneous but vague associations of what it feels like when the heads of two true lovers touch—abrupt check (it is not just touch, it is a bump)—instantaneous but vague associations of the efficacy of personal violence in sexual excitement—second check, reinforcing the first (are they hurt?)—instinctive movement to repress or overlook pain—the check overcome (they are not seriously the worse)—laughter.

The second episode is the breaking of a piece of porcelain. This is certainly much less amusing than the former episode. For it to be amusing at all, two conditions must be fulfilled. On the one hand, the phrase 'highly prized' must not be allowed to lead the reader's mind off along such associations as—*objets d'art*, unique specimens, impossible to replace, etc. On the other hand, the same phrase should arouse vague associations such as—knick-knacks, sentimental presents, women's lavish care of useless ornaments, women's fads in general. If we turn to the original we find that these two conditions are met; my translation was too loose, for the French reads: "Une porcelaine, très estimée dans la maison," as much as to say: "Prized by these two women (who are all we know of the house), but then you know what women are!"

The third episode is a fall, accompanied by the breaking of a mirror. I propose to consider falls, as occasions for laughter, at greater length later. With regard to the mirror I suspect that various unconscious associations are not unimportant in the total behaviour of the spectator, but I am very uncertain about them, and would not stress the point. For what they are worth, I make the following suggestions: The first free association to mirror in all normal persons is 'seeing oneself.' This would seem to lead straight to Narcissism of one kind or another, which again leads to sex. I think it very possible that the delight with which children—to say nothing of adults—view their bodies, unclothed, or only partly clothed, in a mirror, does fix down very strong associations in the unconscious, which are ready to take their share in behaviour at the most unexpected moments. The distress with which Liza, in Mr. Shaw's *Pygmalion*, discovered a large mirror in the bathroom when she was sent to take her first real bath, is only the reverse side of such associations; and closely linked to them also is, I have no doubt, the popular superstition that it is unlucky to break a mirror.[1]

The fourth episode is the disaster to the guitar. Why a guitar rather than any other musical instrument that might be hung on the wall? Surely, because the guitar is, to the European mind at least, an instrument particularly associated with love serenades. I do not pretend that a violin would not have done for the purpose; the whole story being a love story, any interruption would do. But one does *better* than another, and it is just by such little, unconscious, apparently trivial differences that all true artists are distinguished from mere craftsmen.

This analysis of the story from Michiels is not offered as exhaustive. It only indicates the lines on which any full analysis would have to be carried out.

STREET MISHAPS.

Writing of 'small misfortunes' which may occasion laughter, Sully instances "the loss of one's hat, a fall due to a slip, or a tilting against another pedestrian."[2] I propose to take these instances in the reverse order.

[1] To the unconscious mind, as to the primitive mind of the savage, one's reflection in a mirror, like one's shadow, is a part of the self. Any injury to the reflection is an injury to the self.

[2] *An Essay on Laughter*, p. 96.

1. *Bumping against another Person.*

Tilting against another pedestrian has been already dealt with, by implication. To tilt against is to charge against, some degree of violence being implied, and laughter at such an encounter is to be explained in the same way as laughter at other forms of physical violence. The differentiæ lie in intention, as in the case of the naïvely sexual and the obscene. The manager of the circus ring intends to hustle the clown out of the way, but one gentle pedestrian does not intend to hustle another in the street. The suggested behaviour in the spectator of the street scene is weaker altogether than that of the spectator at the circus, and the laugh, when it occurs, is feebler. But, essentially, the behaviour is the same in both cases.

2. *Tumbles.*

Amusement occasioned by a fall that is due to carelessness on the part of the faller, is less easy to account for. It is simple enough if the mishap occurs to a person towards whom the laugher may be presumed to be closely bound by ties of affection, or the reverse. The funniest sight he ever saw, according to one of Dr. Kimmins' small informants, aged seven, was his mother's falling out of a hammock : "but she did not hurt herself much," the youngster made haste to add.[1] On the other hand, we all laugh frequently enough at the downfall of those towards whom we feel hostile in the main, though examination of each case as it occurs will indicate that hostility is never pure, but always qualified and restrained in some way, usually by the opposite tendency of mild affection—sneaking affection, we should probably call it in such circumstances—that, in short, our attitude, when we laugh, is ambivalent. The more difficult cases to understand are those when the child or the adult laughs at the falling down of a stranger, a person to whom he may be supposed completely indifferent.

[1] Kimmins, *op. cit.*, p. 295.

But is this supposition accurate? Is it true that we are ever completely indifferent to anyone at whom we go the length of laughing? Before one can laugh at a stranger one's attention must be called to him; that is obvious. But to call attention is to start behaviour. The individual whose attention is called prepares for action; and if laughter is to eventuate, time and space must permit this preparation to be brought to some degree of precision. One is much more likely to laugh at the discomfiture of a stranger if one's attention has been fixed on him for some measurable period of time previous to that discomfiture. It is a better joke if the old gentleman who slips on the banana skin has been coming down the street in full view for some time, than if he suddenly turns a corner and plumps down at your feet. Similarly, the amusing incident must not be too far away from us. We must have no doubts, for example, that it is a human being that is falling off a bus, and not just a 'cello case. More than that, we must be able to tell with some degree of certainty what sort of a human being it is. In other words, before we laugh at a stranger he must have ceased to be a stranger in some measure; we must have had time and opportunity to adjust ourselves to him.

There is no doubt that this process of adjustment is going on all the time, whether we are aware of it or not. We never remain utterly indifferent to anyone into whose presence we are thrown; we begin at once to like or dislike him, in a mild degree. Sitting in a tramcar and absorbed in metaphysical speculation, we nevertheless take in the people sitting opposite, and may surprise ourselves later on by remembering quite a lot about them, and by realizing that, quite irrationally, as we say, we bear some of them much goodwill and others not a little antipathy.

By the time we have grown up, this continual stocktaking of our fellows has become very largely unconscious. As children, we carry it on for the most part quite consciously. And the tendency to like strangers—the positive instinct of love—is on the whole stronger in children than the opposite tendency. Their likings are more intense while they last, and their dislikings less ambivalent.

It is not surprising, therefore, to find children much more ready than grown-ups to laugh at the fall in the street of strangers against whom they bear no grudge whatever, and much less ready to laugh at those towards whom they feel decidedly hostile.

Freud has suggested that a fall is specially associated with love in the child, from the fact that he has been so often picked up and fondled by his near relatives and nurse, after coming to grief in this way.[1] If this is true, it is a reinforcement of laughter; but I should hesitate to make much of it.

What is certain, however, is that the fall has sexual associations for the adult. With women generally, and probably with men also, though not so generally, falling in dreams symbolizes the performance of the sexual act, just as we speak of a fallen woman when we mean a prostitute. In this connection we may recall the idle chatter of the Nurse in *Romeo and Juliet.*[2] Juliet at the age of three fell and cut her brow, and the Nurse's husband—" 'A was a merry man "—picked her up, and made a joke about the incident.

> " Yea," quoth he, " dost thou fall upon thy face?
> Thou wilt fall backward when thou hast more wit;
> Wilt thou not, Jule?"

The husband, like the unconscious mind in dreams, was merely applying the proverb, ' When a maiden falls, she falls on her back.'

The characteristic feature of epilepsy to the ordinary person is the falling of the sufferer: the English name for the disease is, or was, ' the falling sickness.' Recent medical research appears to be establishing beyond dispute the importance of sexual factors in its causation,[3]

[1] *Interpretation of Dreams*, English translation, London, George Allen & Unwin, p. 239.
[2] Act I, scene 3.
[3] Cf. Ernest Jones, *op. cit.*, chap. xxv.

and the curious thing to note is that primitive peoples seem dimly to have glimpsed the same fact. One has only to consult any full record of popular cures for epilepsy, such as, for example, the record given by Sir James Frazer in *Balder the Beautiful*,[1] to be struck with the remarkable unanimity shown in different parts of the world and in different ages in prescribing to the patient objects, like mistletoe or the domestic fowl, or actions, like thrashing or hammering a nail into mother earth, which can be, and I think must be, interpreted as sexually symbolic.[2]

3. *The Loss of a Hat.*

Sully's third example was the loss of one's hat. Now a hat that is blown off somebody's head has generally to be chased by the owner or by an obliging passer-by, and one ingenious American writer on comedy has gone so far as to assert that unless the hat is recovered and returned to its lawful owner, no fun is to be got out of the incident.[3] If this is true of the United States, I am afraid it is not true of the Old World, where we are perhaps less anxious to uphold the rights of private property. I wish to consider separately the two parts of the episode, the blowing of the hat away, and the chase of it down the street. Each part may be amusing in itself, and for somewhat different reasons. The chase must be postponed to the next chapter, the blowing off is to be considered now.

[1] Vol. ii, pp. 78 ff. Cf. also Frazer, *The Scapegoat*, pp. 52 ff., 68, 260, and 330. In fairness to this eminent ethnologist it should be said that he gives no hint of a sexual interpretation to the popular cures for epilepsy he records. Probably such an interpretation would not commend itself to him. But to anyone familiar with recent work in psycho-analysis such an interpretation is irresistible.

[2] I think some interesting psychological investigations could be carried out on the descriptions of epilepsy given by the great writers. One might well begin with the work of Dostoevsky, himself an epileptic. Cf. the description put into the mouth of Prince Myshkin of the moments before the fit, culminating in the final moment of unendurable ecstacy, " the acme of harmony and beauty . . . the highest synthesis of life."—*The Idiot*, Mrs. Garnett's translation, pp. 224–5.

[3] H. M. Kallen, " The Æsthetic Principle in Comedy," in *Amer. Journ. Psychology*, vol. xxii, 1911.

In discussing accidental falls in the street, I suggested that before they can provoke noticeable laughter the laugher must have had opportunity to adjust himself tentatively towards the person who falls. This does not appear to be equally true of laughter at the loss of a hat. The situation is, no doubt, much more effective if the victim of the wind is not a total stranger to the laugher, but it is apparently enough that a human being should be involved. This leads me to suspect that there must be something in the mere uncovering of a human head more apt to provoke laughter than in the mere falling of a human being, and this suspicion is strengthened again by the evidence of dreams and popular customs. In dreams, removal of the hat is frequently made use of to symbolize removal of clothes in general, chiefly for sexual purposes; and the hat itself is constantly employed as a phallic symbol. The history of headgear from the time when mankind first began to wear anything on the head down to the present day, illustrates the same unconscious sexual associations; fashions change, but the shapes of hats, caps, bonnets, mutches, which are continually recurring, are shapes that recall the sexual to the unconscious mind.[1] Among primitive peoples also, even among those who do not normally wear anything on the head, the head must be carefully covered at sexual crises. Especially is this true of young girls at puberty.[2] Similarly, peasant women in many parts of Europe to-day, notably in certain parts of Russia, would regard it as shameful to be seen out of doors without some covering for their heads, and will undergo no little discomfort on this account when working in the fields. The same curious twist of modesty is shown more than once in the fabliaux and in Renaissance jest books, as witness the following story from the collection known as *Merry Tales and Quick Answers*.

[1] And not to the unconscious mind only. There is an obscene name not uncommon among men for the soft felt hats they have taken to wearing during the last dozen years or so.

[2] Cf. Frazer, *Balder the Beautiful*, vol. i, chap. ii.

As a woman, that for a certayne impedimente had shaued her head, sat in her house bare head, one of her neighbours called her forth hastely into the strete, and for haste she forgotte to putte on her kerchefe. When her neighbour sawe her so, she blamed her for cominge abrode bare heed: wherfore she whypte vp her clothes ouer her heed. . . . They, that stode by, beganne to laugh at her folysshenes, whiche to hyde a lytell faute shewed a greatter.

Strange though it may sound, therefore, I think the blowing of a man's hat off by the wind is a stimulus of sexual behaviour in the spectators, in exactly the same way as, though of course in a much milder form than, the uncovering of the obscene, and is provocative of laughter for essentially the same reason. The spectator unconsciously interprets it as a sort of obscene exposure of the person. Partly for this reason, and partly because it is so much more unusual and therefore a better interruption, it is much more amusing—other things equal—to see a woman's hat blown off than a man's. It is only because women are so careful to fasten their hats on with pins that we get so few opportunities of enjoying this kind of a joke at their expense.

To forestall the criticism that the essence of the joke at the loss of a hat lies in the man's having lost it against his will, I would only remark in passing that the sight of a man walking down the street with his hat in his hand is often gently amusing. And the vision of such a figure, called up in the mind of the reader, is, I suspect, one of the minor factors contributing to the comicality of Johnson's famous parody of the ballad stanza:

I put my hat upon my head,
  And walked into the Strand,
And there I met another man,
  Whose hat was in his hand.

The Physical in General.

We cannot go on indefinitely, discussing each part of the body in turn, else this chapter would drag its weary length through volumes. "Any incident is comic," says Bergson, "that calls our attention to the physical in a person, when it is the moral side that is concerned."[1] I am not prepared to accept this statement exactly as it stands, and would rather revise it to read: 'Any incident is potentially comic that calls our attention to the physical in a person, (i) when this serves to check or interrupt love behaviour in us, or (ii) when this brings to focus hate behaviour in us that is still discoverably ambivalent, and/or (iii) when the physical is consciously or unconsciously interpreted in terms of sex.' It is quite true that the sudden direction of our attention to the physical in a person when we are concerned with the moral side, may be comic. The moral side is the 'higher,' not only in an ethical sense, but psychologically also. To keep on the moral (or the intellectual) plane of behaviour is more of a strain; it uses up more psycho-physical energy. The calling of our attention to the physical diverts our behaviour on to a lower level, and is felt as a *drop*. There is a temporary surplus of energy, dammed back, and the transference of attention to the physical is felt to be inopportune. We may, if we are of a serious cast or are deeply engaged in what we were thinking about, refuse to have our attention led away; in that event, we decline the opportunity to laugh: or we may accept the invitation to come down from our upper levels. Then, if, as almost invariably happens, the physical can be used consciously or unconsciously as a stimulus of sexual behaviour, we are in a specially favourable condition for laughter. There is a certain momentum behind our behaviour; it is abruptly switched into love channels, well worn with use, and whatever minor interruptions it happens to meet stand no chance against it.

At the same time it must not be forgotten that the physical is not an equally good stimulus of love behaviour at all points. Some parts of the body and some bodily processes are more heavily loaded than others. The

[1] *Laughter*, p. 51.

child has less decided preferences in this respect than the adult, because love in the child is much more diffuse, much less closely tied to special organs and functions. He gets the pleasures of love out of nearly the whole of his body indiscriminately, and he therefore takes his fun out of nearly the whole of his body also. Though unconsciously the adult is at one with the child, his experience of love is at once richer and more definite, and if the physical reference on which the joke turns can be linked more or less closely to specifically sexual functions, so much the better. The obscene and the indecent may be too direct for his growing modesty and disgust, and so he makes shift with the sexual at still further removes, taking his pleasure and cracking his jests at references to those parts of the body which seem quite harmless and inoffensive, but which have nevertheless borrowed their load from other parts which are not so inoffensive. It is those parts of the body especially which we find employed as sexual symbols in dreams, in folk-lore, and in the customs of primitive man, and turned into sexual fetishes by the abnormal, which are constantly used for laughter.

Further, the possible varieties of human behaviour are so innumerable, that the reference to the physical may be used not so much to provoke love behaviour as to check love behaviour already functioning. This has been illustrated several times already in the course of the present chapter, but I cannot resist quoting one further instance from a recent playlet, entitled *Suppressed Desires*,[1] produced in the autumn of 1921 at the Everyman Theatre in Hampstead. The sub-title of this playlet is *A Freudian Comedy in two Scenes*, and it is a clever and most amusing parody of psycho-analysis. As one who am psycho-analytically inclined, I propose to take a mild revenge on the authors of the skit by quoting one of their jokes that brought down the house, and then analysing it. A joke that is analysed is no longer a joke. I quote from memory.

[1] By George Cram Cook and Susan Glaspell.

"A complex, what do you mean by a complex?" asks the innocent sister-in-law.

"Dear me!" exclaims the husband, who is hostile to the psycho-analysts, not without reason; "don't you know what a complex is? It's a kind of ingrowing mental toe-nail."

That this was a hit, a palpable hit, the whole house testified by rocking with laughter. For myself, I laughed louder than most, and made a mental note to discover why I did so, at a more convenient season. For what it is worth, I give the explanation that seems to me to meet the case. The whole play turns on love in various forms, and on hate that is mixed and restrained by love. The wife is obsessed with psycho-analysis, reads, talks, and thinks about nothing else. She flings psycho-analytic terms recklessly at her long-suffering husband, and has no sooner got her harmless sister into her house than she discovers in her repressed libidinous wishes and torturing sexual complexes. The husband, who would like to be an architect if his wife would only allow him peace to work, has exhausted his patience with psycho-analysis, and very nearly (but not quite) exhausted his patience with his wife. The behaviour of the audience, therefore, is continually oscillating round love issues. Sexual terms are being continually flung across the footlights at them, but the effect of these is being as continually nullified by their prevailing sympathy with the husband and their suggested dislike of the wife, and of those disturbers of domestic peace whom she represents. Into this well-prepared behaviour is suddenly tossed the heavily loaded word 'complex.' There is a short pause, to allow it to act. The audience being generally familiar with the terminology of the new psychology, it does act, unmistakably, arousing vaguely but effectively all the usual sexual associations of the word, as employed by the Freudians. And then, suddenly, all these associations are blocked, headed off, by the comparison of a complex to so trivial and irritating a thing as an ingrowing toe-nail. Again there is a pause, brief, practically instantaneous, then the audience realizes the triviality of the interruption thrown into their behaviour, and out-breaks their laughter. This in its turn gains in vigour as the released energy is reinforced by the stimulation of the tendencies of hostility to psycho-analysis, which had been temporarily in abeyance, but which are called back again into activity by the contemptuous simile.

CHAPTER VII

COMIC DEVICES

In the second chapter of his book on laughter, M. Bergson suggests that many of the stock devices of comedy are developments of familiar childish games, and that the pleasure we take in them is largely reminiscent.[1]

Of comic devices, derived from childish games, Bergson himself considers only three, the jack-in-the-box effect, the dancing-jack effect, and the snowball or nine-pin effect, and he uses these only to extract from them the principle of mechanism, being content thereafter to work out the implications of the principle rather than the implications of the toys. Thus he finds that repetition, inversion, and reciprocal interference of series, are specially characteristic of mechanism as contrasted with the organic, and adds the truly astonishing statement: " Now, it is easy to see that these are also the methods of light comedy, *and that no others are possible.*"[2]

It is one of the penalties of being a distinguished writer to have one's suggestions taken up and turned to other uses than the one for which they were originally intended. I do not believe that Bergson's hint, that comic situations borrow much of their force from their association with children's games, when fully worked out, can be made to support his theory of laughter; but I think it is not so difficult to bring it into conformity with the theory so far upheld in this book.

Peep-bo and Jack-in-the-box.

In the third chapter I attempted to show how the peep-bo situation and the toy jack-in-the-box become estab-

[1] *Laughter*, p. 68.

[2] *Op. cit.*, p. 89 (italics mine).

lished in the life history of the child as at least potentially laughable. Objects (generally persons), to which the child is closely attached, are continually peeping-bo with him, intentionally or unintentionally, and exciting his laughter; and as his experience widens, an ever-increasing number of objects are brought within the net of this behaviour, so that at the end of a few years the peep-bo scheme, if such a phrase may be pardoned, covers a very extensive field, and many a situation, the laughableness of which would be difficult if not impossible to explain directly, takes its meaning for the child from some other situation which it somehow resembles, and which is nearer to the original and simple form of peep-bo. Within this wide scheme the jack-in-the-box holds a special place. It is not merely peep-bo, but peep-bo with additional attractions. The clue to these additional attractions may be found in the shape the jack usually has: he is a little Punch, complete with nose, chin, hat, and hump. He is a little man that pops out of a dark closed box.

Bergson has cited the classic examples of the jack-in-the-box effect from the comedy of Molière. The first and perhaps the best occurs in the sixth scene of *Le mariage forcé*, where Sganarelle attempts again and again to close the lid on the philosopher Pancrace, only to see him spring out and go on talking. The scene is like a fugue. First Sganarelle tries to shut Pancrace's mouth: "Sganarelle impatienté ferme la bouche du docteur avec sa main à plusieurs reprises; et le docteur continue de parler d'abord que Sganarelle ôte sa main."[1] Then Sganarelle tries to drive the babbler from the stage, but Pancrace puts his head out of a window, still babbling, and eventually returns to the stage itself. Finally, the philosopher takes it upon himself to act the jack-in-the-box without assistance. Still furiously chopping logic, he makes as if to walk away, returns, walks away again, and again returns, at long last disappearing behind the scenes in a torrent of words. Bergson's other instances are: the scene in *Tartufe*, where Orgon repeatedly interrupts the

[1] Stage direction.

story of his wife's illness with the question " Eh Tartufe ? " ; the scene in *Les Fourberies de Scapin,* where Géronte, being pressed to ransom his son from the Turkish galley, keeps on repeating " Que diable allait-il faire dans cette galère ? " ; the scene in *L'avare,* where Harpagon meets all objections to the proposed marriage of his daughter with the phrase " Sans dot ! " ; and the scene in *Le misanthrope,* where Alceste, urged to give a frank criticism of the sonnet composed by Oronte, begins each speech with " Je ne dis pas cela. Mais . . ." In conformity with his general theory, Bergson maintains that the central element in all these comic incidents is repetition, and concludes : " In a comic repetition of words we generally find two terms : a repressed feeling which goes off like a spring, and an idea that delights in repressing the feeling anew."[1] At the same time he admits that there is nothing essentially comic in mere repetition, apart from the associations aroused by the repetition,[2] though according to his theory of laughter, repetition, being characteristic of mechanism and not of life, *ought* to be comic on its own account and not solely because it recalls a toy that pleased us as children. Besides, in all but the first of the comic scenes quoted, Bergson unduly emphasizes the jack-in-the-box effect. Other elements are more important. On the whole, the most amusing of the incidents—measured by the outward and audible behaviour of the spectator—is probably that between Sganarelle and Pancrace. Here the mingled sources of laughter are many. The interminable babbling of the philosopher is a delay in the arrangements for the marriage of Sganarelle ; it also gives us the occasion to work off some of our every-ready hostility against the philosophers and all who set up to be more learned than the average. The form of the incident is strongly reminiscent of the jack-in-the-box, a toy with love associations of more than one kind. And added to this, and, as it were precipitating the whole behaviour, Sganarelle uses a certain amount of personal violence towards Pancrace.

[1] *Op. cit.,* p. 73. [2] *Loc. cit.*

In the remaining incidents, the jack-in-the-box effect is of minor importance. The degree to which they vary in amusement does not depend on the degree to which they recall that toy, consciously or unconsciously, but on other factors altogether. Harpagon's "Sans dot!" and Géronte's "Que diable allait-il faire dans cette galère?" are more provocative of laughter than Orgon's "Eh Tartufe?" and one important reason at least for this is that both remarks stand for a sort of cumulative interruption which is being put in the way of love stories in which we as spectators take some interest.

The truth seems to be that the jack-in-the-box effect is a good provocative of laughter in farce, or *low* comedy, where no great appeal is made to the wits, and the audience can safely revert to childish attitudes of mind; but of much less importance in high comedy, where even if it provides the rough outline of the comic incident, it is so transformed by the admixture of other elements that it may be practically neglected in the explanation of laughter.

The Dancing-jack.

"All that is serious in life comes from our freedom," says Bergson. To turn life into a comedy we have "merely to fancy that our seeming freedom conceals the strings of a dancing-jack, and that we are, as the poet says:

> . . . humble marionettes
> The wires of which are pulled by Fate."[1]

At no other point in his brilliant book does the weakness of Bergson's theory of laughter show more clearly. All that is serious in life comes from our freedom, without doubt; but our freedom is made possible for us by the almost complete mechanization, through habit, of whatever activities we have thoroughly acquired. Were it not for the action of what Samuel Butler called 'unconscious memory,' we should be in a sorry plight; no sort of freedom would be possible for us, since we should be for

[1] *Op. cit.*, p. 79.

ever beginning all over again, with no chance of attending to anything except the crude but perplexing affairs of moving, feeding, and propagating our kind. The action of unconscious memory is a hundred times more mechanical than anything to be found in comedy, and this mechanism is the very first condition that makes social life possible. Nor is there anything necessarily comic in the image of human beings handled and controlled by Fate. There is nothing necessarily tragic in it either, but on the whole it is more likely to be taken as a tragic than as a comic theme.

It may be true that children get fun out of the dancing-jack. Out of what may they not get fun? But it is surely arguable that the dancing-jack is then a source of childish laughter not simply because it is manipulated, but because, being manipulated, it dances, and dances not in the way children are accustomed to, not as human beings dance, with a certain attempted regularity and smoothness of rhythm, but jerkily, unaccountably, irregularly. If the dancing-jack is a toy, loved as a toy, and shaped as a clown, or as a Punch, or as a monkey, or in any other way already familiar to the child, and if when the strings are pulled he jumps about in a wild fashion, unlike the fashion in which human beings are known, and monkeys supposed, to behave, all the conditions are present that make laughter possible, without taking into consideration at all the fact that the child or someone else is doing the pulling. It is certainly not on the pulling of the strings that the laughing child's attention is fixed, but on the antics of the jack which happen to result therefrom. A child, to whom such a jack is displayed, may be extremely anxious to get it into his own hands, and do the pulling himself. But in that event he is not laughing at the jack, and probably will not be laughing at all.

In point of fact, the dancing-jack as such is hardly worth considering in the present connection. The occasions in adult life and on the stage when its childish associations are unequivocally aroused are few, and on all such occasions the causes of laughter can safely be sought elsewhere.

It is well, however, to note in passing that dancing may be, and constantly is, used by the comic writer to encourage the laughing mood, though not actually to provoke the laugh. How frequently comedies are interspersed with dances of one kind or another, is too well-known to need many words. Comedy and ballet are always closely linked. And without entering into the subject in detail—for it would require a book in itself—we may say dogmatically that the two purposes for which dancing has always been used by the human race are—love and war. It is markedly effective either to raise and intensify love or to raise and intensify hate, and it is not markedly effective for any other purpose, whether the subject be a South Sea islander, a Greek of the time of Pericles, a chorus girl in a modern revue, or the most captivating of all the fox-trotters in a modern ball-room. If the men of the twentieth century have given up using the dance to stimulate their hatred of neighbouring tribes, they go on using it, and improving upon it, as an aphrodisiac.

Nine-pins.

The game of nine-pins, or bowling, so popular in the times of Charles I and Pepys, is still popular in America and elsewhere, though it has been crowded out of favour in England by the allied game of bowls. Like all games of this kind it depends for a great part of the pleasure it brings on unregarded personification of the inanimate objects played with. The pins are 'men,' just as the figures used in draughts and chess and halma are 'men,' and as the small white ball in bowls is the 'jack,' or little man. With children this personification is obviously much more fully conscious than with adults; all toys tend to come alive, even if they begin by being dead. The nine-pins—or 'men'—have to be toppled over, and the reason why this may be a source of merriment to the child is the same as the reason why the toppling over of real persons may be amusing. To this extent its laughable effect is at second-hand. What is specially characteristic of the game, however, is that the knocking down of one pin often results in the knocking down of others; the effect is passed on. As we should expect, Bergson looks upon this as a mechanical propagation of movement, and comic because it is mechanical. What actually happens, however, is that with a slight expenditure of energy the child achieves a considerable result. Once the ball is released from his hand he has nothing further to do except watch; the game goes on of itself, and he is absolved from further muscular exertion. That is a saving of energy, a favourable condition for laughter. Moreover, the result achieved is spread over a period of time, is not strictly continuous, and is not therefore evenly pleasant to watch. There is always an element of uncertainty in the spectator's behaviour, for the next pin may not be toppled over after all. In such behaviour, shot through and through with love associations aroused by the personification of the pins, we have all the conditions fulfilled which we have found necessary for laughter in the child.

Transferred to the comic stage, the nine-pin device brings with it effective, if unnoticed, associations with the childish game. At the same time it turns back upon itself, returning to the original pattern, dealing once again with human beings and not merely with their representatives in wood. The comedian therefore gets nearer to the primary sources of laughter, though he has to make something of a detour to reach them. Examples from farce are familiar to everyone. One character, receiving a kick or a blow, passes it on to another, who passes it on to a third, who passes it on to a fourth, and so on, for just so long as the patience of the spectator will hold out.

The Chase.

In the third chapter I chose, as the most typical laughter-provoking incident of the chase, that in which a small child is pursued down the street by his mother or nurse, and I called attention to the fact that the moments of greatest laughter were when the child was almost, but not quite captured. This incident seems to establish such strong associations that it remains throughout life the norm to which all comic chases more or less conform. The hat that is blown off a head and goes gambolling along the gutter touches off these associations. If we are *inclined* to laugh all the time it is being pursued, we laugh aloud when the pursuer stretches forth his hand to lay hold upon it, only to see it elude his grasp and fly away again faster than ever. The circus clown produces this effect deliberately by surreptitiously kicking his hat away from him at the same instant as he stoops down to seize it. The producer of the funny film also has worked the device threadbare; every funny film must finish up with a wild pursuit of the chief comedian, round corners, down stairs, over walls, and through windows; and observation of the children in the audience, to whom this is a never-failing occasion for noisy laughter, will show that it is just when the comedian is within an ace of being caught, but escapes, that laughter is noisiest. The device, on a grand or a small scale, makes the main or the sub-plots of many an amusing comedy. We may recall, as one of the most hilarious, Labiche's *Un chapeau de paille d'Italie*, the whole five acts of which are taken up with the chase over Paris of a hat of special straw which is required to match exactly a hat that has been eaten by a horse before the play commences. Fadinard, the hero, dashes headlong from place to place in his wild search, dragging at his heels the whole of his wedding party.

DISGUISES.

While there is nothing necessarily comic in disguise, as such, this is perhaps the commonest device of all in comedy, because it gives such unrivalled opportunity for that doubleness of view, those opposing trends of behaviour in the spectator, which may be so easily exploited into laughter. Given a situation that hinges on love excited now, or uncertain and incomplete hate excited now, or on love associations built up in the past and vaguely active in the present, one has only to lay a disguise over some of the characters in the situation, a disguise which deceives the others but does not deceive the spectators, and all the materials of laughter are ready prepared. If the disguise is concrete, a change of clothes, a mask, a false beard, so much the better; it is open, palpable. But the disguise need not be so concrete. It may be represented rather by some error of vision on the part of one or more of the characters in the comedy, it may adhere to the seer rather than to the thing or person seen. It is all one, so long as the spectator is not permanently the victim of the same error; he must, sooner or later, be permitted to see behind the disguise. Thus the device of mistaken identity is for practical comic purposes the same as the device of disguise.

The original of this device is really to be found in the peep-bo situation also, with which we are already familiar. A member of the family circle of the child disguises himself in some fashion, it matters little how, and appears before the child transformed. If the disguise is complete, it must be short-lived, or it will missfire. It is best that it should not be complete, that the child should be thrown into a state of uncertainty between the conflicting beliefs that this strange object is, and is not, his father, or mother, or elder brother. Then with the removal of the disguise doubt vanishes, and the love trends in behaviour already set hesitatingly in motion carry all before them.

There is no disputing the frequency with which this tiny comedy is played in the life history of *all* young children. The disguise need not be consciously assumed by the elder relative. Not yet perfect in the business of seeing and recognizing, the child is for ever being thrown into a state of uncertainty by the appearance of his relatives, at a distance from him, in new suits of clothes, or with unwonted expressions on their faces. And this uncertainty is for ever being resolved the moment after.

This familiar incident takes firm root in human experience, setting up associations that remain for the rest of life easy to stir again. Thus the mere seeing through of a disguise and the recognition of the person behind it, tends always to be greeted by laughter, even though we may be comparatively indifferent to the person, and even though love behaviour is not directly stimulated in other ways. I say 'tends to be greeted with laughter.' It is seldom that we get an actual laugh out of such an incident in adult everyday life or on the comic stage, unless love behaviour is directly stimulated in other ways. Laughter that is no more than mnemic is usually too faint to be heard.

If we think of the endless disguises that are assumed and eventually discovered in the comedies of Shakespeare, we shall realize how dependent on the simultaneous direct excitement of love behaviour is this comic device. Julia, Viola, and Rosalind wear doublet and hose for one purpose or another, according to their own statements, but for one purpose only in the intention of the dramatist: their disguise is a hindrance to the smooth development of their love stories. Bottom is 'translated' that Titania may make love to an ass. Three parts of the fun in *The Comedy of Errors* arises from the confusion introduced into the marital relations of the Ephesian Antipholus and Dromio by the sudden intrusion of their Syracusan twins. So fond indeed was Shakespeare of the device of a transparent disguise that he did not always refrain from making use of it on inappropriate occasions. When he set out to write *Much Ado about Nothing*, he had several versions of the original story to choose from. He need not have put Hero to the indignity of being married off, disguised as someone else, to the "scambling, out-facing, fashion-monging boy," Claudio. But the temptation to fall back on the old trick of the disguise in love was too strong to be resisted.

When Molière chose to write a comedy which should turn on the device of mistaken identity the result was *Sganarelle, ou le cocu imaginaire*, the theme of which is clearly enough indicated in the sub-title. When Aristophanes dressed up Mnesilochus in women's clothing and sent him to the Thesmophoria, it was with three aims in view, to furnish the necessary setting for jibes at women, to let off squibs at Euripides, and to lead up easily to a succession of obscene jests.

In short, disguises are potentially comic from their deep-rooted childish associations with love. But no comic poet who aims at laughter trusts only to these old associations. He reinforces them by making a direct and immediate appeal to the sympathetic love behaviour —or ambivalent hate behaviour—of his audience.

Moral Delinquencies.

The transition from comic devices of incident and plot to the comic portrayal of character is easy. A disguise that is put on with a change of clothes leads straight to a disguise that is put on with a change of manners. Hypocrisy is a mask, behind which the spectator, if he is to turn it to laughter, must be permitted to peep.

The comic treatment of vices will be discussed in detail in the next chapter. For the present I wish only to consider in a very general way, and mostly from the point of view of technique, how the comic writer handles such material.

To be accepted as comic, immorality must neither fail to arouse opposition in some measure nor arouse opposition that is too fierce. It is now customary to insist that in the proper approach to a work of art moral judgment is to be altogether suspended. What exactly does that mean? Formulating a moral judgment on some person or thing is, in effect, a preparation to act towards him or it in special ways. The judgment may not issue immediately in overt action, the opportunity for which may have passed, and may never recur. But it is of the essence of the judgment that, as soon as the opportunity serves, action of some sort shall take place. In relation to an art object, be it a sonata, a statue, a painting, or a character in a play, this is no longer true. We can hardly be said to formulate a moral judgment on such an object, for though we may prepare to act towards it, it is of the essence of such preparation that its issue in overt action shall be indefinitely postponed. We cut the behaviour short at an earlier stage. But though it is cut short, the behaviour must be complete *so far as it goes*. In relation to a vicious person in a comedy, both the suggested behaviour his words and actions set on foot in us and the resistance we oppose to this behaviour must be started. While we need not treat Falstaff as if he were a real person capable of interfering with us in our daily lives, as if he lived round the corner and might any day lead our sons astray, yet Falstaff's evil living is not comic to us unless it momentarily stimulates in us both impulses to eat, drink, and be merry, and impulses to control the desires of the flesh; and unless, both sets of impulses being, so to speak, hung up indefinitely, the former are allowed to go a little further on the road to satisfaction than the latter. We must sympathize with the temptation of sack and sugar, and sympathize also with him who eschews sack and sugar, but our first sympathy must carry it off as against the second.

It is when the second takes precedence of the first that laughter is killed. Then, and not before, are we ready to acquiesce in the sombre criticism of Victor Hugo on Falstaff—" Falstaff, glouton, poltron, féroce, immonde . . . marche sur les quatre pattes de la turpitude; Falstaff est le centaur du porc." [1]

For the good, honest, sober, peaceable folk that most of us are, it is not easy to catch the proper mood. It takes practice in art.[2] Very laboriously, for the practical business of living in society, we have built up laudable sentiments in relation to cakes and ale, and these sentiments assert themselves, from force of habit. But in the approach to comedy, this everyday behaviour has to

[1] *William Shakespeare*, p. 263.
[2] Not necessarily practice in the making of *new* works of art, but practice at least in the remaking of *old* works, which is true criticism.

be reversed. We must counter-march against our own education, taking it unawares in the rear.

The comic poet must help, of course. We are all potentially drunkards, gluttons, cowards, hypocrites, liars, libertines, brawlers, thieves; and the comic poet who sets undesirable characters to gambol their hour on the stage can depend upon their appealing directly to the sympathies of the audience. But this appeal will be overwhelmed by opposition, nature will be successfully repressed by nurture, unless the comic poet neutralizes the opposition by various technical devices. Some of these must be briefly noticed.

One device is haste. If the audience is kept on the run, it has less leisure to be moral. As every motorist and airman knows, there is a certain hypnotic virtue in mere speed; it lulls the higher centres. A comedy that goes with a swing has something of the same effect.[1]

A second device is vigour. If the vicious characters go about their nefarious work with verve and enjoyment, they infect the spectators the more irresistibly. The Gadshill robbery in *Henry IV* is made tolerable by the exuberance of Falstaff; who cares for the travellers when he is dancing round them?

FAL. Strike; down with them; cut the villains' throats. Ah! whoreson caterpillars! bacon-fed knaves! they hate us youth: down with them: fleece them.

TRAVELLERS. O, we are undone, both we and ours, for ever!

FAL. Hang ye, gorbellied knaves! are ye undone? No, ye fat chuffs; I would your store were here! On, bacons, on! What, ye knaves? young men must live. You are grand-jurors, are ye? We'll jure ye, i' faith.

And so in every other scene of the play in which the young-old knight appears. His capacity for enjoyment is prodigious. We pant after him, and have no breath

[1] A similar device can be used in tragedy, as in *Macbeth*. To prevent this tragedy from becoming sordid Shakespeare had to exert himself. One of the means he used was leaving the spectator little time to think of 'the deep damnation' of Duncan's murder.

with which to make the protests of virtue. And again, who can resist the full flow of Rabelaisian joy in life, as it comes rushing and tumbling forth in an endless torrent or words? If a man should speak plainly, Panurge is little better than one of the wicked, and Friar John of the tribe of Beelzebub. But who gets a chance to speak at all, let alone speak plainly, once Rabelais has cast his spell? The author does all the speaking there is opportunity for, and more. The Aristophanic, Rabelaisian, Shakespearean vigour was lost for a time in the comedy of France, when common sense, incarnate in Molière, watered it down. Some of it has been recovered in light comedy; the best of the plays of Labiche sweep the audience off their feet. Some of it has been recovered also in the romantic comedy of Rostand; the swashbuckling Cyrano is in the older tradition. In England, the stage tradition of vigour in comedy died with the last of the Elizabethans, was revived in another form in the novel by Henry Fielding, and in that form has maintained itself, somewhat precariously at times—under the chilling influence of Henry James, for instance—down to the present day. The best modern English stage comedies—*The Importance of being Earnest, You Never can Tell, The Cassilis Engagement* for example—depend upon the tradition of vigour hardly at all.

Another method by which the comic writer forestalls the spectator's habitual tendency to pass moral judgment on the vicious characters, is to gloss over or tone down the criticism which the other characters pass on them. Again there is no better example to be found than Shakespeare's management of the associates of Falstaff. The skill with which Shakespeare plays, first on our sympathies with Falstaff in his wickedness, and then on our sympathies with those who stand for law and order and fair dealing among men, all the while keeping Falstaff in the ascendant, is a perpetual wonder and delight to those who have glimpsed, however faintly, the means by which it is done. Act Second, Scene First of the Second Part of *Henry IV*, shows this perhaps most clearly. Falstaff has eaten and drunken the Hostess out of house and home, and has the best of reasons for being in the disfavour of the Lord Chief Justice. No doubt we of the twentieth century, being superficially more chivalrous to women and more law-abiding than were our Elizabethan ancestors, are more inclined than they to take to heart the complaints of the Hostess and the rating of the Lord Chief Justice. But it is not to be supposed that the groundlings of Shakespeare's theatre were indifferent to what these two worthy persons had to allege against the hero, Sir John Paunch. And so Shakespeare, having given this hero-worship a brisk shaking up, allows it to have its freedom again by reconciling the Hostess to Falstaff, and by scoring a final hit to Falstaff against the Lord Chief Justice.

CH. JUST. What foolish master taught you these manners, Sir John?
FAL. Master Gower, if they become me not, he was a fool that taught them me. This is the right fencing grace, my lord; tap for tap, and so part fair.
CH. JUST. Now the Lord lighten thee! thou art a great fool.

Falstaff triumphs, not only over the woman and the officer of state, but also over the scruples of conscience that trouble his admirers. If those he has wronged are disarmed, why should we be offended?

As Mr. John Palmer has shown at some length in his book on *The Comedy of Manners*, it is the general acceptance by all the characters within the play—and therefore by the audience as well—of the a-moral rules of the game, that gives the peculiar dry taste to the best of Congreve's and Wycherley's work. These writers did not trouble themselves to stimulate vigorously the behaviour of their spectators. The times in which they wrote were too fundamentally lazy for that. But neither did they stimulate vigorously opposition to this behaviour. And the one method brings about much the same result as the other, except that in the one case laughter is hearty, and in the other it is thin and weak. At the best, one does no more than snigger at Restoration drama; Shakespeare's laugh was:

> broad as ten thousand beeves
> At pasture.

It is not without cause, then, that philosophers have found laughter the mark of the god and the mark of the beast in man. Were there no evil in the world, says the moralist Laprade, there would be no laughter, no anger, no tears.[1] The poet Baudelaire is arrested by the thought: "Le sage ne rit qu'en tremblant," and he expands this saying into: "Le Sage par excellence, le Verbe incarné, n'a jamais ri."[2] "Comme le rire est essentiellement humain," he continues; "il est essentiellement contradictoire, c'est à dire, qu'il est à la fois signe d'une grandeur infinie et d'une misère infinie, misère infinie rélativement à l'Être absolu dont il possède la conception, grandeur infinie rélativement aux animaux. C'est du choc perpetuel de ces deux infinis que ce degage le rire."[3] Reason does not laugh, says Emerson; for reason sees the whole. It is only the intellect that laughs, isolating the object of laughter, and seeing in it some discrepancy with the ideal.[4]

Were man always in the strictly moral mood, there would be no laughter at vice. For such laughter is *with* vice, growing out of sympathy with the impulses that issue in vice. It is a confession of our common humanity, an acknowledgment that we too suffer the tyranny of the flesh.

Yet, were man incapable of morality, he would be equally incapable of laughter at immorality. Laughter with vice is also laughter with the counter forces that restrain vice. If it testifies to the primitive nature of man, it testifies also to his power of controlling

[1] *Questions d'art et de morale*, p. 327.
[2] *Curiosités esthétiques*, p. 362.
[3] *Ibid.*, p. 370.
[4] "The Comic," in *Letters and Social Aims.*

this primitive nature in the service of a social purpose.

Laughter is like the passage of Janus. It has two doors, opening, the one towards the darkling past, and the other towards the brightening future of mankind.

CHAPTER VIII

THE COMIC TREATMENT OF VICES

FROM the days of Aristotle down to the present time it has been maintained, with varying emphasis and in various keys, that it is the business of comedy to lay bare vice in its less aggressive shapes, and, by exposing it, to improve the morals of the age. Let us leave open for the moment this question of the corrective aim of comedy, and, by taking up certain vices in turn, try to discover how it is that they actually conduce to the laughter of men.

Frailties of a specifically sexual nature have been already dealt with. It remains to consider others not so directly linked with sex.

DRUNKENNESS.

A drunken man may well become amusing to the child in the first instance, not so much because he is drunken, but because, being drunken, he falls, or loses his hat, or bumps into other people, or performs, unintentionally, many of the other antics which the circus clown and the pantomime comedian perform intentionally to raise a laugh. Drunkenness as such has then no meaning for the child. But as soon as it acquires meaning a new complication is introduced into his behaviour. This new complication is linked to love in either or both of two ways. In the first place, drunken actions are felt as interruptions of affection, if the child is disposed to like the man on the whole, or as points on which dislike can fasten, if the child is disposed to dislike him on the whole. So much is obvious. In the second place, drunkenness would appear to acquire meaning for the child—the middle-class child of Western Europe at least—in a less obvious way also. He is told that drunkenness is wicked, and is not told why; it is doubtful if he could be made to understand why. What he notices, however, is the behaviour of his grown-up relatives: when he is with them and a drunken man appears, they pretend not to see the offender, or attempt to distract the child's attention from what he finds a very interesting spectacle. With no real knowledge of the matter, all the child can do is to interpret it in the light of his own limited experience. Before ever he learns anything about drunkenness, his interest in sexual affairs has been very similarly treated by the Olympians, who have impressed on him as best they can that sex is something secret, naughty, and shameful, something that all 'nice' little boys and girls do not notice. Now, however we may disagree about the detailed consequences of this repression of sexual interest in the young child, we have to agree that it is important, that he takes it very seriously, and that it does have serious consequences in after life. Is it altogether fantastic to suggest that the attempted repression of a child's interest in drunkenness is taken by him to mean that drunkenness is practically the same as indecent exposure or whispering about the forbidden topic of sex, that, in fact, a firm association is established for him between drunkenness and the sexual, and that a drunken man becomes a substituted stimulus of sexual behaviour?

Whether the association between the sexual and drunkenness is established in childhood in the manner outlined or not, there is no doubt about its establishment in adult behaviour. It is unnecessary to enlarge on the text, 'Women and Wine.' I have already quoted M. Couat's saying, which puts the matter succinctly enough: "Le vin et l'amour vont ensemble, l'un prépare à l'autre."[1] Macbeth's porter held the same opinion, and expressed it more bluntly.[2] The cult of the Wine God all over the world confirms it.

To put the matter dogmatically: the underlying, unregarded reason why drunkenness always tends to be

[1] See p. 97 above. [2] Act II, Scene 3.

amusing is that it is a substituted, unconscious stimulus of sexual behaviour in the spectator.

GLUTTONY.

I do not think any similar association is established between sex and gluttony, and it is not surprising, therefore, that this vice is less frequently exploited for the purposes of laughter than the companion vice of drunkenness. It is seldom, of course, that the one is displayed without the other—except in the case of the small boy who has eaten too much at a party. The small boy does not present any very serious difficulties. If he is one of our acquaintance, and we like him—if we do not like him, it is improbable that we shall laugh at his plight, we shall be too busy being shocked at his bad manners—his greediness will simply act as a minor disturbance of our liking, to be laughed off and away. Even if he is not of our acquaintance, the joke may still appeal to us feebly, by relying on our mildly affectionate attitude towards children in general, or, more effectively, by directing attention in some unusual way to the physiological consequences of over-eating. "Carry me home," said the small boy weakly; "but don't bend me." For an infinitesimal fraction of time we are deceived: our pity is made ready. The instant after, we are undeceived, we have a vision of the distended little belly, tight as a drum; this is at once an interruption to the former behaviour and a redirection of it towards physical facts. The instant after again, the whole incident, as it takes place in us, is dissipated, for it is absurd; we recognize the absurdity, and our energy, directed into love channels, escapes through a non-contributory love channel, the laugh.

The gluttony of Falstaff—what is it but the greediness of a child we like? We continue to like him, in spite of his resemblance to a sow that has overwhelmed all her litter but one. It disturbs us only momentarily to hear him called 'that trunk of humours, that bolting-hutch of beastliness, that swollen parcel of dropsies, that huge bombard of sack, that stuffed cloak-bag of guts, that roasted Manningtree ox with the pudding in his belly.' It would take more than that to bear down our affection for the man.

Thieving.

It is instructive to observe how Shakespeare introduces his pet thief, Autolycus. He brings him on the stage singing. And what a song!

When daffodils begin to peer,
  With, heigh! the doxy over the dale,
Why, then comes in the sweet o' the year;
  For the red blood reigns in the winter's pale.

The white sheet bleaching on the hedge,
  With, heigh! the sweet birds, O, how they sing!
Doth set my pugging tooth on edge;
  For a quart of ale is a dish for a king.

The lark, that tirra-lirra chants,
  With, heigh! with, heigh! the thrush and the jay:
Are summer songs for me and my aunts,
  While we lie tumbling in the hay.[1]

By the time he has sung these three stanzas Autolycus may do with the audience what he pleases; he has given them medicines to make them love him,[2] and a two-penny matter, like the picking of the clown's pocket immediately after, is no real disturbance of this love. They bear the clown no ill-will, but they bear Autolycus much good-will, and that comes to the same thing, for laughter.

Molière's methods, in *Les Fourberies de Scapin*, are less subtle, less poetic, depend less on the unconscious influence of rhythm and melody and rhyme; but the results are the same. All is fair in love and war, 'tis said, and Scapin is actively engaged in furthering two

[1] *The Winter's Tale*, Act IV, Scene 3.

[2] Note what may be called the ancillary love suggestions, more specifically sexual; 'the doxy,' i.e. thieves' slang for a mistress, and 'me and my aunts (i.e. doxies) while we lie tumbling in the hay.'

love affairs ; we, the spectators, will allow him many privileges on that score. Argante and Géronte, the hard-hearted fathers, arouse our hostility by their opposition to the love affairs of their childern. It is therefore doubly amusing when Scapin wheedles two hundred pistoles out of the former and five hundred crowns out of the latter, for these acts of knavery achieve a double purpose. They assist Octave and Léandre and they vex their miserly parents.

Lying.

What is true of thieving is true also of lying. While we do not approve of lying as a habit, even in our friends, and the particular lies our friends tell therefore come upon us always with some slight shock, we are prepared to condone them, either because we are much too well-disposed to the liars or sufficiently ill-disposed to the victims of the lie. Not a little ink has been wasted on the problem of whether or not Shakespeare intended us to believe Falstaff when he asserted to the Prince and Poins, after they had tried to put him down with the plain tale of the Gadshill robbery, that he had recognized them under their suits of buckram. What does it matter ? Falstaff's lies were all open and palpable, deceiving nobody except those whom we are quite pleased to see deceived, like Justice Shallow. And if they had deceived better folk, it would have made little difference, for Falstaff could take us with him in everything. On the other hand, it is not Pecksniff's lies but the discovery of them that is amusing.

Cowardice.

It was the height of Shakespeare's daring, in comedy, to show Falstaff a coward at the Battle of Shrewsbury. It has been too much for most of the critics, whose hearts have not been large enough to overlook cowardice in a friend. With many it has distorted their whole outlook on Falstaff, leading them to assert that he is an object of derision, a character to be laughed *at*, and laughed *down* a ridiculous and disgraceful figure. Is he not a coward, and is not cowardice the lowest degradation to which a knight and a soldier can sink? Maurice Morgann felt this so keenly, and yet felt so keenly also the extraordinary attractiveness of the man Falstaff, that he set out boldly to maintain that Shakespeare did not intend him to a appear a coward, and that all indications of cowardice can be explained away. Since the publication of Morgann's essay, in 1777, critics have been of two minds in the matter, though it would seem that the orthodox opinion now, in England at least, is Morgann's opinion. I confess to being heterodox; it is time that Morgann's thesis was duly docketed and put away along with all the other curiosities of Shakespeare worship.

There is some justification for Morgann, however. Study of the first part of *Henry IV* leads one to suspect that Shakespeare was himself uncertain at the beginning whether Falstaff was to turn out a coward or not. The other delinquencies of this hero presented little difficulty; they were manly vices and could be carried off with a swagger. Cowardice is a different matter. It has become one of the deepest of social traditions that men must act as though they did not fear death; the impulse to fear death being so strong, the resistance opposed to this impulse has had to be correspondingly strengthened. Our indignation at an act of cowardice is fierce, because the temptation to be cowards ourselves is fierce. It looks as though Shakespeare was not sure whether or no he dare risk provoking this indignation against a character to whom he purposed that our attitude should be affectionate on the whole. He therefore leaves the question open in the earlier scenes. It is not until Falstaff has proved himself so infinite in resource, so impossible to put down, that Shakespeare makes up his mind. One can almost hear him saying, 'By heavens! this fat-bellied rascal may do what he will. A good wit will make use of anything. He shall be a very coward, and yet be not damned for it.'

The decision taken, Shakespeare still walks warily.

He prepares us for the severe shock of the battle scene by lesser shocks. He is determined that we shall acquire the knack of seeing Falstaff base without ceasing to esteem him. And so he gives us first the witty catechism on honour, then the pointing of the moral by the death of Sir Walter Blunt and Falstaff's commentary on it, then the discovery that Falstaff's pistol case is loaded with 'that will sack a city,' and then, and not till then, Falstaff's shamming death to avoid death.

Why all this preparation? Apart from the obvious fact that Shakespeare turned the preparation itself to account for laughter, it was advisable, if not actually necessary, that the audience should get into the way of brushing aside increasingly solid obstructions in the path of their affection and esteem for the astonishing knight. Provided the obstruction can be brushed aside at all, then the more weighty it is the louder may the laugh be made. It is easier to turn a jest on a cowardly action, if we have no reason to respect and like the coward. That is Shakespeare's way with Parolles, Jonson's with Bobadil, and Beaumont and Fletcher's with Master Humphrey. Shakespeare's way with Falstaff was different, and much the more adventurous. He took the risk of turning the audience against his favourite, and, to judge by the subsequent course of Shakespearean criticism, the risk was too great. In this respect the character of Falstaff failed. It requires not a little of Shakespeare's wide tolerance to accept cowardice in a man of gentle birth and royal associates, and to laugh it off without undue hostility. We are few of us big enough in the heart for that.

On the other hand, cowardice can be laughed away easily enough if bravery is not of the essence of what we expect from a character. Don Quixote and Pantagruel must be courageous: it does not matter about Sancho Panza and Panurge. When the great storm overtook Pantagruel and his companions, "Panurge alone sate on his Breech upon deck, weeping and howling."[1] He

[1] *The Fourth Book of Dr. Francis Rabelais*, chap. xix.

was but a pitiful rascal in any event. What does it matter if our liking for him is mingled with contempt?

None the less, cowardice always needs delicate handling if it is to remain comic. In his essay on *Stage Illusion* Charles Lamb points out how the actor may collaborate with the author, or, it may be, supply the defects of the author, in making cowardice tolerable in comedy. The actor may establish friendly relations with the audience, and keep up a 'perpetual sub-insinuation' to them that he is not such a chicken-livered rogue as he appears. Lamb goes on to say that the actor may perform the same pious office for yet another odious vice, avarice, thereby disarming "the character of a great deal of its odiousness, by seeming to engage *our* compassion for the insecure tenure by which he holds his money bags and parchments." To put this in other and more clumsy words: if the author, aiming at a comic effect, has aroused too strongly the hostility of the audience, the actor may counteract this by appealing to the affection of the audience; and out of the ambivalent behaviour so provoked, laughter may be snatched.

Hypocrisy.

Perhaps the most famous, or infamous, hypocrite in literature is Tartufe. I have already expressed the opinion that the comedy to which he has lent his name is not specially designed to evoke laughter, not even the laughter of the mind. Except for certain incidental scenes—such as that between Valère and Marianne, when the indefatigable Dorine plays peacemaker—the atmosphere of the play is indeed sombre. Molière, it would appear, was too bitter against the religious hypocrites—not without cause as the event proved—to take that detached view which comedy of his special kind requires. But, however that may be, it is evident that the audience is not left to discover, in an outburst of laughter, that the hero is 'the exact reverse of what he affects,' which is how Fielding explained laughter at hypocrisy. On the contrary, Molière takes extraordinary pains to set the audience right on the true character of Tartufe before ever he brings him on the stage, in the third act, after every other important character has delivered an opinion on him. The unmasking of Tartufe to Orgon and to Madame Pernelle, the only two persons to whom his hypocrisy is not plain from the beginning, is by no means comic. Indeed, though the whole action turns on the deception which Tartufe is able to practise on Orgon, such mildly comic incidents as the play contains depend hardly at all on hypocrisy. When they are related to it, they draw their comic force from another source, namely from the fact that Tartufe makes love to Orgon's wife. Remembering Tartufe's outward allegiance to extra-mundane things, one smiles at the sight of him protesting his fleshly desire for Elmire, and remembering that, one smiles again when Orgon the husband encourages him to spend as much time as possible in the company of his wife. Is it not significant that Molière, as if in a forlorn attempt to extract some elements of comedy from a plot and a character that are in themselves inimical to laughter, has recourse to situations vaguely reminiscent of stories of cuckoldry, that unfailing fountain of human mirth ?

The truth seems to be that hypocrisy, like cowardice, arouses too fierce and unmixed an opposition from those who watch it, to be really fruitful in laughter. It may be, as Fielding says, more *ridiculous* than vanity; let us not dispute about words. What is certain is that it is more appropriate to satire than to comedy.

The laughter aimed at the clergy or priests in almost all ages, and especially in the Middle Ages, confirms this statement. It has been asserted that the laity were glad of every opportunity to vent their suppressed hostility to the Mediæval Church, and that the endless stories against the priests gave such an outlet. I am not concerned to dispute this, but only to point out that when the real or supposed hypocrisy of the clergy was turned to laughter the discrepancy between profession and performance was not felt to be very severe. It was, after all, chiefly about the lesser clergy that the jokes were made, and only when not very much was expected of them. According to M. Bédier, the satirical bent of the fabliaux has been much exaggerated.[1] Their general aim was to promote health and forgetfulness. As the author of *Le Pauvre Mercier* put it[2]:

> Se je di chose qui soit belle,
> Elle doit bien estre escoutée,
> Et par biaus diz est oubliée
> Maintes fois ire et cuisançons . . .
> Car, quant aucuns dit les risées,
> Les fort tançons sont oubliées.

On the whole, the tone of the fabliaux is good-humoured, and usually when the jongleur raises a laugh at the failure of the priesthood to live up to their professed standards of morality it is evident that he is not really scandalized. On the other hand, when the jongleur is hostile, he must do one of two things to avoid killing the laughter of his hearers. Either he must qualify his hostility by its opposite, or he must cast the tale into a sexual mould. The latter is, of course, the easier of the two methods, and the more usual. The proportion of anti-clerical fabliaux with sexual motives is very high indeed.

It is the same in the jest-books, the continuations of the fabliaux in a later age. The people were tolerant of the fleshly errors of the priests and priestesses, at least when these were such as the generality of mankind fall into.

Vanity.

If hypocrisy is a difficult vice to manage for laughter, because the opposition it arouses is usually too intense, vanity is among the easiest. It is a hackneyed theme in comic literature.

Vanity is self-love, carried beyond the normal in some direction or directions. Psychologists of the Ribot-McDougall school prefer to make a separate instinct of

[1] *Les Fabliaux*, p. 326. [2] Quoted by Bédier, *op. cit.*, p. 310.

self-love—positive self-feeling, as it is often clumsily called. For my own part I can see no real justification for this. It is so much simpler to take the hint contained in popular speech, and classify self-love with all other kinds of love. Havelock Ellis, Freud, and other writers on the sexual, have made us familiar with auto-erotism, in the strict sense, i.e. sexual behaviour that, to find satisfaction, does not require any object outside the person who behaves. We need only widen the meaning of auto-erotism to take in all the phenomena of self-love, normal and abnormal. That is to say, the performance of some functions not merely brings the pleasure which all successful functioning brings, but also stimulates in the performer love behaviour which, instead of being projected outwards, is turned inwards on himself as object, thereby achieving a secondary satisfaction which may blend with the first, but is nevertheless distinguishable from it. Such auto-erotism is universal in the human race, not uncommon in many other animals, and the *sine qua non* of evolution from lower to higher. It is due to this twisting of behaviour upon itself that man is able, not simply to live, but to live well. From one point of view, it is the whole aim of culture to make an increasing number of functions auto-erotic, so that an individual shall miss the full satisfaction of their performance unless he can feel 'proud' that they were well and worthily performed.

On this showing, self-love in the widest sense, like auto-erotism in sexual affairs, is of supreme importance in human development, and remains healthy so long as it remains proportionate in the total behaviour of the individual. It ceases to be healthy when it passes into the so-called harmless vanity on which comedy seizes, and it becomes dangerous when it passes into the over-weening or dominating vanity of the insane. Vanity is self-love, attached to certain functions,[1] which takes up too much of the time and energy of the vain person,

[1] It might seem better to say, 'attached to certain qualities,' but a quality is only a capacity and a capacity is a function. Not to lose sight of the essentially dynamic character of the whole process I prefer to speak simply of a function.

preventing him from devoting himself adequately to all the activities his situation demands from him.

It is because vanity is a lop-sided but harmless development of self-love, which is universal, that it is so easily turned to laughter. We are ready on the instant to accept the suggestions of self-love which the figure of the vain person offers us; it needs only the lightest trigger-pressure to release that kind of behaviour in us. Immediately afterwards we are made to realize that what we see is not healthy self-love, but rather that the vain person is, like Malvolio, 'sick of self-love.' Such realization is interruptory to the facile behaviour already started; it checks it. The occurrence or failure of the laugh will then depend on whether the original behaviour, helped out with behaviour of any other kind that will coalesce with it, can overcome the check or not. And if this description of the behaviour is, so to speak, turned over on its face, the reverse side shows the same result. Observation of vanity may excite behaviour that is predominantly hostile, but this hostility is limited and checked by the contradictory tendencies of self-love, suggestively induced. Either our feeling *with* is hindered by our feeling *against*, or our feeling *against* is hindered by our feeling *with*. It comes to much the same thing either way, for laughter.

With the comic writers of France it is usually easy to decide whether, on the balance, hostility or affection prevails in our responses towards their vain characters. It is the glory of French literature that it is so precise and clear: everything in it is either this or that, seldom confusedly both this and that. Thus, in the comedy to which M. Perrichon gives his name, though we come in the end to like him well enough, it is mainly because he provides us with so many opportunities of laughing at him. Our liking is extraneous; it is not the reflection of the author's attitude. On most, if not all, of the separate occasions when he shows in a comic light, his conduct provokes in us behaviour which is ambivalent, it is true, but in which dislike prevails. His vanity is best shown in his turning against Armand, who has saved his life, in favour of Daniel, 'ce bon Daniel,' whose life he has saved. Witness the excellent scene in the third act of this comedy, where Perrichon discovers that the account of his life-saving exploit in the Alps has found its way mysteriously into the Press. The vain-glorious Perrichon is an object of hostility, of ridicule. That is to say, although his self-love is easy to understand and acts suggestively on us, the readers or spectators of the play, yet it is generally off-set and borne down by a stronger feeling, contempt. We deride this 'bon bourgeois,' and there is in our attitude a certain coolness and hardness, a cutting equanimity of temper, that the French alone seem able to induce.

Yet examples of a different attitude are not wanting in French literature, especially perhaps in modern work. Cyrano de Bergerac, in Rostand's romantic play, is vain of his swordsmanship, M. l'Abbé Coignard, in Anatole France's *La rotisserie de la reine pédauque,* is vain of his learning; yet these trifling vanities hardly ripple the surface of our profound esteem for these gracious shadows of imagination.

It is not the habit of writers of the British race to be quite so certain in their likes and dislikes. If they are contemptuous on the whole, their contempt is always apt to turn itself inside out and expose the human sympathy and affection with which it is lined. J. M. Synge had strong affinities with the French, among whom he spent much of his short life, but when he came to write a comedy that took vanity as its theme he was not at all sure at the end of it, and consequently left his readers not at all sure either, whether the hero was more to be despised than liked or more to be liked than despised. The universal, if veiled, hostility of a son to his father, is not perhaps so likely to drive a twentieth-century Englishman to parricide as it was to drive Christy Mahon[1] to—up with a loy and lay flat his da. Nor would the Englishman be so proud of the feat that a whole comedy

[1] *The Playboy of the Western World.*

could be made out of his vanity. Rather are we in England vain of being more *civilized* than the villagers of Mayo. Yet Synge's play would fail altogether of its effect on us, did it not get under our conscious guard and touch off age-old impulses that we may be loth enough to acknowledge. There is never a son of us all who has not at some period of his fettered childhood wanted bitterly to get rid of his father, or some other male relative standing in the place of a father, and who would not have been vain enough of the feat had it been accomplished. Christy claims to have done it for us, and he boasts of it; which gives us a vicarious, if unconscious satisfaction, checked all the time by sentiments that are more uniformly conscious, like filial affection and respect for human life. So evenly balanced are the opposite groups of tendencies in us that even after we discover that old Mahon has suffered nothing worse than a broken head, we should find it hard to decide whether our contempt for Christy, such as it is, is not due to the same causes as Pegeen Mike's when she turns on him with: "And it's lies you told, letting on you had him slitted, and you nothing at all. . . . And to think of the coaxing glory we had given him, and he after doing nothing but hitting a soft blow and chasing northward in a sweat of fear. Quit off from this."[1] Truly, *The Playboy* is a perplexing comedy, an altogether unaccountable comedy if we omit to take stock of the unconscious motives in us to which it makes its whimsical appeal.

The case of Malvolio has been touched on so often by critics that nothing more need be said on it here. Shakespeare treated him in a truly Shakespearean way; he refused to take sides permanently with or against him. For all his foppery the man had dignity, which makes us at the last rather ashamed that we began by agreeing so light-heartedly with Maria and Feste and Sir Toby Belch to bait him.

[1] Act III.

The Devil.

A desultory discussion of this kind on some of the human frailties which have been exploited for comic purposes would be incomplete without some reference to the devil. A full and satisfactory history of demonology as it has been used to provoke the laughter of men has yet to be written, and no attempt can be made here to treat the subject in detail. We must be content with hints.

The first problem is that of the psycho-genesis of evil. Evil, we may say, is that which is believed as a result of experience to be harmful, that which has been found to bring displeasure. In ordinary speech even to-day no rigorous distinction is drawn between physical and moral evil; and the lower we descend in the scale of civilization the less frequently is the distinction drawn at all. The only final test to which man can bring evil is feeling; evil is ultimately identical with the unpleasant. Now displeasure arises, as we saw in an earlier chapter, from the hindrance of behaviour, and this hindrance may be either internal or external. Yet this distinction again is not so clear-cut for the childish and primitive mind as it seems to be to us. Even when the hindrance is definitely located externally it is at once interpreted in accordance with what the person hindered would or might have done himself. If the hindering object is non-human it is interpreted anthropomorphically; if human, it is interpreted in the light of the experience, however limited that may be, of the person it hinders. Thus in any event evil is a projection from within, and takes shape in men and women, or in gods, devils, fairies, elves, or what not, who are moved by like impulses to those of man.

For the individual at any age and level of culture, the devil-in-chief, the Prince of Darkness, or whatever polite or impolite name he may be given, will be the more or less completely organized projection of those hindrances to the individual's behaviour with which he is most familiar. The child's devil is a simple person, with only a few ways of saying 'Don't.' The highly sophisticated adult of modern times needs a very complicated devil, to match himself. Thus Ivan Karamazov's projection was a shabby-genteel poor relation, indolent, sceptical, "qui faisait la cinquantaine," who was unable to conceive how he could ever have been anything so exalted as an angel, who was subject to rheumatism and colds in the head, and whose unrealized ideal was to be "incarnated once and for all, irrevocably, in the form of some merchant's wife, weighing eighteen stone," and believing implicitly everything that the Church told her to believe.[1] And for any group of men—a tribe, a religious sect, a race—the devil will be the mean of the individual projections, a being much simpler than the devil any one adult might construct for himself, and approximating more nearly to the devil of the child.

Once again, however, it is important to emphasize that a hindrance to behaviour takes whatever character it possesses from the behaviour it hinders. Whatever may be the ontological truth about evil, the psychological truth is that it is the negative of good, something so irrevocably bound up with good that in the last resort no description of it is possible except in terms of the good which it obstructs. Here, as always, behaviour shows a double face. Evil is both a hindrance and an incentive. It says 'Don't' and 'Do' at the same moment. The devil is the enemy of man, and the tempter of man. He repels and attracts. God and the devil begin by being identical, then the devil becomes the servant of God, and then at length the devil becomes the enemy of God. This development in the idea of the devil is well illustrated by Hebrew literature. Satan does not figure in the Pentateuch, in which all recorded acts of evil are the work of Jehovah, no less than all recorded acts of good. By the time we reach the Book of Job, Satan has taken his place as an emissary of Jehovah, and it is not until much later in the history of the Jewish religion that we find God and the devil set over against one another in

[1] Dostoevsky, *The Brothers Karamazov*, English translation, pp. 686 ff.

opposition. The fundamental identity of good and evil is also symbolized in the fall of Lucifer, once the greatest of the angels. Faced with this ambiguity in the devil, the grand equivocator, the theologians tend to simplify all difficulties by maintaining that he troubles the spirit and tempts the flesh, that he facilitates one kind of behaviour and hinders another. Such a doctrine may be good theology; it is only a half—or quarter—truth in psychology. For the devil in the first instance is both a hindrance and a provocation *to the same behaviour*.

Now though the devil is a composite figure, the incarnation of all sorts of hindrances and temptations, he shows certain predominating traits derived from the particular kind, or kinds, of behaviour he most energetically obstructs and, simultaneously, excites. Dr. Ernest Jones has advanced the hypothesis that the devil is the projection of the child's thoughts about the father, the first person in the child's experience to interfere seriously with his impulses.[1] This is an interesting and not improbable hypothesis, which fits easily into mythology and folklore, and which finds support in a curious way from the story of the Karamazov family, the greatest of the Dostoevsky novels. The devil, whom Ivan refuses to acknowledge as anything but a projection of his own imagination,[2] appears to him when he had tortured himself into delirium with the thought that, though he did not actually murder his father, Fyodor Pavlovitch Karamazov, with his own hands, yet he was equally guilty with the murderer because he had *wished* his father dead. Now the psycho-analyst contends that the main cause of the hatred which a child, especially a male child, conceives for the father, is sexual jealousy, the father being regarded as a rival in the love of the mother; and though

[1] *Papers on Psycho-Analysis*, p. 233. Jones appears to have elaborated the hypothesis elsewhere, but I have not seen the fuller discussion, and should therefore hesitate to pronounce any more definite opinion on it than that given in the text.

[2] Ivan says: "I sometimes don't see you and don't even hear your voice as I did last time, but I always guess what you are prating, for it's I, *I myself speaking, not you*."—Dostoevsky, *op. cit.*, p. 688 (italics in the original).

this opinion has excited indignation, it has received confirmation so often and so unmistakably in the practical work of psychotherapy that there is no escaping it.

But even if we refuse, for good reasons or for none at all, to follow the psycho-analysts in this direction, we are still bound to admit that the idea of the devil has always been predominantly, though not exclusively, sexual. Ordinary speech betrays this pre-occupation of the mind: when we say simply that so and so is an *immoral* or *vicious* person it is ten chances to one that we mean a sexually immoral or vicious person. And when the devil was at the very top of his power over the popular imagination, in the Middle Ages in Europe, it was mainly his relation to sexual behaviour that gave him meaning. This is clearly indicated in the ecclesiastical writings. In mediæval belief man walked in constant peril on the earth. The sins that he committed and the unhappy accidents that befell him were alike the devil's work, and if the devil could not always get his due, in the eternal damnation of man's soul, he could at least make this world a place of irritation to the faithful. (This notion was not altogether an inconvenience. It enabled the abbot Richalmus to lay at the devil's door such unpleasantnesses as the itching of flea bites, stomach-ache after a heavy meal in the refectory, and unsteadiness in the legs following a bout of drinking.) Arrayed against the devil and eager to intervene on man's behalf, especially if asked, were the Virgin and the saints. If man fell into mortal sin and so forfeited his soul to the devil, the latter might still be cozened out of his bargain with the assistance of these higher powers. Now the surprising fact to notice is that in all five examples of the outwitting of the devil by the Virgin, the saints, or by the mere use of a sacrament of the Church, which Mr. H. O. Taylor selects as typical from the *Dialogi miraculorum* of Cæsar of Heisterbach, the *Exempla* of Étienne de Bourbon and Jacques de Vitry, and the *Miracles de Nostre Dame*, it is a sexual fault which the sinner who is saved from the devil has committed at his instigation. It is not to be supposed that sexual sins were the only dangerous sins in the eyes of the chroniclers. Yet it is surely not just an accident that the historian of *The Mediæval Mind*, who is not—like the present writer—attempting to prove a theory, should choose these as the best illustrations he can find of the mediæval attitude towards the devil and his ways. Such was the attitude of those who took sides against the devil. But he was not without followers, in those who renounced Christianity and gave themselves to his worship. Writing of this religion of the devil in her *Witch Cult in Western Europe*, Miss M. A. Murray maintains the thesis, I think successfully, that this religion was the survival of fertility cults immensely older than Christianity. "Looked upon in the light of a fertility cult," she says, "the ritual of the witches becomes comprehensible. Originally for the promotion of fertility, it became gradually degraded into a method for blasting fertility, and thus the witches who had once been the means of bringing prosperity to the people and the land by driving out all evil influences, in process of time were looked upon as being themselves the evil influences, and were held in horror accordingly."[1] Fertility cults are all based on the principle of sympathetic magic: however elaborate their rites may become in the passage of centuries, these can all be traced back to a common origin, the performance of the sexual act by a man and a woman in order that it may be *suggested* to animals and plants to bring forth their kind. The central fact in the ritual of the witch cult, to which all else was accessory, was *giving oneself to the devil.* The gift was of soul and body, and the devil, or his mortal representative, ratified the bargain in a forthright manner, by performing the sexual act with the devotee.[2] From this important part of the ritual grew the belief in incubi and succubi, so widely held in the Middle Ages,[3] the belief of which M. Anatole France makes such pleasant use in *La rotisserie de la reine pédauque.*

[1] *Op. cit.*, p. 24.

[2] Often, of necessity, as Miss Murray suggests, with an artificial phallus.

[3] It was fully set forth by Thomas Aquinas.

After what has been said it is not surprising to find the devil so often turned all to a jape in mediæval and later times. It is clear in the first place that he will not be accepted as laughable when he excites fear or hatred to the virtual exclusion of all other reactions. If the doctrines of the Church fathers had been rigorously adopted, that is to say, acted on at all times and places, it would have been impossible for the devil to play the large and amusing part he did in fabliau, morality, and interlude. It is only a devil who is not altogether terrifying or altogether hateful who can be used for comic purposes. The audience may be glad to see him worsted, because they have been taught to hate and fear him as the enemy of mankind. But before this gladness can be shot with laughter their hostility must be qualified by the belief that after all he is not so black as he is painted.

If the outline I have given of the psychogenesis of evil is accurate, it will be seen that this belief in the equivocal character of the devil is fundamental, and that if nothing special conduces to exaggerate one side or the other, the side of repulsion or the side of attraction, the attitude of the normal person when confronted with one whom he believes to be the devil in person, or an actor playing the devil, or when suddenly called on to react to a story in which the devil plays the leading part, will be truly ambivalent, and what is more, ambivalently sexual. The devil will appear both as an invitation to sexual behaviour and an obstruction of it. This is the best of all foundations on which to build up jests. Much of what the devil is set to do and suffer, in the fabliaux, in the moralities, and in the interludes, would be amusing if an ordinary person took his place. Much of the farce is simply knock-about, as between the devil and his attendant 'vice,' with his dagger of lath. The pitiful but boisterous incidents with which Marlowe endeavoured to mitigate the horror of *Doctor Faustus* would have set the groundlings in a roar even if Mephistophilis and his attendant imps had not been concerned. But we must recognize that there is something specially suitable in the devil for the provoking of laughter, the effect of which is missed if a mere man is substituted for him. For the devil contains within his own ambiguous person all the materials of laughter ready for use.[1] He has the power of simultaneously touching off deep-seated sexual associations and strong resistances to these associations. What more can a jester ask for?

[1] "The Devil is not, indeed, perfectly humorous; but that is only because he is the extreme of all humour."—Coleridge, *The Literary Remains*, vol. i, lect. ix, p. 138.

CHAPTER IX

SATIRE AND HUMOUR

Derision.

To a theorist like Mr. Max Eastman, for whom laughter "is a definite affirmation of hospitality and delight,"[1] derision presents a serious difficulty—or would do so, if he faced it. Instead of facing it, Eastman skips nimbly away from it. He blames philosophers for not clearly distinguishing laughter from the curling of the lip in scorn, and maintains that the temper of these two acts is opposite and their neural machinery distinct[2]; and he therefore dismisses the topic of scorn from his consideration of laughter.[3] This is very graceful and convenient, but, I am afraid, not very convincing. We have somehow to face the undoubted fact that we all resent being laughed at. The surest way to an understanding of this fact lies through an examination of satire.

The Genesis of Satire.

Satire is a weapon of offence, used originally for private quarrels. It is a weapon forged by hate.

Hate, as we have seen, is ultimately a derivative of love; it grows out of the frustration of love. But it may, on occasion, so possess a man as virtually to obliterate all signs of its connection with love. It is then as nearly whole-hearted as human behaviour can ever be. More usually, hate is restrained and modified, on the one hand by fear, and on the other by the reinforcement of its

[1] *The Sense of Humor*, p. 4.

[2] Why distinct? Because, says Eastman, we laugh with both sides of our face and sneer only with one!

[3] *Op. cit.*, pp. 6–7.

inherent love strain. The hater is then not so cocksure of his intentions; his whole behaviour is, or tends to be ambiguous. At some stage in the progressive modification of hate the ambiguity or ambivalence becomes manifest, for the hater begins to laugh at his opponent, instead of setting upon him with unmitigated vigour. To speak in metaphor, the love strain in his behaviour is now continually resting itself against one minor obstruction after another, and with their aid dams back the impulse of hate for an instant. With the bursting of the momentary dam comes the laugh.

The process by which the hater himself comes eventually to laughter is obviously much longer than that by which the mere spectators of a contest come to it. They are from the first in a position to take both sides, and are in fact compelled to take both sides to follow the contest properly. Their pleasure at a clever thrust by one party is given just that touch of bitterness which makes it the more welcome, by displeasure at the discomfiture of the other party; and when, on the balance, their attitude is impartial, or, to speak more accurately, oscillating, so that they are prepared at any time to agree that the better man should win, the watching of the contest may bring them regular bouts of laughter, as one side or the other gains a temporary advantage. Their suggested hostility fastens first on A and then on B, but even while it is fastened on A it is qualified both by present affection for B and by the active if unconscious memory of immediately past affection for A himself.

This primitive enjoyment by the spectator of a fight, as a fight, is to be traced in the most civilized of adults whenever a battle of the wits is in progress, provided the effect of this battle is to direct attention to the antagonists rather than to the things they say. During a philosophical argument the listener, however impartial he may be, has no leisure for laughter so long as his interest is absorbed by the matter in dispute. Yet sub-consciously he follows the debate, not as a search for truth, but as a contest between men, and any gesture or remark directing his attention to the disputants may lift his interest in them out of the sub-conscious, suspend for the moment his interest in truth, and set him laughing. In such circumstances it is always some direct or indirect personal allusion that releases the laugh.

With the growth of culture, however, the spectator becomes more exacting. He is less prone to enjoy a quarrel, simply because it is a quarrel; his moral training asserts itself, making him cautious lest he appear to lend support to an unjust cause. To overcome these scruples, to entice and hold a following, the satirist is compelled to make use of various devices. Almost invariably he must make it appear that his private quarrel is really a public one, that the individuals he is satirizing are enemies of the people or types of a recurring public danger. Instead of being only a private lampoon, satire then becomes the intimate concern of a group. Either it braces itself to the attack of some poet, like Euripides, or Addison, or Southey, some prominent statesman, like Cleon, or Shaftesbury, some representative of a numerous and powerful political or religious party, like Socrates the pretended Sophist, Zeal-of-the-land Busy and Hudibras the pretended Puritans, Gladstone the Home-Ruler, and Joseph Chamberlain the apostle of Tariff Reform; or, if the figures the satirist presents are not already well known, he must nevertheless invest them with a certain grandeur, and give them public standing, by the vigour and technical skill with which he turns them to ridicule. At the same time, as Mr. Chesterton has so justly pointed out,[1] the successful satirist must always show a certain respect for his enemies, and temper his attack upon them. It is not wise for him to pretend that they are wholly despicable persons; rather should he admit their good qualities, and on this admission, as on a background, paint in their bad. The result is not merely that the bad qualities stand out the more clearly; the mixture of bad and good renders the behaviour of the persons to whom the satire is addressed definitely ambivalent, so

[1] "Pope and the Art of Satire," in *Twelve Types*.

that their suggested dislike has to push always against the opposite tendency. Without this opposite tendency to be continually overcome there is no chance for laughter.

Supplementary Laughter in Satire.

Laughter is not the chief aim of the satirist, nor is the effect of great satire to provoke loud laughter. Indeed, the satirist, and the comic poet in the mood of the satirist, when laughter is their purpose, generally take care to precipitate it by incidents which are potentially laughable independently of the general satirical purpose, and which, when used to further that purpose, cause the behaviour of the audience to twist round, so to speak, upon itself. This may be illustrated from both Aristophanes and Anatole France. In the hilarious scene before the house of Pluto in *The Frogs* where Æacus attempts, by whipping them, to discover which of the two strangers, Dionysus and his servant Xanthias, is really the immortal, each blow as it is delivered comes as a shock to the spectators. And if our previous analysis is correct, the shock is of a peculiar kind, for whipping is unconsciously a sexual stimulus.[1] Yet in this case it is not so much the blows that matter as the responses they elicit from the victims; whoever cries out with the pain is to be set down the impostor. The force of the shocks is therefore carried over until the spectators hear what effect the blows have on god and man. It is the ejaculations of the whipped that release the laugh. But the effect of these is to show Dionysus in a ridiculous light. The spectators turn against him for the sorry rogue that he is. We may say, therefore, that the positive though aimless love behaviour,

[1] As the Greeks well knew. Only a few lines earlier in this scene Xanthias warns Æacus not to whip Dionysus with "scourges made of leek or young shalott." The reference here—the point of the joke—is to various ceremonial scourgings, incidents in fertility rituals. Thus, Pan's statues were beaten with squills, and the *pharmakoi* were beaten with squills and branches of the fig tree. Similar customs, again, were followed at the Roman celebration of the *Nonæ Caprotinæ*. See Gilbert Murray, note to this passage in his translation of *The Frogs* (p. 118), and Frazer, *The Scapegoat*, pp. 252 ff.

set going by the sexual stimulus of whipping, twists round and unites with the negative, and aimed, love behaviour, hostility to Dionysus. Together they explode. Again a similar effect may be observed in reading the story of the queen Glamorgane and the pious young monk Oddoul, as told by Anatole France in *L'île des pingouins.*[1] Glamorgane, having attempted to seduce the monk and been repulsed, turns against him, as Potiphar's wife turned against Joseph, and causes him to be shut up in prison, pending execution. The rest of the story must be told in the words of the original.

Mais Dieu ne souffrit pas que l'innocent pérît. Il lui envoya un ange qui, ayant pris la forme d'une servante de la reine, nommée Gudrune, le tira de sa prison et le conduisit dans la chambre même qu'habitait cette femme dont il avait l'apparence.

Et l'ange dit au jeune Oddoul :

— Je t'aime parce que tu oses.

Et le jeune Oddoul, croyant entendre Gudrune elle-même, répondit, les yeux baissés :

— C'est par la grace du Seigneur que j'ai résisté aux violences de la reine et bravé le courroux de cette femme puissante.

Et l'ange demanda :

— Comment ? tu n'as pas fait ce dont la reine t'accuse ?

— En vérité ! non, je ne l'ai pas fait, répondit Oddoul, la main sur son cœur.

— Tu ne l'as pas fait ?

— Non ! je ne l'ai pas fait. La seule pensée d'une pareille action me remplit d'horreur.

— Alors, s'écria l'ange, qu'est-ce que tu fiches ici, espèce d'andouille ?

Et il ouvrit la porte pour favoriser la fuite du jeune religieux.

Oddoul se sentit violemment poussé dehors. A peine était-il descendu dans la rue qu'une main lui versa un pot de chambre sur la tête ; et il songea :

— Tes desseins sont mysterieux, Seigneur, et tes voies impénétrables.

Let us neglect for the moment the continuous, ironical treatment of official Christianity in this passage, and take it simply as a tale of two women and a man. The dominant *motif* is obviously sexual, yet, let the moralists say what

[1] Bk. III, chap. i.

they will, we are conscious in reading it of a growing hostility towards the too pious Oddoul. This hostility is brought suddenly into clear focus by the ignominious drenching he receives at the end, an incident which is itself sexually determined. The full force of the reader's balked sexual behaviour is therefore turned against the virtuous monk; in our turn we repeat—with the proper 'distance' and with reservations—the violent change of front suggested to us by the actions of the queen Glamorgane and her disappointed maid Gudrune.

Satires on Religion.

This story introduces the topic of anti-religious satires, consideration of which makes still plainer what we may call the alternative moods of laughter. Anatole France's treatment of Christianity in *L'île des pingouins, La révolte des anges,* and incidentally in other works, is in the one mood, the treatment of the gods by Aristophanes, and of the angels and saints by the jongleurs, is in the other mood. If we approach Anatole France in the proper spirit, retraversing as best we can for ourselves the emotional paths which he has trodden, and of which he has left us the map in his pellucid and finely drawn prose, our prevailing mood is one of disbelief in the dogmas of the Christian Church, and of antagonism, subdued, ironical, well mannered, to all those persons, both human and supposedly divine, who have tried to force these dogmas on the world. That is the prevailing mood, and it is gentle. But dappling it is a lingering and haunting affection for just those same persons, human and supposedly divine, a shadowy regret that they were not right. How absurdly false is the belief in the efficacy of baptism! Yet—how absurdly attractive is the venerable Saint Maël! How quiet and untroubled is the old age of Pontius Pilate, in retirement in Sicily! He does not even remember the Jewish fanatic whom it was his official duty to condemn to death by crucifixion. But Anatole France, and we, remember; and the active memory, whatever may be our explicit religious opinions, flecks the serenity of the story with the shadow of blasphemy.

It is in another mood that Aristophanes pokes fun at the immortals, Dionysus, Herakles, Iris, very Zeus. Himself a conservative in temper, distrusting the Sophists because they were undermining the established convictions of the Athenians, Aristophanes had no intention of unsettling the religious beliefs of his people when he wrote *The Frogs* and *The Birds*. It is not to be supposed that he was a fervent believer in the gods; for all that he was no sceptic. It may be said, indeed, that his faith in Zeus was staunch enough to stand the test of a little ridicule thrown at the father of the gods and men. To recapture the Aristophanic point of view is for us difficult in the extreme. For better, for worse, Christianity has killed the religion of the Greeks, and Aristophanes, as someone has said, is "the hierophant of a now unapprehended mystery."[1] But we shoot wide of the mark if, because we find it difficult to believe, even for the playful purposes of comedy, in the divinity of Dionysus the coward, and Herakles the glutton, we imagine that Aristophanes did not believe in their divinity either.

Similar to the mood of Aristophanes is that of the jongleur who cracks a jest at the expense of Saint Peter, and the nameless poets of the Middle Ages who parody incidents in the Gospel story. One of the best of the fabliaux explains why no more jongleurs are allowed in hell. Time was when a jongleur was left in charge of the damned in that place of torment, and so far abused his trust as to gamble all their souls away to Saint Peter. Irritated at his bad luck with the dice, he boldly accused the saint of cheating, and pulled his carefully trimmed whiskers. Two metrical Latin poems of the Middle Ages are mentioned by Wright, in his *History of Caricature and Grotesque*.[2] One, entitled *Cœna*, is a parody of the wedding feast at Cana in Galilee. It tells of a great feast to which all

[1] I think this excellent phrase belongs by rights to J. A. Symonds, but I have lost the reference.

[2] Pages 45–7.

the famous persons in sacred history were invited. Moses came too late and had to stay outside, Esau and Paul had to stand, Job grumbled dreadfully because he was required to sit on a dunghill. After the feast each guest contributed to the entertainment, according to his ability:

> Tunc Adam poma ministrat, Samson favi dulcia.
> David cytharum percussit, et Maria tympana.
> Judith choreas ducebat, et Jubal psalteria.
> Asael metra canebat, saltabat Herodias.

In a MS. of the eleventh century is related how a certain man visited heaven and hell in a dream, and afterwards recounted his adventures there to the Archbishop of Mainz. In heaven he saw Christ sitting at a table eating, waited on by St. John the Baptist as butler, and by St. Peter as cook. The visitor does not appear to have been very hospitably received, for he sat in a corner, and when he saw his opportunity, stole a piece of liver, ate it, and departed. Unfortunately he did not keep this part of the story to himself, and the worthy Archbishop had the dreamer tied to a stake and flogged as a punishment for stealing from heaven!

When Anatole France writes of religious persons and creeds, then, he writes in the vein of satire. Thin and lingering wisps of belief pass like clouds, throwing pale shadows on the wide field of scepticism. It was otherwise with Aristophanes and the mediæval jesters. Their writing, when it treats of religion, is not properly in the vein of satire. They are not hostile for all their boldness; rather is their faith robust enough to withstand and enjoy the shock of the ludicrous.

Caricature and Parody.

It is a truism that the stock method of caricature is exaggeration. And as Gaultier has pointed out, of the two possible kinds of exaggeration, upwards or downwards, it is only the latter which excites laughter and is effective in caricature. "Pour faire naître le rire, l'exageration est . . . obligée d'enlaidir et de rabaisser la nature."[1] We need not follow him in the quaint explanation which he goes on to give of this fact. Ugliness, he says, is chosen not for its own sake but out of contrast to the ideal, " par colère d'idéal froissé."[2] " La charge, loin de provenir d'une condescendance au mal, ne rabaisse la nature que pour mettre mieux en évidence ce qui la sépare de l'idéal rêvé."[3] That this may ultimately be the effect of caricature is possible, though, I think, improbable; that it is the avowed or unavowed aim of the caricaturist, is certainly untrue. Caricature is an attack on an individual or an institution, and exaggeration downwards is simply a weapon of offence.

It is obvious that caricature and parody lose the greater part of their effect unless the original, or object of attack, is known, and unless the spectators already take, or can be persuaded by the artist to take, an interest in this original. Other things equal, the most laughable caricatures and parodies are those which 'take off' well-known persons or well-known works of art.

Now the interest taken in the original is, at least in part, either affection or the reverse. If it is affection, the attack of the successful caricaturist or parodist merely ruffles the surface, leaving the interest essentially unchanged; provided always the attack is not too fierce. We do not need to be of the same political party as the cartoonist to relish his political cartoons; nor do we need to be anti-Tennysonian to laugh at the innumerable parodies which have been made on his poems. " A lady of *bas bleu* celebrity," writes Isaac D'Israeli, in *Curiosities of Literature*, . . . " had two friends, whom she equally admired—an elegant poet and his parodist. She had contrived to prevent their meeting as long as her stratagems lasted, till at length she apologized to the serious bard for inviting him when his mock *umbra* was to be present. Astonished, she perceived that both men of

[1] Gaultier, *Le rire et la caricature*, p. 34.
[2] *Ibid.*, p. 35.
[3] *Loc. cit.* Cf. the opinion of Alfred Michiels, expressed in *Le monde du comique et du rire*, summarized in Appendix, pp. 262–3 below.

genius felt a mutual esteem for each other's opposite talent; the ridiculed had perceived no malignity in the playfulness of the parody, and even seemed to consider it a compliment, aware that parodists do not waste their talent on obscure productions; while the ridiculer himself was very sensible that he was the inferior poet. The lady-critic had imagined that PARODY must necessarily be malicious; and in some cases it is said those on whom the parody has been performed have been of the same opinion." [1] Nor, it must be confessed, have they been invariably wrong. If the interest in the original is often affection, and the caricature or parody only a mock attack or easily interpreted as such, the same effect for laughter may be achieved when the interest is chiefly hostility. But in this event, if a laugh is to be provoked, hostility must be limited by real or pretended affection.

It is surprising how much the effect of a parody of a poem, for instance, is enhanced by the reader's retaining a subconscious picture of the poet whose work is being parodied. There is no doubt that a good deal of the enjoyment which the nineteenth century took in parodies of Tennyson's work was due to this cause. The figure of Tennyson the man is fading now, and parodies of *Locksley Hall, The May Queen,* and *Break, Break, Break* lose some of their piquancy in consequence. Thus, when Mr. Stephen Leacock turned to the second of these famous poems, he wrote, not the usual kind of parody, on the poem itself, but a parody on Tennyson *and* the poem. This is entitled *How Tennyson killed the May Queen.*[2] Here is Part I:

As soon as the child's malady had declared itself the afflicted parents of the May Queen telegraphed to Tennyson: "Our child gone crazy on subject of early rising, could you come and write some poetry about her?"

Alfred, always prompt to fill orders in writing from the country, came down on the evening train. The old cottager greeted the poet warmly, and began at once to speak of the state of his unfortunate daughter.

[1] *Op. cit.,* p. 345. [2] *Literary Lapses,* pp. 227–8.

"She was took queer in May," he said, "along of a sort of bee that the young folks had; she ain't been just right since; happen you might do summat."

With these words he opened the door of an inner room.

The girl lay in feverish slumber. Beside her bed was an alarm-clock set for half-past three. Connected with the clock was an ingenious arrangement of a falling brick with a string attached to the child's toe.

At the entrance of the visitor she started up in bed. "Whoop," she yelled, "I am to be Queen of the May, mother, ye-e!"

Then perceiving Tennyson in the doorway: "If that's a caller," she said, "tell him to call me early."

The shock caused the brick to fall. In the subsequent confusion Alfred modestly withdrew to the sitting-room.

"At this rate," he chuckled, "I shall not have long to wait. A few weeks of that strain will finish her."

It is perhaps not unnecessary to add, as a reminder, that though the general effect of a caricature or a parody depends on reference to the original, the particular laughable details within it may be quite independent of this reference. A parody may well have an independent comic life of its own. Usually, of course, the dependent and the independent effects are too subtly interwrought to be consciously distinguished in the reading. Take, for instance, the following burlesque on Keats' ballad, *La belle dame sans merci*, ascribed by Walter Hamilton [1] to Bayard Taylor.

Oh, what can ail thee, seedy swell,
Alone, and idly loitering?
The season's o'er—at operas
No "stars" now sing.

Oh, what can ail thee, seedy swell,
So moody! in the dumps so down?
Why linger here when all the world
Is "out of town?"

I see black care upon thy brow,
Tell me, are I.O.U.'s now due?
And in thy pouch, I fear thy purse
Is empty, too.

[1] *Parodies*, vol. vi, p. 193.

"I met a lady at a ball,
Full beautiful—a fairy bright;
Her hair was golden (dyed, I find!)
Struck by the sight——

"I gazed, and longed to know her then:
So I entreated the M.C.
To introduce me—and he did!
Sad hour for me.

"We paced the mazy dance, and too,
We talked thro' that sweet evening long,
And to her—it came to pass,
I breathed Love's song.

"She promised me her lily hand,
She seemed particularly cool:
No warning voice then whispered low,
'Thou art a fool!'

"Next day I found I lov'd her not,
And then she wept and sigh'd full sore,
Went to her lawyer, on the spot,
And talk'd it o'er.

"She brought an action, too, for breach
Of promise—'tis the fashion—zounds!
The jury brought in damages
Five thousand pounds!

"And this is why I sojourn here
Alone, and idly loitering,
Tho' all the season's through and tho'
No 'stars' now sing!"

Here it is obvious that the story might easily have been made funny, apart from any reference to the original poem; it is simply a love story comically twisted.

Irony.

Of all the methods which satire may use none is more generally effective than irony; it is ambivalence reduced to a technique. For reasons that are somewhat obscure Eastman classifies irony under the humour of quantity, and contrasts it with exaggeration, which may also be the humour of quantity. Irony, he says, at first signified stating less than was meant, just as exaggeration signified stating more than was meant.[1] Yet immediately afterwards he admits that the two "cannot in many cases be distinguished." "And so by a little perceptive shift or casuistry any exaggeration may be viewed as irony, and any irony as exaggeration, and the view that actually prevails in a given example is not always easy to determine."[2] In the etymology of the word there is no hint of this quantitative significance.[3] Irony simply says one thing and means another, generally the opposite. Both what it says and what it implies are present to the minds of the audience, whose behaviour is thus determined in different, and generally opposing directions. When Gulliver visited the Academy of Lagado he professed to be greatly disturbed at the teaching of the professors of politics.

> In the school of political projectors I was but ill entertained, the professors appearing in my judgment wholly out of their senses, which is a scene that never fails to make me melancholy. These unhappy people were proposing schemes for persuading monarchs to choose favourites upon the score of their wisdom, capacity, and virtue; of teaching ministers to consult the public good; of rewarding merit, great abilities, and eminent services; of instructing princes to know their true interest, by placing it on the same foundation with that of their people; of choosing for employments persons qualified to exercise them; with many other wild, impossible chimeras, that never entered before into the heart of man to conceive, and confirmed in me the old observation, that there is nothing so extravagant and irrational which some philosophers have not maintained for truth.

In this passage it may be said the ironical intention is so evident that no reader can be deceived by it. True, no reader is ever permanently deceived by effective irony, for a pretence must be seen through. But a pretence misses fire altogether unless it is a continuous stimulus

[1] *The Sense of Humor*, p. 52. [2] *Ibid.*, p. 54.

[3] εἴρων, a dissembler.

to behaviour in the wrong direction, requiring the continuous stimulus to behaviour in the right direction to overpower it. Eastman quotes a saying of Mr. Dooley: "Ye thought he was a bad man, but I knew him for a single-minded innocent ol' la'ad who niver harmed anny man excipt f'r gain an' was incapable iv falsehood outside iv business." Could one imagine a more effective thrust at someone towards whom one was hostile?

The Sting in Laughter.

We are now better able to understand the displeasure we all feel on being made the object of laughter. The laugh betokens an interruption to behaviour that has been overcome, quickly, and with comparative ease—an interruption of a trivial kind. Strictly, the trivial interruption is within the behaviour of the laugher, but when the laugh seems to be aimed at us, the triviality passes over from the laugher to us, the supposed cause of it, making us, as we appropriately say, 'feel small.' This is no affair of reason, but of feeling. By taking thought we may satisfy ourselves that the triviality of which we are guilty is narrowly circumscribed, of no real consequence in comparison with all our other capacities for greatness. Then, reconstructing the incident, we may echo the laugh against ourselves, albeit more quietly. The same result is secured if the triviality is manifestly localized in some activity in respect to which we are not really auto-erotic. The golfer who does not pretend to be a cricketer, while he may well resent being laughed at for missing his drive at golf, is quite likely to join in the laugh against himself when he plays a wild golf stroke at cricket and sends the ball into the sky. The social utility of ragging is that it keeps vanity within bounds and teaches men to accept laughter against themselves, if not always without feeling it, at least without showing their feelings; the social danger of ragging is that it may also kill auto-erotism in respect to functions of which men ought to be proud. When men resent being laughed at, resentment does not wait to take thought. It is felt immediately, because it marks an obstacle, serious for the moment, thrown into the path of self-love.

Laughter, as we have seen, occurs in alternative moods, in a mood of love and in a mood of hate. The immediate effect of being laughed at is essentially the same into whatever context we fit the laugh: we feel belittled. Yet, obviously, the greater part of the sting may be taken out by the realization, at the time or afterwards, that the foolishness of which we have been guilty is no lasting impediment to the affection our friends bear us. "You may estimate your capacity for Comic perception," says Meredith, "by being able to detect the ridicule of them you love, without loving them less: and more by being able to see yourself somewhat ridiculous in dear eyes, and accepting the correction their image of you proposes." [1] It is when we interpret the laugh as evidence of hostility that it is so bitter. Partly this is due to its catching us unawares, unprepared to retaliate. Still more is it due to our recognizing, not perhaps explicitly, the equivocal character of the laugh, or, more accurately, the equivocal character of the behaviour of which the laugh is the outward sign. To be hated thoroughly is not always unpleasant. We know then what to expect, we are able to brace ourselves for the counter-attack. When the hatred is not thorough, and the attack of our enemy is not pressed home, we are thrown into uncertainty and confusion of feeling. Instead of saying bluntly: 'I hate you, and will do all I can to injure you,' the supposed enemy says, suavely: 'I hate you on the whole, but of course you have good points all the same which I am forced to admit.' That clouds the issue. It leaves us in the peculiarly helpless state of not knowing exactly what to do next, a state uniformly unpleasant to experience.

[1] *Essay on Comedy*, p. 78.

LAUGHTER AS A CORRECTIVE.

Since laughter is usually unpleasant to its object, the later result of it may be a change in the object. Few writers on the subject have failed to emphasize the corrective function laughter and comedy may exercise. Some few of the moralists, it is true, have been doubtful. Of these the most famous was Jean Jacques Rousseau, who expressed his doubts forcibly, eloquently, and for the time being effectively, in his *Lettre à M. d'Alembert*. Comedy, he says boldly, has never bettered the world. Less famous, yet even more emphatic, was the opinion of Victor de Laprade, who asserted that self-reform is much too difficult and serious a process to be effected by laughter.[1] But the burden of these moralists' complaints against the theatre was that comedy did not address itself to the reform of those failings which they most wished to see reformed. It cannot be seriously maintained that laughter—and comedy in so far as it depends on laughter—has no effect on the behaviour of those it is aimed at. There is only one sure way of avoiding the unpleasantness of being laughed at, and that is to avoid doing the things that laughter fastens on.

It does not follow, of course, that the laugher is always æsthetically, morally, or even socially right. The dust has settled now on the old controversy: Is ridicule the test of truth? It is to be hoped no one stirs it again. Ridicule is a test of what the laugher believes at the moment to be truth. Fortunately it is not the primary business of the psychologist to equate that with objective truth.

Nor does it follow that comedy is of necessity less disinterested than other forms of art. Arguing from the supposedly invariable corrective purpose of comedy, Bergson places it midway between art and Nature, in the zone of artifice.[2] Now it is not to be denied that the comic poet may sometimes be intentionally didactic. Then he seeks deliberately to bring about a change in the

[1] *Questions d'art et de morale*, p. 313. [2] *Laughter*, p. 66.

object he presents to himself. Often, it is true, such a motive has very little to do with his work, while it is in the making, and is only thought of afterwards, when he is called to account for his work. So it was with Molière. As an artist, the comic writer has no concern with any such motive. Art is achieved by the postponement of all those external reactions to an object, which, if immediately carried out, would result in a change in it, or in the artist's relation to it. If the comic poet shows men their form and image, it is well; his work as artist is done. If they, in their turn, not liking the form and image they are shown, set about to change themselves for better or for worse, that is strictly not the artist's affair. He cannot prevent their changing, and indeed as one who, besides being an artist, has to live a practical life among them, he may well be glad to see them change. But change is no part of his artistic purpose. In his capacity as artist he is content with men as they are, and it is just this contentment which impels him to place his impressions of them on record, so that others coming after him may enjoy impressions as nearly similar as possible. This is art in its pure or essential form. Men may not always attain to it, and may not always strive to attain to it. They may allow the beliefs of practical life to mingle with the beliefs of art, they may insert too little 'distance' between themselves and the object. There are degrees in art.

It is a mistake, however, to suppose that because the satirist always and the comic writer sometimes are hostile to the objects they present to themselves, therefore this hostility implies intention on their part to have these objects removed or altered in some respect. It no more implies this intention than the love of another artist implies his intention to approach closer to the object of his love. It is not true to say with Bergson, "In laughter we always find an unavowed intention to humiliate, and consequently to correct, our neighbour, if not in his will, at least in his deed."[1] Humiliation and correction

[1] *Op. cit.*, p. 136.

are practical motives. The laugher may be governed by neither, or he may be governed by the first without being governed by the second. It all depends on the degree to which he is able to become an artist. In truth, the functioning of hostility brings the maximum of assured pleasure just when it is suspended at the point of passage into overt action. If the behaviour of the artist oversteps that boundary, he plunges at once into the turmoil of practical life, where he must take his chance with others and suffer displeasure that is not always of his own choosing. If he stops short at that boundary, he remains master of his own feelings, immune in a magic circle that he has drawn round himself and that none other may enter except at his free beckoning.

HUMOUR.

Few English words have had a more interesting history than the word 'Humour,' and few in everyday use are given more hack work that is not their business. The history of the word has been written often and well, and I do not propose to rewrite it here. Nor do I propose to discuss the subject itself at any length, for that, too, has been done fully and adequately, twice at least in English. The *locus classicus* on humour is Meredith's *Essay on Comedy*; to this Sully has added most of what was still left to say, in the concluding chapters of his *Essay on Laughter*. My purpose here is only to show the bearings of their views on the general theory of laughter set forth in this book.

Speaking of the ridiculous person: "If you laugh all round him," says Meredith, "tumble him, roll him about, deal him a smack and drop a tear on him, own his likeness to you and yours to your neighbour, spare him as little as you shun, pity him as much as you expose, it is a spirit of Humour that is moving you."[1] "The humorist of mean order is a refreshing laugher, giving tone to the feelings and sometimes allowing the feelings to be too

[1] *Op, cit.*, p. 79.

much for him. But the humorist of high has an embrace of contrasts beyond the scope of the Comic poet. . . . The stroke of the great humorist is world-wide, with lights of Tragedy in his laughter."[1] Humour, says Sully, epigrammatically, "is a kind of binocular mental vision. . . . We enjoy pensively the presentation of Don Quixote, of Uncle Toby, and the other great humorous characters just because we are in a mood in which, while giving ourselves up to an amusing spectacle, we nevertheless embrace in our reflective survey, and are affected by, something of its deeper meaning."[2]

The fact of humour presents an insuperable difficulty to all those theorists who treat laughter as an affair of the intellect alone, and who understand by the intellect something into which emotion does not enter. Humour being more characteristic of the English than, perhaps, of any other European people, purely intellectual theories of laughter have been more common in France and Germany than in England, and so far as they are to be found in England at all, date especially from the eighteenth century, the century in which Englishmen were prone to be afraid of their own emotions. The most emphatic statement of the intellectualist position is that of Bergson. "The comic," he says, "appeals to intelligence pure, and requires a temporary anæsthesia of the heart."[3] This, after all, is only a twentieth-century paraphrase of Horace Walpole's epigram: "The world is a comedy to those that think, a tragedy to those who feel." Now it has been many times pointed out,[4] that this generalization may hold in the main for classical French comedy, for the comedy of Ben Jonson, and for the comedy of Congreve, but that it breaks down immediately we attempt to apply it to the comedy of Shakespeare, Fielding, Sterne, and Dickens in English, Cervantes in Spanish, and Rostand in French.

The truth is that if, in an examination of laughter, we

[1] *Op. cit.*, pp. 83–4.
[2] Sully, *op. cit.*, p. 302.
[3] Bergson, *op. cit.*, p. 5.
[4] By Meredith, Sully, and Palmer especially.

start with the laugh as an emotional experience, there is no great difficulty in reaching the laugh of Molière, from which all emotion *seems* sometimes to have been evaporated; whereas, if we begin with Molière, by no means can we reach over to the laughter of Cervantes at Don Quixote or even to that of Anatole France at l'Abbé Coignard. Actually, of course, it is wrong to suppose that emotion has been entirely evaporated out of the laughter of Molière.

Purely intellectual behaviour, by which is meant behaviour that contains no feeling, is quite mythical. Man is so constituted that whatever he does, he feels as he does it; this is true whether he passionately kisses his beloved on the lips or dispassionately thinks out a problem in higher mathematics. The difference, in terms of feeling, between these two kinds of behaviour is real enough, but in accounting for this difference we must move from love to mathematics and not from mathematics to love. A man may love a woman, or sing a love song, or write a scientific treatise on the instinct of sex. In the first case, his conduct is said to be emotional; in the second, to be still emotional, though intellect is presumed to have some small share in it; in the third, to be unemotional, intellect alone being active. When a man does nothing but think, his emotions are supposed to be having a rest. When he does nothing but love, it is his intellect that is supposed to be having a rest. This would be a most convenient arrangement, if it were possible. Unfortunately, it does not happen.

Thinking is never just thinking; it is always thinking *about* something. The something thought about may be vague enough, but it is always related immediately or mediately to the impulses which drive man to action. The force of thought is the force of instinct, nothing more and nothing less. Loving a woman and thinking about love seem utterly different kinds of behaviour. Fundamentally they are the same behaviour, to be classified under the instinct of love. Progress from the one to the other is made by the process of *leaving out*. Loving a woman is love on the plane of practice; the behaviour is as complete as possible, in respect to all its responses. The whole organism is implicated. Singing a love poem is love projected on to the plane of art; the behaviour is considerably thinned down, for the object towards which it is addressed has been pushed away into the distance, and most of the characteristic overt responses of the behaviour have been arrested. Thinking about love is love projected on to the plane of science; the behaviour is still further thinned down, its object has receded to a still greater distance, the remaining overt responses have been arrested, and an indefinite number of the internal responses also. Organic resonance is at its minimum. Out of life, which is present action, is developed art, which is the arrest of outward action, and out of art is developed science, which is the arrest of outward and a great part of inward action. Nevertheless, just as art and science grow out of action, which is the beginning, so they point towards action, which is the end. Art is nearer to practical life; it carries the preparations for the completion of behaviour to a more advanced stage; like life, it still deals with the concrete. In science the completion of behaviour is so remote that sometimes it is hardly envisaged at all; the preparations are like those made for a journey that may never be taken, or like those made by one person for a journey to be taken by another; science deals with the abstract, which is the concrete denuded of just those qualities which most strongly tempt to immediate action.

As behaviour is thinned down, feeling is thinned down too. The man who holds his beloved in his arms thrills through every nerve.[1] The man who only thinks about the love of "the male" for "the female" has but a limited number of nerves in action, and the consequent thrill, it must be confessed, is a trifle weak. Yet for all that, feeling remains essentially the same in both cases.

[1] Physiologically, it might be more accurate to say 'nearly every nerve.' It would be interesting if the physiologists could tell us roughly *how* many.

Be it extensive or narrow, behaviour that succeeds is felt as pleasant, behaviour that fails is felt as unpleasant.

After this shameless digression it is time to return to humour. Having refused to admit the possibility of pure intelligence, devoid of feeling, or of pure intelligence that is not driving along in the path of some instinct, we should not find it difficult to relate the so-called unemotional laughter of high comedy to the obviously emotional laughter of Shakespeare picturing the deathbed of Sir John Falstaff. Just as there is no hard line between practical life and play, or between play which is not art and play which is, so there is no hard line between art and science. High comedy is nearer to science than romantic comedy; it tends, by special devices, to insert more 'distance' between us and the characters in it. Artistic distance may be increased or diminished in a variety of ways; the tragic writer, for instance, raises his hero above the level of common humanity, so that the audience shall respond to him not simply as to one like unto themselves, but as to one greater than themselves in those capacities they yet share with him.[1] The comic writer has other methods. Some of these have been already discussed in an earlier chapter; two more are indicated by Bergson. Speaking of comedy in general, to which his remarks do not strictly apply, instead of limiting himself to high comedy, to which they do apply, he says that the comic writer lulls the sensibility of the spectators, first by isolating the specially comic quality in the comic character, giving it thereby a kind of independent existence; and second by directing the spectators' attention to gestures rather than to actions.[2] The effect of both these methods is, in Bergson's opinion, to intensify the illusion of mechanism—a conclusion we may take the liberty of doubting. What is less open to doubt is

[1] How difficult it is to produce the proper tragic illusion unless the *circumstances* of the tragic character are also raised above the common level may be illustrated from Mr. Masefield's *Nan*; it is excessively difficult to write a tragedy about a wash-house.

[2] Bergson, *op. cit.*, pp. 140 ff.

that the effect of both these methods is a diminution of concreteness in the comic character. Instead of being rounded and complete, a true *person*, such a comic character is shown, as it were, in only two dimensions. You cannot step round behind him, for he always rotates on his vertical axis so as to present himself to you, full face. A continuation of this tendency of high comedy would lead, on the one side, to a substitution for comic persons of true abstractions or types—analogous to the abstractions of science, the electron, the colloid, the instinct, for example—and, on the other side, to such a rarefication of the spectators' emotions that it is much to be doubted if laughter could be traced with anything less delicate than a galvanometer. To be contrasted with this are the many-sidedness of the humorous character, and the consequent wide responsiveness of the humorist. The humorist comes into touch with his characters at almost as many points as he would were they real persons. And, more than this, he comes into touch with their different sides not successively, as in real life, but simultaneously. In practical affairs we are concerned at any one moment with only what is relevant to our immediate business; we neglect the rest. As soon as we are relieved of the need to carry our behaviour to its normal conclusions, we are enabled to pack more into it. There is no hurry, and we can both take in a wider range of vision, and examine every part in more detail. An apt illustration of this is given by Mr. Roger Fry. "I remember," he says, "seeing in a cinematograph the arrival of a train at a foreign station and the people descending from the carriages; there was no platform, and to my intense surprise I saw several people turn right round after reaching the ground, as though to orientate themselves; an almost ridiculous performance which I had never noticed in all the many hundred occasions on which such a scene had passed before my eyes in real life. The fact being that at a station one is never really a spectator of events, but an actor engaged in the drama of luggage or prospective seats, and one actually sees only so much as will help to the appropriate action."[1] To be an artist is to be a spectator, and of all spectators the great humorist has the widest range of vision.

To know all is to pardon all, for to know all is to be responsive, to be sympathetic. The strict meaning of sympathy is responsiveness to suggestion, as shown in feeling. By a further development of the word—a development with which the French equivalent has not kept pace—it has come to be specially applied to suggestively induced sorrow, in this sense being equivalent to pity, compassion, commiseration. This development in meaning of the word 'sympathy' might be taken as the outline of the development of the humorist. Widely responsive to the varied behaviour of men, emotionally quick at all points, he comes at the last to show as the most striking feature in his attitude a large pity for the follies, the weaknesses and the sufferings of mankind. Thus Walter Pater, writing of Charles Lamb, speaks of humour as proceeding from the amalgam of mirth with pity.[2] And it is this readiness of the humorist to respond out of the largeness of his heart simultaneously to the joyous and the grievous, and to mix his laughter with his tears, that seems so natural to the illogical English and so preposterous to precise thinkers of the Latin races.

Yet, if our analysis of laughter is correct, the amalgam of pity with mirth is not perplexing at all, for pity is love obstructed by sympathetic displeasure, often by sympathetic pain. The continuous chequering of love by displeasure, sympathetically induced, is the first condition of humour. The humorist does not dissipate our pity, but urges us to rise above it by taking a wider view. The sting of pity is gone, for the mere event that provokes it is set in a context of relations that takes us beyond it.

[1] "An Essay in Æsthetics," in *New Quarterly*, vol. ii, 1909.
[2] *Appreciations*, p. 108.

The great humorists do not laugh. They are too fully occupied. But the possibility, the tendency, of laughter is in them, because they gaze steadily on the contradictions of life, its pleasures and distresses, and their love for man is trammelled.

CHAPTER X

WIT

THE text for this chapter is Professor Freud's *Wit and its Relation to the Unconscious*, and what I have to say is little more than a commentary, sometimes a criticism, on special points brought out in that astonishing book, which is undoubtedly the fullest and most illuminating work yet published on the subject.

Two Kinds of Wit.

Developing a distinction already made, though not in precisely the same words, by previous German writers, Freud distinguishes two main species of wit, which he calls harmless wit and tendency wit. Harmless wit, he considers, is enjoyed for its own sake; it manipulates words and manipulates thoughts for the pleasure to be got from such manipulation; it serves no purpose beyond itself; it is not aimed. Tendency wit, while it makes use of the same techniques as harmless wit, and thereby produces similar pleasure, is, in addition, serving a sexual or a hostile impulse—a sexual or a hostile *wish*, to use the misleading Freudian term—and thus, in so far as this impulse is satisfied, reaches to deeper sources of pleasure than mere technical manipulation. Above all, it is aimed at some person or group of persons.

This distinction appears self-evident. I believe, however, that it is false, for reasons which I hope to give in the sequel. I believe that harmless wit is like Sairey Gamp's alleged friend, Mrs. Harris—nothing but a convenient fiction.

The Tendencies of Wit.

Leaving this question open for the present, let us consider what Freud has to say about tendency wit. The kernel of his book is here, as all his critics, friendly and unfriendly, have recognized. Indeed, some of his followers, in their ardour, have elaborated what he has said into something much wider in scope. There is no necessary harm in so doing, provided the responsibility is not laid on him; but it is to be feared that not all the Freudians have been as careful in this respect as they should have been. For instance, in his book, *The Freudian Wish*, Mr. E. B. Holt writes: "After reviewing the long list of theories and definitions of humour, which is as dense a jungle of misconception as anywhere exists, Freud caps them all with his simple formula that every form of wit or humour is nothing but a means of 'letting the cat out of the bag.' But what cat, what bag, and what are the means? The cat is one of those suppressed wishes, the bag is the confinement imposed by the vigilant censor, and the means are a variety of devices to trick the censor, particularly by taking advantage of the latter's weak points."[1] Whether this is a true summary of what Freud ought to have said of 'every form of wit or humour' might, presumably, be discussed; it is certainly not a true summary of what he actually has said. To begin with, Freud does not review a long list of theories and definitions of humour, but confines himself strictly to examining a few—a very few—definitions of *wit*; and throughout his book he is careful never to confuse wit with the comic or with humour. It is only his conclusions on tendency wit which could be legitimately summed up in the formula: 'Letting the cat out of the bag,' and it is only of this species of wit that we are justified, if we wish only to interpret Freud and not to develop our own views, in describing the cat, the bag, and the means of letting the one out of the other, in the lively fashion of Holt.

[1] *Op. cit.*, pp. 17–18.

Tendency wit, then, on Freud's view, is either sexual or hostile, either a sexual advance or a more or less vigorous attack. If the word *love* is substituted for the word *sex*—for reasons I indicated in the third chapter—I have no comment to make on this, the central thesis of Freud's book, beyond accepting it, and acknowledging the real debt I owe to him for enunciating it so clearly and supporting it with such a wealth of instance. I do not wish to go laboriously over the same ground as he has already traversed with a light heart and a vigilant eye, because the reader, be he psychologically trained or not, who is not to be convinced by Freud's reasoning, is not likely to be convinced by anything I could add to it, and it is a great deal better that anyone interested in the discussion of the question, and not already familiar with Freud's work, should make himself familiar with it at first hand without further delay, than that he should waste time over a second-hand and probably inadequate transcript from me. I propose to take it as proved, therefore, that tendency wit, whatever other characteristics it may have, is either love behaviour, or hate behaviour, or an uncertain compound of both, and that the primary satisfaction of such wit is the satisfaction of love or hate impulses. It may also be remarked in passing, that hate impulses seem to predominate on the whole.

Eluding the Censor.

So much for the *cat.* The *bag,* Holt says, is the confinement imposed by the vigilant censor.

This concept of the endopsychic censor is attractive, and, pragmatically at any rate, of considerable value. It does seem to tell us something useful, when we say that the love or hate impulses which we have found to be at the root of wit are denied crude expression by the action of an agent, like a censor, who sub-edits unconscious wishes to make them conform to the laws of conscious life. Yet I think the majority of psychologists, especially in England and France, agree with the late Dr. W. H. R. Rivers that this concept has serious drawbacks. It is "based on analogy with a highly complex and specialized social institution. . . . It would be more satisfactory if the controlling agency which the facts need could be expressed in some other form. Since the process which has to be explained takes place within the region of unconscious experience, or at least on its confines, we might expect to find the appropriate mode of expression in a physiological rather than a sociological parallel. It is to physiology rather than to sociology that we should look for the clue to the nature of the process by which a person is guarded from such elements of his unconscious experience as might disturb the harmony of his existence."[1] This suggestion goes to the root of the matter. The most hopeful line of advance for psychology is towards physiology. Our physiological knowledge may be still too meagre to tell us much of what happens when we behave in particular ways, and we are therefore forced to go on using very general, and very vague, concepts, like feeling, intelligence, the unconscious, psychical 'distance,' and so forth. These concepts, when honestly used, are confessions of ignorance, as well as confessions of faith. Nothing is to be gained, and a great deal is to be lost, if we mask our ignorance by choosing metaphors and analogies that point in the wrong direction, when we might instead have chosen those that point, no matter how indecisively, in the right direction. The social sciences are still notoriously unstable, and this instability is infectious. It is only too common, as the history of the psycho-analytic movement shows, for metaphors and analogies to be carriers of the infection.

Yet if we refuse, for prudential reasons, to adopt Freud's concept of the endopsychic censor, we cannot refuse to admit the facts this concept is intended to cover. Impulses, especially perhaps those of love and hate, are prevented from running a smooth course by counter-forces from within as well as from without behaviour. These sometimes inhibit impulses altogether, sometimes

[1] Rivers, *Instinct and the Unconscious*, 2nd edition, p. 229.

stop them before they have gone far towards satisfaction, sometimes merely hinder them. Of the counter-forces from within behaviour, it is those a man feels no shame in acknowledging, those by which he attempts to regulate his waking life, which Freud indicates by the term 'endopsychic censor,' and which Rivers alternatively and more convincingly proposes to indicate on the analogy of the higher (genetically more recent) levels of the nervous system controlling and transforming the lower (genetically older).

Tendency wit is aimed love or hate behaviour which has been obstructed in some way, but the obstruction to which has been circumvented. It enables us to make love or to attack, surreptitiously, in situations where open, frank, unrestricted love-making or hostility would be dangerous, or at the very least unpleasant. The concept of the censor, applied to wit, emphasizes those occasions when the obstruction is internal, when the author of the witticism is restrained by the counter-forces of modesty, kindliness, and so on. And in the last resort the obstruction is always internal, though it is sometimes primarily external. An example of a witticism struck off against mainly internal resistances has already been given in an earlier chapter. With a person of average culture—even in Vienna, a city that strikes the Englishman as somewhat lax in its morals!—it would be well-nigh impossible, bluntly and publicly, to proffer the advice: 'If your wife does not satisfy your sexual needs, find a prostitute.' It would not merely shock the audience, it would shock the author before he could get it said. The internal resistance, however built up, would be too strong. But the temptation to say it being strong also, this cynical remark assumes a disguise, and slips out in the form: 'A wife is like an umbrella, at the worst one may take a cab.' By disguising itself it has become wit—of a kind. Its very obscurity in the new form is a sign of the strength of the resistance it had to get past.

Again, the obstruction may begin by being external to the author. If we make love wittily to a woman, she may let it pass; the return stroke of her modesty is parried. If we set about it more plainly, she may summon her husband or her brother to trounce us. To attack a man with wit is to snipe at him from behind a pile of sandbags; his possible superiority to us in the open need not greatly disturb us.

Besides, not only is wit aimed, it is generally intended to be overheard. The author must have his audience as well as his victim in mind, and must dodge or overpower the resistances in them which would otherwise throw them into opposition to him. It may be that Samuel Butler (the elder) had no personal scruples preventing him from belabouring the Puritans without stint, but in writing *Hudibras* he had to think continually of his readers. Few of them would have been fanatical enough to go on reading an attack on the Puritans, unless it were tricked out with fantastic rhymes, the thin, momentarily deceptive pretence of irony, and other graces of verse supererogatory to the topic. If no other resistance had to be overcome, there was at least the resistance of boredom, one of the most constant from which the reading public of the Restoration suffered. What courtier of Charles II, be he never so indifferent, could resist having his fling at Hudibras, as a representative of his class, when he read what Butler had to say of his religion?[1]

> For his religion, it was fit
> To match his learning and his wit:
> 'Twas Presbyterian true blue;
> For he was of that stubborn crew
> Of errant saints, whom all men grant
> To be the true church militant;
> Such as do build their faith upon
> The holy text of pike and gun;
> Decide all controversies by
> Infallible artillery;
> And prove their doctrine orthodox,
> By apostolic blows and knocks;
> Call fire, and sword, and desolation,
> A godly, thorough reformation,

[1] *Hudibras*, Part I, Canto 1, ll. 189–218.

Which always must be carried on,
And still be doing, never done;
As if religion were intended
For nothing else but to be mended:
A sect whose chief devotion lies
In odd, perverse antipathies;
In falling out with that or this,
And finding somewhat still amiss;
Most peevish, cross, and splenetic,
Than dog distract, or monkey sick;
That with more care keep holy-day
The wrong, than others the right way,
Compound for sins they are inclin'd to,
By damning those they have no mind to:
Still so perverse and opposite,
As if they worshipp'd God for spite.

Usually, of course, it is not simply the tendency of his readers to be bored that the witty author has to get past. When he is attacking some public person, he must forestall the resentment of his victim's acquaintances, even though he risks the resentment of his victim's friends. This has been already discussed in the chapter on satire, but I cannot refrain from quoting, as perhaps the finest example in English, Pope's famous lines on Addison. It is hostile wit at the highest reach.

But were there one whose fires
True genius kindles, and fair fame inspires;
Blest with each talent and each art to please,
And born to write, converse, and live with ease;
Should such a man, too fond to rule alone,
Bear, like the Turk, no brother near the throne,
View him with scornful, yet with jealous eyes,
And hate for arts that caus'd himself to rise;
Damn with faint praise, assent with civil leer,
And without sneering, teach the rest to sneer;
Willing to wound, and yet afraid to strike,
Just hint a fault, and hesitate dislike. . . .
Like Cato, give his little senate laws,
And sit attentive to his own applause;
While wits and templars every sentence raise,
And wonder with a foolish face of praise—
Who but must laugh, if such a man there be?
Who would not weep, if Atticus were he?

Harmless Wit.

It is very easy to give examples of tendency wit; it is very difficult to give examples of really harmless wit, in Freud's sense of that term. The idea itself is elusive. It is very difficult to give any psychological meaning to the statement that harmless wit is pursued for its own sake. Indeed, the more one thinks over the idea of harmless wit, as developed by Freud, the more incomprehensible it gets. Implicated in it are the ideas of intellectual behaviour as being somehow of a radically different kind from all other kinds of behaviour, somehow exempt from the impulses that stir to manifest action, and of words being able to give pleasure by some mysterious quality in them which is not associated with their meaning. Such ideas appear to me to be altogether at variance with the fundamental ideas on which Freud's psychology rests, and I can only account for his retaining the notion of harmless wit on the assumption that he has failed in this particular case rigorously to apply the solvents he has so fearlessly applied on other occasions.

In the hope, perhaps forlorn, of clearing up the difficulty, let us take four examples of wit, cited by Freud. The first two illustrate tendency wit, which has been already discussed, the second two would, presumably, be classified by him as harmless. The four are given here together for purposes of comparison.

Wendell Phillips, according to a recent biography by Dr. Lorenzo Sears, was on one occasion lecturing in Ohio, and while on a railroad journey going to keep one of his appointments met, in the car, a number of clergymen returning from some sort of convention. One of the ministers, feeling called upon to approach Mr. Phillips, asked him: "Are you Mr. Phillips?" "I am, sir." "Are you trying to free the niggers?" "Yes, sir; I am an abolitionist." "Well, why do you preach your doctrines up here? Why don't you go over into Kentucky?" "Excuse me, are you a preacher?" "I am, sir." "Are you trying to save souls from hell?" "Yes, sir, that's my business." "Well, why don't you go there?"

Two unscrupulous Americans succeeded in amassing a large fortune, and then attempted to establish themselves in good society. They had their portraits painted by one of the leading artists of the day, had them hung side by side on the wall of a salon, and gave an evening reception to show them off. Among the guests was a celebrated art critic, who was asked by the two plutocrats to give his expert opinion on the portraits. After examining them carefully for a long time, he pointed to the bare space of wall between them, and asked: "And where is the Saviour?"

Commenting on the saying: "Never to be born would be best for mortal man," the *Fliegende Blätter* remarked: "But hardly one man in a hundred thousand has this luck."

"January," said Lichtenberg, "is the month in which one extends good wishes to his friends, and the rest are months in which the good wishes are not fulfilled."

The first two of the above examples need not delay us. There is no doubt about the arousal and gratification of a hostile tendency, or tendencies, against definite persons figuring in the stories. It is the third and fourth examples which call for elucidation. If the wit here is not harmless, what tendencies can it be said to arouse and gratify? If it is not aimless, against whom can it be said to be aimed? Let us take the two examples separately, and, at the risk of explaining them away—a risk to which we should by this time have grown thoroughly accustomed—try to describe what happens in us when we hear them for the first time.

The first effect of the editorial comment in the *Fliegende Blätter* is to send us back to read again the original statement that called it forth. This original statement has an assured air of wisdom about it, warranted to carry the casual reader over it the first time, at least, without his realizing its inherent absurdity. It seems to enunciate a profound, if melancholy, truth. It is the aim of the editorial comment to slip behind this solemn façade, and expose the emptiness behind. Now this emptiness having been exposed, it is a hundred chances to one that the next act of the reader will be to ask himself, or any one else who is convenient, who the would-be philosopher was who was first guilty of this pretentious nonsense. It is not at all necessary that this question should be answered, in order that we may appreciate the joke. But the fact that it should rise so immediately into consciousness is, I believe, significant; because it indicates the general directions of the reader's behaviour as he fastens on the point of the joke. Somewhere, as a kind of vanishing point towards which the lines of his behaviour converge, is the misty figure of 'a pseudo-philosopher,' and just as the draughtsman is able after a very little practice to draw correctly in perspective without first marking down precisely the vanishing point in which his lines would meet if produced, so after a very little practice in wit we are able to behave accurately towards a given witticism without knowing anything more about the person against whom it is aimed than simply that he exists.[1] We lend him all the character he needs to have for our immediate purposes, out of our experience of similar pseudo-philosophers whom we have known more intimately in the flesh, and we work off on him, whether he deserves it or not, some of our ready antagonism to all those who set themselves up to be wiser men than we are, yet turn out in the event to be less wise. We load the sins of his fellows upon him for our pleasure.

In reading Lichtenberg's witticism our behaviour appears more obvious, but is actually less so. This witticism carries more in it, as if in a state of solution, than a mere crude psychological litmus test will show. It is capable of being interpreted in three ways: either as a gibe at Fortune, the personified sum of forces that sometimes help and sometimes hinder man in his lawful and unlawful endeavours; or as a flicker of humorous compassion for man the hindered; or, more prosaically, as a polite thrust at those gushing people, whose acquaintance we share with Lichtenberg, and whose charity is mostly verbal. Which is the correct interpretation?

[1] It is, of course, no matter if he be really dead. He is alive to us, in the same way as Polonius is alive when we are engaged in reading *Hamlet*.

Properly speaking, all three are correct, for the psychological content of any statement is the sum of meaning that is in fact taken out of it, whether that agrees or not with the meaning the author intended should be taken out of it. I conjecture that in first reading this witticism we are vaguely aware of all three of these interpretations as possible, though we may not bring any one of them into clear focus and decide that it is the objectively correct interpretation. And it is probably due to this uncertainty on our part that our behaviour carries on beyond the point of the witticism, and continues to *use*, in puzzling the thing out, some at least of the energy that might have escaped in laughter, had it been less complex. However that may be, there seems little doubt that in reading this, as in reading the former witticism, we are fumbling after persons of one kind or another, in order that we may gratify hostile impulses towards them. And this, if Freud's words are to be taken strictly, is what harmless wit does not do.

It may be objected that, even supposing the above analysis, wire-drawn as it sounds, to be accurate, yet a great part of wit consists in nothing more subtle than a bandying to and fro of words, words being treated for the nonce as independent entities. Children, it would seem, handle words very much as they handle their toys, tossing them about, catching them, turning them round and over, setting them in queer and unaccustomed postures, lopping off pieces from them, and patching them again with odds and ends taken from other words that do not properly belong to them; and grown men and women —especially perhaps men—in the mood of play revert to these childish habits, and toy with high-sounding or fantastic words, 'pour rien, pour le plaisir.' As the late Professor Sir Walter Raleigh said somewhere, writers have not merely to find words for a meaning, but sometimes also to find a meaning for words; for words sometimes roll sonorously off the tongue or snap viciously as they are spoken, imposing themselves for the mere sound of them and compelling the writer, willy nilly, to take them into his service. In so far as this juggling with words constitutes wit, it is usual to dismiss it as 'intellectual play.' Unfortunately, however, that does not dispose of it.

It may be said bluntly at once that there is no possibility of divorcing the sound of words from their meaning in the fashion indicated. Ultimately, their sound is part, and a strikingly important part, of their total meaning. But accepting for the moment the usual distinction between sound and meaning, we may say that both children and adults, especially children, are incapable of treating words as mere sounds. Whenever we examine the tricks children play with words we discover unmistakably that the meaning of the words they seem to toss about so carelessly is always present in the back of their minds. It may be, objectively, quite a wrong meaning, but that is immaterial. It is meaning for the child. The flurry of words is amusing to the child himself because he realizes that he is misusing them, and in order to realize that, he must have some sort of notion of what the correct use, for him, would be. If he suddenly takes a fancy to call every article on a dining-table a plate, he is yet well aware that 'plate' is not the correct name for a pepper caster, even though he may not know that 'pepper caster' is. His purpose in miscalling common objects is simply to tease his elders. His wit, such as it is, is aimed, and what is amusing to him is the effect it has on his adult relatives. On other occasions, it is true, the intention to tease may be absent, and a child, having been attracted by a word, may apply it promiscuously and laughingly, whatever may be the observed effect on other people. But it is safe to say that what is then amusing to him is the visual imagery called up by the misapplication of the word. And that, for psychology, is meaning, whatever it may be for logic.

Passing to adults, we may well pause for a moment to discuss the pun, that poor relation in the family of wit, so often buffeted and despised. According to Kuno Fischer, as quoted by Freud, a pun is a poor form of wit because it does not really play on words but only on the sound of words. A real play on words "transfers itself from the sound of the word into the word itself."[1] I confess that the distinction between a play on words and a pun is somewhat too finely drawn for me to follow. To do nothing but play on the sound of words a pun would have always to be made in a foreign language we did not understand, and then we should be blissfully ignorant that it was a pun. You may, if it pleases you to be critical, call a pun a bad play on words, but all plays on words, good or bad, depend for their effect on the conjunction of similar sound with different meaning, and require us to attend to both sound and meaning. The goodness or badness of the play on words consists, not in the words abstractly taken, but in what they signify. It is the situation they suggest that contains the possibility of laughter, and it is the business of the witty technique, directing attention to similarity or identity of sound, to touch off this laughter.

When a pun misses fire, one of three things must have happened. Either the audience has failed to *imagine* the situation the pun hints at; or this situation, when imagined, has turned out not to be a laughable one; or too much effort has had to be expended in picking up the similarity of sound on which the pun depends. Failure to imagine the situation may be the fault of the audience or the fault of the punster. Their minds may be too sluggish, or he may not have said enough. To get the full effect of a pun it is sometimes necessary to amplify it. No one knew this better than Charles Lamb, himself an inveterate punster. In discussing *Popular Fallacies*, No. 9—'That the worst puns are the best,' he repeats a favourite joke of Swift's.

> An Oxford scholar, meeting a porter who was carrying a hare through the streets, accosts him with this extraordinary question: "Prithee, friend, is that thine own hare or a wig?"

Lamb undertakes to defend this pun against possible critics, and it is highly instructive to notice how he sets

[1] Quoted by Freud, *op. cit.*, p. 56.

about his task. With the sharp visual imagination of an artist he *expands the situation.*

> There is no excusing this [he says] and no resisting it. . . . We must take in the totality of time, place, and person; the pert look of the enquiring scholar, the desponding looks of the puzzled porter; the one stopping at leisure, the other hurrying on with his burden; the innocent though rather abrupt tendency of the first member of the question, with the utter and inextricable irrelevancy of the second; the place—a public street not favourable to frivolous investigations; the affrontive quality of the primitive enquiry (the common question) invidiously transferred to the derivative (the new turn given to it) in the implied satire; namely, that few of that tribe are expected to eat of the good things which they carry, they being in most countries considered rather as the temporary trustees than owners of such dainties, which the fellow was beginning to understand; but then the wig again comes in, and he can make nothing of it; all put together constitute a picture: Hogarth could have made it intelligible on canvas.

"The totality of time, place, and person"—therein lies the secret which was revealed to Lamb, which is an open secret to every artist, but which is denied to every theorist on wit who searches for it, with his eyes shut, in such phrases as 'the sound of words,' 'the technique of words,' or 'playing with words for their own sake.'

When a situation is too tragic, or too intense for laughter to be a normal reaction, a pun will either be overlooked altogether by the audience, or, if noticed, will jar unpleasantly on their ears. How many ordinary readers are aware, while reading, of that ghastly jingle in her words, when Lady Macbeth, after the murder of Duncan, says:[1]

> If he do bleed,
> I'll gild the faces of the grooms withal;
> For it must seem their guilt.

And of those readers who have noticed this of their own accord, how many have not felt it to be one of those unpardonable conceits to which Shakespeare, like the other Elizabethans, was only too prone? This pun,

[1] Act II, Scene 2.

however, has been defended, and I believe justly, on the ground that in situations so intense as that in which Lady Macbeth had placed herself, situations which strain the mind to the verge of insanity, there is a tendency for it to catch wildly at jingling words, as if in a forlorn attempt to lower the tension by following out their associations. If that is true, the reason why the reader who notices the pun is offended at it, is simply that he is failing to re-live the experience of Lady Macbeth, even artistically, as Shakespeare lived it. The reader's behaviour is at once too intense and not intense enough for a pun to be accepted.

The Technique of Wit.

In conformity with his distinction between harmless and tendency wit, Freud is compelled to make the technique of wit account for its own laughter, or, at the least, for its own pleasure. After examining this technique in great detail, and classifying it in the most exhaustive way, he comes to the conclusion that what is characteristic of it is " a compressing or—to be more exact—an economic tendency."[1] The parenthesis strikes me as most unhappy. If Freud had left the matter at " a compressing tendency," adverse criticism would have had little to pounce on. By transposing " compression " into " economy " he has secured not the greater accuracy he desired, but greater confusion.

He has to admit, first, that not every economy in expression is witty, and second, that the economy is often more apparent than real. " The economies of wit," he says, very aptly, " remind one of the manner in which many a housewife economizes when she spends time and money to reach a distant market because the vegetables can there be had a cent cheaper. What does wit save by means of its technique? Instead of putting together a few new words, which, for the most part, could have been accomplished without any effort, it goes to the

[1] *Op. cit.*, p. 50.

trouble of searching for the word which comprises both ideas. Indeed, it must often at first transform the expression of one of the ideas into an unusual form until it furnishes an associative connection with the second thought. Would it not have been simpler, easier, and really more economical to express both thoughts as they happen to come, even if no agreement in expression results? Is not the economy in verbal expression more than abrogated through the expenditure of intellectual work?"[1] These questions are pertinent; Freud does not answer them immediately after asking them, and when he returns to them at a later stage in the book he still fails to answer them satisfactorily. Pleasure in harmless wit, that is to say pleasure in the technique of wit considered by itself, may be traced, he supposes, to economy in psychic expenditure. In plays on words, for instance, the technique consists in "directing the psychic focus upon the sound instead of upon the sense of the word, and in allowing the (acoustic) word disguise to take the place of the meaning accorded to it by its relation to reality."[2] Again: "If we experience in wit an unmistakable pleasure because through the use of the same or similar words we reach from one set of ideas to a distant other one . . . we can justly refer this pleasure to the economy of psychic expenditure."[3]

I confess I do not understand what this means. Nor am I much helped by consideration of Freud's own examples of plays on words. A witticism of which he is very fond—not without reason—and which he quotes more than once, is the one levelled against Napoleon III when he saw fit to confiscate the estates belonging to the House of Orleans. As it was one of the first acts of this Gilbertian emperor after coming to his throne, some obscure wit remarked of it: "C'est le premier vol de l'aigle." This is far from being harmless wit; Freud would not for a moment pretend that it is harmless; but, according to his view, the pleasure to be had from it is not to be traced to one source only, but rather to

[1] *Op. cit.*, p. 53. [2] *Ibid.*, p. 181. [3] *Ibid.*, p. 182.

two sources. It is pleasure from successful hostility to Napoleon III, *plus* pleasure from the technique, and this latter pleasure would seem to be due to our saving psychic expenditure by passing easily and quickly from the idea of flight to the idea of theft, the bridge for this passage being the word *vol,* which contains both ideas.

The apparent economy in this and similar witticisms is not in dispute; one word is made to do duty for two ideas. But it is quite incorrect to suppose that this apparent economy corresponds to any real economy of psychic—or psycho-physical—expenditure. On the contrary, it would seem to require additional expenditure, and that, not simply on the part of the author of the witticism, but on the part of the reader also, whose behaviour is a quick repetition of the author's, instigated and helped out by him. Whether we take the author or the reader, behaviour has, so to speak, to cover the ground three times, instead of twice; once to catch the first meaning of *vol,* once to catch the second, and yet once again to realize that both meanings have been compressed into a word, or, rather, that two words with different meanings have exactly the same sound. The rapidity with which the third operation is carried out must not disguise from us that it is actually carried out against habit, and therefore, comparatively, with an effort. It is quite true, as Freud alleges, that children incline to expect the same meaning from words with the same sound, but it is not true that adults have any such normal inclination. A child is still listening, or tending to listen, to the sound of words, as is an adult when he is straining his ears to follow a conversation in a foreign language he does not know very well. But in everyday speech adults do not pay attention to the sound of their own language—unless, of course, there is some special reason why they should. They hear the sound of words, but do not listen to it. Their habit patterns are set, the words are heard subconsciously, sometimes unconsciously, behaviour passes instantaneously to meaning, and it is there that attention is fixed. In listening to wit one must always let behaviour run its course up to the point when meaning is apprehended, since, to be effective, wit obviously must be *understood*. And in wit which involves a play on words attention must pause twice instead of once; it must pause on meaning and it must pause on sound. And that, quite simply, requires additional effort.[1]

The misconception of wit as economizing psychic expenditure arises through confusion of speed with force. We have it on good authority that brevity is the soul of wit. A really effective witticism does its business in a flash. But speeding up behaviour in this way is not the same as economizing effort; quite the contrary. More has to be got through in a given time, and that can only be done, in human behaviour as with a piece of machinery, by increasing the pressure in it. It is precisely for this reason that wit is notoriously fatiguing.

This speeding up of behaviour prepares for laughter, though in itself it cannot provoke laughter. It compels us to have ready more psycho-physical energy than usual, and that is a predisposing condition for laughter. It only remains to apply the match and explode the charge.

A Word on Metrical Technique.

I have purposely refrained from making a detailed examination of the techniques of wit, for the same reason that I refrained from discussing at length the tendencies of wit: it has been so well done already by Freud. And though I do not agree with him that the various techniques are all designed to economize psychic expenditure,

[1] How difficult it is to break into firmly established habit patterns in this respect is strikingly illustrated in a tonic language, like Chinese. Sounds which the unpractised European ear accepts as identical, so far from being accepted as identical by illiterate Chinese, are heard by them as *totally different*, because the meaning of these sounds is totally different. In other words, they hear the slight, tonic *difference* in sound, and are incapable of listening to the great *similarity* in sound. For example, *ma* (in the third tone) means *horse*, *ma* (in the fourth tone) means *hemp* (in Pekingese). Being entirely preoccupied with this difference in meaning, the illiterate Chinese farmer will probably refuse to admit any similarity whatever in sound between these two words.

I am full of admiration for the way he has analysed and classified them. I wish only to add a word on metrical technique in relation to wit, confining myself entirely to English verse.

It is generally agreed that the wittiest period in English poetry is that which stretches roughly from Waller to Goldsmith, and that of all the poets during this hundred odd years the greatest, in respect to those qualities which were then most valued, chiefly the qualities of wit, was Alexander Pope. This is not to say—as I should be unwilling to do—that Pope was a greater poet than Dryden, but only that he was a more witty poet than Dryden or than any of his contemporaries. I think this would be admitted to be what the lawyers call 'common ground.' Now it was Pope who brought the decasyllabic, antithetical, rhymed, and end-stopped couplet to its highest pitch of technical perfection, and it is 'common ground' also that this verse-form, whatever may be its limitations, has been proved, chiefly by the use Dryden and Pope made of it, to be unsurpassed for the purposes of satire, which depends very largely on hostile wit. It might be plausibly argued also that it is unsurpassed for wit in its other tone, and the polite badinage of *The Rape of the Lock* might be quoted in support of this argument. But something might be said against such an opinion, and I am not concerned to press it. What is certain is that English satires which have used other verse-forms than the heroic couplet have on the whole suffered in effectiveness thereby. Byron was a trenchant satirist, and had a witty tongue; but, striking as *The Vision of Judgment* and *Don Juan* are in these respects, one cannot help regretting that he cast them into *ottava rima.* Jokes in the body of the stanza are apt to miss-fire; it is only when they are saved up till the end and brought out with a snap in the concluding couplet that they hit the mark unerringly.

The heroic couplet has been found, then, empirically, to be the most appropriate for wit—at least for hostile wit. It is worth while trying to give some psychological account of this fact. It may help us to clarify our ideas on wit in general.

And first a word on rhyme. It is usual, when psychologists undertake to discuss rhyme, to describe the pleasure in it as resulting from the discovery of the familiar at a time when the unfamiliar is to be expected. That may be so, but it is not the point I wish to make at present. I think it is too often overlooked that in the best verse it is not merely the words which rhyme. The chiming of the words marks the chiming of that which the words signify. The great metrists seem to secure, in some subtle way—too subtle for the prosaic psychologist, I am afraid—that thought shall rhyme with thought, when word rhymes with word. At any rate, whether this is intentional or not, the result of coming on the rhyming word is to send the reader back for an instant to the word in the earlier line with which it rhymes, and therefore to the thought of which that word and its fellows are the signs. When it is a rhyming couplet that is concerned, this return of the thought upon itself is much more clearly marked than if lines rhyme alternately. The rhyme acts as a binder. It is as though we took an extra turn of a rope round the bundle of thoughts contained in the couplet, and jerked it tight.

End-stopping the couplet is the logical development of this tightening up, for if the couplet enjambs with the next, the rope is at once loosened again. Running the couplet on into a triplet, and expanding the last line of the couplet into an alexandrine have a similar loosening effect on the couplets that immediately follow, for these devices break into the habit sequence we have developed of turning back at the end of each second line to take the extra twist of the rope round the bundle. When Pope took over the heroic couplet from Dryden, enjambment, triplets, and alexandrines were permissible 'licences,' and by no means infrequent. When he handed on the heroic couplet to his successors, these 'licences' were looked on with disfavour.

This compagination of the couplet made brevity essential. Each bundle, before being laid neatly in its place, had to be complete in itself, and there were only twenty syllables to do it in. Words had to be rigidly economized, and economy of words—though not economy of psychic expenditure—is essential for wit.

A still more rigid economy of words could have been secured, it is true, by dropping two syllables in each line, and turning the verse into rhymed octosyllabics, the form of *Hudibras*. Indeed, it is quite possible, with many of Pope's lines, and with many more of the lines written by his successors, to resort to this pruning without apparently spoiling the sense at all. Among the lesser poets of the Popian school the *gradus* epithet became a hopeless vice. But Pope frequently used these otherwise redundant syllables, and used them for the very purposes of wit. Somtimes it was to clamp the two lines of the couplet still more securely together, more often it was to throw the two halves of a line into opposition. These tricks are only too well known.

Exactly similar in its effect to the last-mentioned device is Pope's regular marking of the cæsura towards the middle of the line. The falling apart of the line into two approximately equal halves encourages the antithetical character of the thought. And that again is of the nature of wit, for while wit must be brief, it must also contain opposition within itself. It must be compact, but if it is an attempt to make love, the attempt must be partly concealed and partly revealed, and both the concealment and the revelation must be evident; while if it is, as Pope's wit generally was, an attack, it must be a defence as well, and both attack and defence must be plain to the reader.

The Relation of Wit to Laughter.

In the light of the preceding chapters of this book, the relation of wit to laughter should be clear. At much of the world's finest wit we do not laugh at all. But the general conditions of laughter are always present, namely, love behaviour interrupted, or hate behaviour restrained, and it depends only on the particular conditions of each witticism whether it shall provoke broad laughter, a gentle smile, or no observable reaction at all. In considering the circumstances in which a pun may missfire, I have already touched on some of these particular conditions which are important for the provocation, or otherwise, of the actual laugh. What is true of the pun is true also, *mutatis mutandis*, of other forms of wit. The author of the witticism must say enough to enable the audience to imagine the situation the witticism hints at, but he must say it elliptically too, or attention is not sufficiently stimulated and pressure in behaviour is not raised high enough. The imagined situation, even though it be of the proper kind, namely a love or a hate situation, must not, once it is imagined, be felt as too intense. It was said also that similarity in sound, on which a pun depends, must not be too difficult to pick out. This remark may now be expanded, so as to take in all the rest of wit. Whenever wit requires that attention shall be paid to the sound of words as well as to their meaning, it is imperative, if laughter is to follow naturally and not simply be forced out by politeness, that this fixing of attention shall take place easily and rapidly.

At the best it calls for additional effort on the part of the listener; it must not call for too severe an effort. Similarly, the fixation of attention on meaning must be rapid and accurate. It is not enough that we should 'blunder round a meaning,' we must catch it as it flies. It need not, as I said before, be objectively correct; it is possible crudely to misunderstand a witticism and still find it amusing. But it must have a sharp and clearly cut meaning for us, however much that misrepresents the intention of the author.

This is only a lumbering way of saying that we must be able immediately to see the point of the joke—not perhaps a very profound remark. But the reason for this plain fact of experience seems to be that the energy at work in following a witticism must suddenly find nothing more to do, before we have had time to adjust ourselves to this new condition of affairs. If we have to continue blundering round a meaning, or straining our ears to catch the sound of the words that we missed at the beginning, we are still using up the energy the author intended us to have at our disposal for a laugh. That is what Kant meant when he said that, for laughter, expectation must be transformed into nothing, and not into the positive opposite of expectation.[1] We must come to something like a dead stop.

"Wit is made, while the comical is found," says Freud,[2] a statement which is epigrammatic, inaccurate, but suggestive. The laughable is that to which we react with momentarily obstructed love or hate behaviour. It is always made by the person who finds it, for the process of finding is of necessity a process of making. But it may also be reproduced for the benefit of others, and the reproduction may take a variety of forms. It may be in words, or paint, or stone, or in a musical score. Wit is a rapid, outline reproduction in words of a laughable situation. What distinguishes it from other forms of comic writing is its brevity, its speed.

[1] *Critique of Judgment*, p. 225.

[1] *Op. cit.*, p. 289.

CHAPTER XI

CONCLUSION

SINCE the bulk of this book was written, Professor R. S. Woodworth has published the best modern text-book on psychology for many years. Of our subject he says: "The most difficult question about laughter is to tell in general psychological terms what is the stimulus that arouses it. We have several ingenious theories of humour, which purport to tell; but they are based on adult humour, and we have as yet no comprehensive genetic study of laughter, tracing it up from its beginnings in the child.[1] . . . One thing is fairly certain: that, while laughing is a native response, we learn what to laugh at, for the most part, just as we learn what to fear." [2]

It may be that the theory I have put forward is merely one more ingenious addition to the many that have preceded it into the shades. But this at least may be claimed for it, that it starts where it should, with the behaviour of children. Examination of the earliest laughter of infants leads to the conclusion that the essential element in the situations provoking it is personal. This in turn suggests that the laugh is a response within the uncertain and ill-coordinated behaviour of the instinct of love. It appears to arise within such behaviour when an obstruction of some kind is first encountered, and then, no matter how, suddenly overcome; it marks the escape of psycho-physical energy mobilized to meet the obstruction, but not actually required for that purpose, and therefore for the moment surplus.

Love is primary, hate is a secondary development out of it; and laughter passes over from the one to the

[1] Woodworth has overlooked Sully's *Essay on Laughter*.
[2] *Psychology, a Study of Mental Life*, pp. 157–8.

other. Yet it never gains that security within the secondary behaviour that it has within the primary, and occurs in a mood of hate only when that mood is equivocal, ambivalent, restrained by a counter-force of love.

I have attempted to trace this double strain in laughter from its simplest to its most complex manifestations; from the smile of the infant in his cradle, to the highest and most ethereal forms of adult wit and humour. At every turn we come, directly or indirectly, on love associations. Some of these are manifest, and would be admitted even by the laugher; others, not so certain, are more or less unconscious, and would probably be denied by the laugher, were they suggested to him by an outside observer of his behaviour. Nevertheless—to put it at the lowest—from whatever side we make our approach, we accumulate evidence pointing to the intimate connection between love and laughter.

Are we to conclude that this connection *might* always be established by analysis? Yes. But this is not to pretend that the analysis is always easy. In a thousand instances we know far too little about the past of him who laughs. All traces of how the connection was first made may have disappeared beyond recall. Dreams may furnish us with hints; hypnosis may assist us still further; but at the last we may well be left with only vague conjectures. There is no end to the obscure and roundabout ways in which stimuli come to be substituted one for another in human existence.

And so the last word, on this as on so many other occasions, is with Bergson. "Many a comic form, that cannot be explained by itself, can indeed only be understood from its resemblance to another, which only makes us laugh by reason of its relationship with a third, and so on indefinitely, so that psychological analysis, however luminous and searching, will go astray unless it holds the thread along which the comic impression has travelled from one end of the series to the other. Where does this progressive continuity come from? What can be the driving force, the strange impulse which causes the comic to glide thus from image to image, farther and farther away from the starting-point, until it is broken up and lost in infinitely remote analogies? But what is that force which divides and subdivides the branches of a tree into smaller boughs and its roots into radicles? An inexorable law dooms every living energy, during the brief interval allotted to it in time, to cover the widest possible extent in space. Now, comic fancy is indeed a living energy, a strange plant that has flourished on the stony portions of the social soil, until such time as culture should allow it to vie with the most refined products of art." [1]

[1] Bergson, *Laughter*, p. 65.

APPENDIX

THEORIES OF LAUGHTER AND COMEDY: A HISTORICAL SUMMARY

THE following pages contain a summary, without criticism, of opinions on laughter and comedy, as expressed by philosophers, poets, critics, and psychologists, from Plato to Mr. Max Eastman. It follows chronological order, and is intended merely for reference. It is by no means complete, particularly in respect to German works. I have tried to make it accurate, so far as it goes, but I should be sometimes sadly at a loss to explain precisely what some of the philosophers, particularly again the German philosophers, mean by statements I have none the less quoted. In the hope that they may perhaps be clearer to others, I have set them down, whether I understand them or not.

PLATO is the first to maintain that malice or envy is at the root of comic enjoyment. Self-deception, or the vain conceit of beauty, wisdom, or wealth, when it is powerful, is to be hated; when it is feeble, and unable to do hurt to others, it is ridiculous and to be laughed at. We laugh at the misfortunes of our friends, and our feeling is mixed pleasure and pain.[1]

"To make a jest of a man is to vilify him in a way," says ARISTOTLE,[2] and comedy should avoid satirizing individuals. "Comedy is . . . an imitation of characters of a lower type [than tragedy]—not, however, in the full

[1] *Philebus*, 47–50.
[2] *Nicomachean Ethics*, iv, 8, 9. (Peters' translation.)

sense of the word bad, the Ludicrous being merely a subdivision of the ugly. It consists in some defect or ugliness which is not painful or destructive. To take an obvious example, the comic mask is ugly and distorted, but does not imply pain."[1] On this very slight foundation an enormous superstructure has been built by later writers, as will be seen in the sequel. Aristotle promised to speak more fully of comedy 'hereafter,'[2] If he ever did so, the passages are lost. But, "taking account of the elements which enter into the idea of beauty in Aristotle, we shall probably not unduly strain the expression [ugliness], if we extend it to embrace the incongruities, absurdities, or cross-purposes of life, its blunders and discords, its imperfect correspondences and adjustments, and that in matters intellectual as well as moral."[3]

CICERO starts from the position of Aristotle. "The ground and as it were the province of the ridiculous . . . lies in a certain baseness and deformity."[4] "All matter for ridicule is therefore to be found in such defects as are observed in the characters of men who are not esteemed, nor in miserable circumstances, nor deserving to be haled to punishment for crimes; such topics neatly handled excite laughter. Jests may be nicely turned also on deformity and bodily defects."[5] Cicero notes also that the defeat of expectation occasions laughter. Summing up, he says: "For it is by deceiving expectation, by satirizing the character of others, by making fun of our own, by comparing a thing with a worse, by pretending,

[1] *Poetics*, v, 1. (Butcher's translation.)
[2] *Ibid.*, vi, 1.
[3] Butcher, *Aristotle's Theory of Poetry and Fine Art*, p. 375.
[4] "Locus autem et regio quasi ridiculi . . . turpitudine et deformitate quadam continetur."—*De Oratore*, ii, 58.
[5] "Quam ob rem materies omnis ridiculorum est in eis vitiis, quæ sunt in vita hominum neque carorum neque calamitosorum neque eorum qui ob facinus ad supplicium rapiendi videntur; eaque belle agitata ridentur. Est etiam deformitatis et corporis vitiorum satis bella materies ad iocandum."—*Ibid.*, ii, 59.

by talking seeming nonsense, and by reproving follies, that laughter is stimulated." [1]

QUINTILIAN doubts if anyone has sufficiently explained laughter.[2] It is, however, always associated with something low (humile). It may take any of six forms: urbanity (urbanitas), gracefulness (venustum), piquancy (salsum), pleasantry (facetum), jesting (iocus), and verbal attacks (dicacitas). "Resemblances conduce most to jests, especially if the allusion is to something meaner and slighter." [3] Following Cicero, he calls attention to the laugh that arises from surprise, or the deceit of expectation, and from the turning of another person's words to express a meaning not intended by him. These are the happiest jokes of all. [4]

All the Italian critics of the Renaissance derive what they have to say on laughter and comedy from the fragmentary remarks of Aristotle, and from the practice of Plautus and Terence. The contemporary *comedia dell'arte,* which might have helped them to complete their theories, was beneath their notice. Thus, TRISSINO makes it the function of the comic poet to represent base actions so as to condemn them. Laughter, he says, comes from the pleasure we take in what is 'low.' [5]

[1] "Exspectationibus enim decipiendis et naturis aliorum inridendis [ipsorum ridicule indicandis et] similitudine turpioris et dissimilatione et subabsurda dicendo et stulta reprehendendo risus movetur."—*Ibid.*, ii, 71.

[2] "Neque hoc ab ullo satis explicari puto, licet multi tentaverint."—*De Institutione Oratoria*, vi, 3.

[3] "In his maxime valet similitudo, si tamen ad aliquid inferius leviusque referatur."—*Loc. cit.*

[4] "Superest genus decipiendi opinione, aut dicta aliter intelligendi, quæ sunt in omni hac materia vel venustissima."—*Loc. cit.*

[5] "Il poeta comico imita le azione peggiori e al solo scopo di condannarle. Come la tragedia consegue il suo fine colla misericordia e colla tema, così la comedia l'ottiene col dileggiare e biasimare le cose brutte e cattive; ma essa non imita ogni sorta di vizi, sibbene quelli che sono ridicoli; cioè, azione comiche di caratteri vili ed oscuri. Il riso vien da diletto e da piacere che si prova di cose che partecipano di brutezza; noi non ridiamo di una bella donna, di una magnifica gioia o di una suave musica; ma una faccia brutta e distorta, una parola sciocca, un movimento goffo ci fa ridere. . . . Onde possiamo conchiudere che un male piccolo, cioè non doloroso ne mortifero, che vediamo in altri e che non crediamo sia in noi ci reca più che tutto piacere o riso."—

MAGGI, who wrote a treatise *De Ridiculis* (1560), modifies the standard Aristotelian maxims by adding the idea of surprise, already noted by Cicero and Quintilian. We do not laugh at the painlessly ugly which is familiar, but only at that which is new and unexpected.[1] MUZIO, writing in 1551, deplores that the comic poets of his day were more intent on making men laugh than on correcting their manners; but MINTURNO (1564), somewhat unexpectedly, takes a milder view, saying that laughter is not to be deprecated.[2] The great SCALIGER (1561) directs attention to form, defining the comic poem as "a dramatic poem made of intrigues, in popular style, and with a happy ending."[3]

In France, PELLETIER and DE LAUDUN take up practically the same position as Scaliger.[4]

A forerunner of Descartes, the French physician JOUBERT, who published his *Traité du ris* in 1579, though unable to break away completely from Aristotle, approaches the problem of laughter from the side of physiology, and hits upon some fresh notions of real value.[5] He defines the ridiculous in the orthodox manner as "something ugly or unseemly, which is at the same time unworthy of pity or compassion," but he qualifies this by remarking that our laughter at the ridiculous has some sadness intermixed with it.[6] The faculty of laughter is not in the brain, but in the heart. "When an object at once pleasant with drollery and sad with ugliness presents itself, the heart is stirred very quickly and unevenly because it wishes to make at the same time two contrary movements, the one of joy, and the other of

Trissino (1563), quoted by J. E. Spingarn, *Literary Criticism in the Renaissance*, Italian translation, 1905, p. 101.

[1] Spingarn, *op. cit.* (English edition), p. 103.

[2] *Ibid.*, p. 104.

[3] *Ibid.*, p. 105.

[4] Pelletier, *Art poétique* (1555), and De Laudun, *Art poétique françois* (1598), quoted by Spingarn, *op. cit.*, English edition, pp. 200, 204.

[5] Not having seen the original (to my great regret), I am dependent on Mr. Eastman's summary in *The Sense of Humor.*

[6] Eastman, *op. cit.*, p. 139.

sorrow. Each one is short, through being suddenly interrupted by its opposite which obstructs the path: at the same time the dilation surpasses the contraction, as in the ridiculous there is always more pleasure than pain." [1] Joubert also connects laughter at the ridiculous with laughter at tickling. "The strange touch brings some pain and annoyment to the parts unaccustomed to it, but being light it causes some kind of false pleasure, namely, that it does not truly offend, and that nature enjoys diversity." [2]

The theories of English writers of the same century, as distinct from the practice of English poets (Jonson chiefly excepted), were nearly identical with those of the Italians and the French, being based on the same sources.

THOMAS WILSON follows Cicero and Quintilian. He honestly confesses his inability to say what laughter is.[3] Its occasion, however, is "the fondness, the filthiness, the deformitie, and all such euill behauiour, as we see to be in other." [4] Wit lies in speaking what is 'clean contrary' to expectation.[5]

GEORGE WHETSTONE praises Menander, Plautus, and Terence, and falls foul of all modern comic poets, of the Italians, French, and Spaniards because they are too lascivious, of the Germans because they are too holy, and of the English because they are "most vaine, indiscreet, and out of order." "To worke a Comedie kindly, graue old men should instruct, yonge men should show the imperfections of youth, Strumpets should be lascivious, Boyes unhappy, and Clownes should speak disorderlye: entermingling all these actions in such sorte as the graue matter may instruct, and the pleasant delight; for without

[1] Eastman, *op. cit.*, p. 212.
[2] *Ibid.*, p. 213.
[3] *The Art of Rhetorique* (1560), reprint 1909, p. 135.
[4] *Loc. cit.*
[5] *Passim.*

this chaunge the attention would be small, and the likinge lesse."[1]

The aim of comedy is clear, according to Sir PHILIP SIDNEY, and is not to excite laughter. "Comedy is an imitation of the common errors of our life, which he [the comic poet] representeth in the most ridiculous and scornefull sort that may be; so as it is impossible that any beholder can be content to be such a one." Comedy handles "the filthiness of evil" in "our private and domestical matters."[2]

Sir JOHN HARRINGTON puts the same opinion in a sentence, urging "that comedies may make men see and shame at their own faults."[3]

BEN JONSON leaves his readers in no doubt as to the theory on which he wrote his own comedies. "The parts of a comedy are the same with a tragedy, and the end is partly the same; for they both delight and teach; the comics are called διδάσκαλοι of the Greeks no less than the tragics."[4] This being the general purpose of comedy, laughter is accessory only. "Nor is the moving of laughter the end of comedy, that is rather a fowling for the people's delight, or their fooling"; and of the work of those poets who, like Aristophanes when he hangs up Socrates in a basket, write for laughter and not to instruct and inform, he says: "This is truly leaping from the stage to the tumbril again, reducing all wit to the original dung cart."[5] The subject matter of comedy should be, first, *real*—

—deeds, and language, such as men do use:
And persons such as comedy would choose,

[1] "Dedication to 'Promos and Cassandra,'" (1578) in *Elizabethan Critical Essays*, ed. Gregory Smith, vol. i, p. 60.

[2] "An Apologie for Poetry" (1591), in *Elizabethan Critical Essays*, vol. i, p. 177.

[3] "A Brief Apology for Poetry" (1591), in *op. cit.*, p. 210.

[4] "Timber, or Discoveries" (1641), in *Works*, Gifford's edition, vol. iii, p. 422.

[5] *Loc. cit.*

> When she would show an image of the times,
> And sport with human follies, not with crimes:[1]

and, secondly, *humorous.* He is careful himself to explain what he means by *humour.*

> It may, by metaphor, apply itself
> Unto the general disposition:
> As when some one peculiar quality
> Doth so possess a man, that it doth draw
> All his affects, his spirits, and his powers,
> In their confluctions, all to run one way,
> This may be truly said to be a humour.[2]

The term retained the meaning fixed down by Jonson for more than a century of literary criticism in England. It is well therefore to be clear about it, and I cannot do better than quote in this connection the best of all Jonson's critics. "The purpose of comedy [according to Jonson] is to note those elements in human character which are either naturally and permanently dominant in each man, or which, on occasion, in the hazard of life, overflow and exceed their limits at the expense of the other contributing elements; to note this in a number of characters differently 'humoured'; and, in the clash of contrasts, to point, with pleasant laughter, the 'moral' of these disorders. A man whom we call avaricious because avarice is to us his most striking characteristic and to him his most absorbing 'humour' may preserve the established proportion of this dominating quality in all his dealings, or he may, as is likely, under stress of living with fools and troublesome persons, be tempted to let it grow at the expense of other qualities, perhaps good, perhaps indifferent. In the one case he may be said to be 'in his humour,' in the other 'out' of it. Both are opportunities for comedy, and the problem is one of degree."[3]

DESCARTES marks a great step forward. He has nothing to say about comedy, but addresses himself

[1] *Every Man in his Humour* (1598), Prologue.
[2] *Every Man out of his Humour* (1599), Induction.
[3] Gregory Smith, *Ben Jonson*, English Men of Letters Series, pp. 82–3.

boldly to the more fundamental subject of laughter. He begins with a physiological account of what causes the audible explosion—the blood passing from the right cavity of the heart to the lungs, filling them, and driving out the air " avec impetuosité par le sifflet, où il forme une voix inarticulée et esclatante."[1] Though it would seem that laughter is one of the principal signs of joy, to cause the laugh joy must not be too strong, and must be mixed with surprise or hate,[2] and sometimes with both.[3] Anything, in short, which suddenly fills the lungs in the manner indicated causes the exterior action of laughter, unless sadness transforms it into groans and cries.[4] Thus derision is a kind of joy, mixed with hate and surprise, at a minor evil. " La Dérision ou Moquerie est une espece de Ioye meslée de Haine, qui vient de ce qu'on aperçoit quelque petit mal en une personne qu'on pense en estre digne. On a de la Haine pour ce mal, et on a de la Ioye de le voir en celuy qui en est digne. Et lors que cela survient inopinement, la surprise de l'Admiration est cause qu'on s'esclate de rire, suivant ce qui a esté dit cy dessus de la nature du ris. Mais ce mal doit estre petit ; car s'il est grand, on ne peut croire que celuy qui l'a en soit digne, si ce n'est qu'on soit de fort mauvais naturel, ou qu'on lui porte beaucoup de Haine."[5]

The most famous English theory of laughter is that of THOMAS HOBBES. It is succinctly stated in the ninth chapter of his *Human Nature* (1650), and still more briefly in *Leviathan* (1651), chap. vi. There is, he says, a passion which has no name, the outward sign of which is the distortion of the face known as laughter, which is always joy ; and this passion " is nothing else but sudden glory arising from a sudden conception of some eminency in ourselves, by comparison with the infirmity of others, or with our own formerly."[6] That which causes laughter must be new and unexpected. And, since " men take

[1] *Passions de l'âme* (1649), Art. 124. [2] *Ibid.*, Arts. 125, 126.
[3] *Ibid.*, Art. 127. [4] *Loc. cit.* [5] *Ibid.*, Art. 178.
[6] " Human Nature," in *Works* (Molesworth, 1840), vol. iv, p. 46.

heinously to be laughed at or derided—that is, triumphed over," it follows that "laughing without offence must be at absurdities and infirmities abstracted from persons, and when all the company may laugh together; for laughing to one's self putteth all the rest into jealousy and examination of themselves."[1] The opposite passion is sudden dejection, causing weeping; it is a "sudden falling out with ourselves."[2] "For no man laughs at old jests, or weeps for an old calamity."[3]

MOLIÈRE theorized about his own art only in self-defence. He fully accepted the moral aim of comedy —to correct through amusement.[4] Ridicule is more effective than set condemnation. "On souffre aisément des répréhensions, mais on ne souffre point la raillerie."[5] "C'est une étrange entreprise que celle de faire rire les honnêtes gens . . . [mais] je voudrois bien savoir si la grande règle de toutes les règles n'est pas de plaire, et si une pièce de théâtre qui a attrapé son but n'a pas suivi un bon chemin."[6] He protests constantly against the accusation of singling out particular individuals for ridicule. "Comme l'affaire de la comédie est de réprésenter en général tous les défauts des hommes, et principalement des hommes de notre siècle, il est impossible à Molière de faire aucun caractère qui ne rencontre quelqu'un dans le monde; et s'il faut qu'on l'accuse d'avoir songé à toutes les personnes où l'on peut trouver les défauts qu'il peint, il faut, sans doute, qu'il ne fasse plus de comédies."[7]

DRYDEN admits himself puzzled by the problem of laughter.[8] But, while recognizing a strange appetite,

[1] *Ibid.*, p. 47.
[2] *Loc. cit.*
[3] "Leviathan," in *Works*, vol. iii, p. 46.
[4] Preface to *Tartufe* (1664), and *Premier placet présenté au roi sur la comédie de Tartufe.*
[5] Preface to *Tartufe.*
[6] *La critique de l'École des Femmes* (1662), Scene 7.
[7] *L'impromptu de Versailles* (1663), Scene 3.
[8] Preface to "An Evening's Love" (1671), in *Essays of John Dryden* (ed. W. P. Ker), vol. i, p. 136.

"like that of a longing woman," for the unexpected, he leans rather to the Platonic opinion that malice is at the root of our pleasure in the laughable. He speaks of "that malicious pleasure in the audience which is testified by laughter,"[1] and asserts that 'low comedy' especially requires much of ill-nature.[2] "Comedy presents us with the imperfections of human nature: Farce entertains us with what is monstrous and chimerical."[3] While the aim of tragedy is to instruct by example, the aim of comedy is primarily to delight, instruction being secondary. The business of the comic poet is to make you laugh. "When he writes humour he makes folly ridiculous; when wit, he moves you, if not always to laughter, yet to a pleasure that is more noble. And if he works a cure on folly, and the small imperfections in mankind, by exposing them to public view, that cure is not performed by an immediate operation. For it works first on the ill-nature of the audience; they are moved to laugh by the representation of deformity; and the shame of that laughter teaches us to amend what is ridiculous in our manners."[4]

THOMAS SHADWELL takes leave to dissent from those who say that the chief aim of the comic poet is to divert and not to instruct. "And for the reformation of Fopps and Knaves," he says, "I think Comedy most useful, because to render Vices and Fopperies very ridiculous is much a greater punishment than Tragedy can inflict upon them."[5]

WILLIAM CONGREVE cannot, or at the least will not, define wit and humour, but can never care for seeing things that force him to entertain low thoughts of his nature. By implication, then, such things cannot be the proper subject-matter of comedy.[6]

[1] "Essay of Dramatic Poesy" (1668), in *op. cit.*, p. 85.
[2] Preface to "An Evening's Love," p. 135.
[3] *Ibid.*, p. 136.
[4] *Ibid.*, p. 143.
[5] Preface to "The Humorists" (1671), in *Critical Essays of the Seventeenth Century* (ed. J. E. Spingarn), vol. ii, p. 154.
[6] "Concerning Humour in Comedy" (1695), in *op. cit.*, vol. iii, p. 244.

JOHN LOCKE influenced later writers, Addison especially, through his famous distinction of wit and judgment. "For *wit* lying most in the assemblage of ideas, and putting these together with quickness and variety, wherein can be found any resemblance or congruity, thereby to make up pleasant pictures and agreeable visions in the fancy; *judgement*, on the contrary, lies quite on the other side, in separating carefully, one from another, ideas wherein can be found the least difference, thereby to avoid being misled by similitude, and by affinity to take one thing for another." [1]

In his *Sensus Communis, an Essay on the Freedom of Wit and Humour*,[2] the Earl of Shaftesbury begins the literary discussion, which vexed so many writers later in the century, whether ridicule can be taken as the test of truth. For his own part he maintains that it can. Humour is "a more lenitive Remedy against Vice, and a kind of Specifick against Superstition and melancholy Delusion. . . . For nothing is ridiculous except what is deformed: Nor is anything proof against Raillery, except what is handsom and just." [3]

JOSEPH ADDISON devoted several numbers of the *Spectator* (1711–14) to the discussion of laughter, wit, and humour. He appears to have been impressed with the thought (which dates at least from Aristotle) that only man of all creation laughs.[4] He accepts in the main the Hobbesian theory of laughter, which he quotes.[5] At the same time, he softens the theory to some degree in two asides. He notes that "a stupid *Butt* is only fit for the conversation of ordinary people: Men of Wit require one that will give them Play, and bestir himself in the absurd part of his Behaviour," [6] thus often getting

[1] *An Essay concerning Human Understanding* (1690), Book II, chap. xi.

[2] First published 1709. Republished in *Characteristics*. I have used the sixth edition of the latter, 1737.

[3] Part IV, sect. i, p. 128.

[4] Nos. 249, 494, and 598. Cf. "Rabelais to the Reader," *Gargantua.*

[5] Nos. 47 and 249.

[6] No. 47.

the laugh on his own side; and again, that the metaphor of laughing, applied to fields and trees in bloom, is universal in all languages, thus showing "that we naturally regard Laughter, as what is both in itself amiable and beautiful."[1] "The two great Branches of Ridicule in Writing are Comedy and Burlesque. The first ridicules Persons by drawing them in their proper Characters, the other by drawing them quite unlike themselves."[2] On wit he quotes Locke, but adds on his own account, first, that a resemblance of ideas, to be witty, must be both delightful and surprising, especially the latter; and secondly, that opposition as well as resemblance of ideas often produces wit.[3] The Jonsonian interpretation of the term 'humour' had persisted throughout the seventeenth century; Dryden[4] had elaborated it, Shadwell,[5] and Congreve[6] had added nothing to it of any importance. Addison represents the transition to a more modern and less restricted interpretation of the term, though he gives his own 'notions' only under the form of an allegory, by supposing Humour to be a person. "Truth was the Founder of the Family, and the Father of Good Sense. Good Sense was the Father of Wit, who married a Lady of a Collateral Line called Mirth, by whom he had issue Humour. Humour therefore being the youngest of this Illustrious Family, and descended from Parents of such different Dispositions, is very various and unequal in his Temper; sometimes you see him putting on grave Looks and a solemn Habit, sometimes airy in his Behaviour and fantastick in his Dress: Insomuch that at different times he appears as serious as a judge, and as jocular as a *Merry-Andrew*. But as he has a great deal of the Mother in his Constitution, whatever Mood he is in, he never fails to make his Company laugh."[7]

[1] No. 249.
[2] *Ibid.*
[3] No. 62.
[4] "Essay of Dramatic Poesy," in *Essays*, vol. i, p. 85 ff.
[5] Preface to "The Sullen Lovers," in *Critical Essays of the Seventeenth Century*, vol. ii, p. 150.
[6] "Concerning Humour in Comedy," in *op. cit.*, vol. iii, p. 248.
[7] *Spectator*, No. 35.

Sir William Temple was the first to suggest that 'humour' is a quality peculiar to the English, the reason he gives being that there is less uniformity of life in England than on the Continent.[1] Swift differed from Temple on this point.[2]

Henry Fielding, considering himself the founder of a new way of writing—the comic epic poem in prose[3] —took the liberty of laying down therein what laws he pleased.[4] "The only source of the true Ridiculous . . . is affectation. . . . Now affectation proceeds from one of these two causes, vanity or hypocrisy. . . . From the discovery of this affectation arises the Ridiculous; which always strikes the reader with surprise and pleasure; and that in a higher and stronger degree when the affectation arises from hypocrisy than when from vanity: for to discover anyone to be the exact reverse of what he affects, is more surprising, and consequently more ridiculous, than to find him a little deficient in the quality he desires the reputation of."[5]

Mark Akenside versifies the standard theory of his day, on "Impetuous Laughter's gay rebuke."

Suffice it to have said,
Where'er the power of Ridicule displays
Her quaint-eyed visage, some incongruous form,
Some stubborn dissonance of things combined,
Strikes on her quick perception. . . .
Ask we for what fair end the Almighty Sire
In mortal bosoms stirs this gay contempt,
These grateful pangs of laughter; from disgust
Educing pleasure? Wherefore, but to aid
The tardy steps of Reason, and at once
By this prompt impulse urge us to depress
Wild Folly's aims.[6]

1 "Of Poetry" (1692), in *Works* (Edinburgh, 1764), vol. ii, p. 346 ff.
2 *Intelligencer*, No. 3 (1728).
3 Preface to *Joseph Andrews* (1742). Cf. "Prosai-comi-epic writing," *Tom Jones*, Book V, chap. i.
4 *Tom Jones*, Book II, chap. i.
5 Preface to *Joseph Andrews*.
6 *Pleasures of the Imagination* (1744), Book. II.

As is well known, the EARL OF CHESTERFIELD considered laughter "illiberal and ill-bred."[1] "Loud laughter is the mirth of the mob, who are only pleased with silly things,"[2] that is, "low buffoonery, or silly accidents."[3] "True wit or good sense never excited a laugh since the creation of the world."[4] He notes also the relativity of wit to class and locality: "Remember that the wit, humour, and jokes of most mixed companies are local. They thrive in that particular soil, but will not often bear transplanting."[5]

Laughter, according to HARTLEY, is "a nascent cry, stopped of a sudden."[6] The first occasion of children's laughter "seems to be a surprise, which brings a momentary fear first, and then a momentary joy in consequence of the removal of that fear."[7] Tickling is a momentary pain and apprehension of pain, with immediate removal of pain.[8] Children have to learn to laugh, as to walk, and also to abate and control laughter. On the whole, he has no high opinion of laughter. "The most natural occasions of mirth and laughter in adults seem to be the little mistakes and follies of children, and the smaller inconsistencies and improprieties which happen in conversation, and the daily occurrences of life; inasmuch as these pleasures are, in great measure, occasioned, or at least supported, by the general pleasurable state, which our love and affection to our friends in general, and to children in particular, put the body and mind into. For this kind of mirth is always checked where we have a dislike; also where the mistake or inconsistency rises beyond a certain limit; for then it produces concern, confusion, and uneasiness."[9]

[1] *Letters to his Son*, Letter 144, 1748. Cf. the opinion of Lord Froth, in Congreve's *The Double Dealer*, Act I, Scene 2.
[2] Letter 146.
[3] Letter 144.
[4] Letter 146.
[5] Letter 147.
[6] *Observations on Man* (1749), Part. I, chap. iv, subsect. (i), 5th edition, p. 450.
[7] *Loc. cit.* [8] *Ibid.*, p. 451. [9] *Ibid.*, pp. 453–4.

OLIVER GOLDSMITH complains that the critics have made comedy impossible by refusing to allow the comic poet to deal with what is *low*. "When a thing is humorously described . . . we compare the absurdity of the character represented with our own, and triumph in our conscious superiority. . . . Thus, then, the pleasure we receive from wit turns on the admiration of another; that which we feel from humour, centres in the admiration of ourselves . . . in other words, the subject of humour must be *low*." [1]

In *Reflections upon Laughter*,[2] FRANCIS HUTCHESON takes elaborate pains to refute the theory of Hobbes. He distinguishes between laughter and ridicule, the latter being only a species of the former.[3] The occasion of laughter is "contrast or opposition of dignity and meanness." [4] Incidentally he notes the relativity of laughter to age and custom, and the different manner in which ridicule is received by the person against whom it is directed, "according as he who uses the ridicule evidences good nature, friendship, and esteem of the person whom he laughs at; or the contrary." [5]

In one of his *Rambler* papers Dr. JOHNSON delivers himself of the following anti-classical opinion: "Comedy has been particularly unpropitious in definers. . . . Any man's reflections will inform him, that every dramatic composition which raises mirth, is comick; and that to raise mirth, it is by no means universally necessary, that the personages should be either mean or corrupt, nor always requisite, that the action should be trivial, nor ever, that it should be fictitious." [6] This is in accord with what Boswell records him to have said about Goldsmith's *She Stoops to Conquer*, namely, "I know of

[1] *Inquiry into the Present State of Polite Learning* (1750), chap. ix.
[2] 1750.
[3] Page 13.
[4] Page 21, *passim*.
[5] Page 29.
[6] *Rambler*, No. 125, May 28, 1751.

no comedy for many years that has so much exhilarated an audience, that has answered so much the great end of comedy—making an audience merry."[1] Johnson, who sets it on record that Swift and Pope never laughed, was of a different habit himself; he laughed "like a rhinoceros."[2]

Malice and surprise are at the root of laughter and comedy, according to DE MARMONTEL, writing in the famous *Encyclopédie*.[3] "La malice naturelle aux hommes est le principe de la comédie. Nous voyons les défauts de nos semblables avec une complaisance mêlée de mépris, lorsque ces défauts ne sont ni assez affligeans pour exciter la compassion, ni assez revoltans pour donner de la haine, ni assez dangereux pour inspirer de l'effroi. Ces images nous font sourire, si elles sont peintes avec finesse: elles nous font rire, si les traits de cette maligne joie, aussi frappans qu'inattendus, sont aiguisés par la surprise. De cette disposition à saisir le ridicule, la comédie tire sa force et ses moyens. Il eût été sans doute plus avantageux de changer en nous cette complaisance vicieuse en une pitié philosophique; mais on a trouvé plus facile et plus sur de faire servir la malice humaine à corriger les autres vices de l'humanité à-peu-près comme on emploie les pointes du diamant à polir le diamant même. C'est là l'objet ou la fin de la comédie."[4] "L'effet du *comique* résulte de la comparaison qu'on fait, même sans s'en apercevoir, de ses mœurs avec les mœurs qu'on voit tourner en ridicule, et suppose entre le spectateur et le personnage réprésenté une différence avantageuse pour le premier."[5] Thus when we laugh at ourselves there is "une duplicité de caractère." The contributor of the article on Laughter (Ris ou Rire) prophesies that no one will ever be able to explain how

[1] Boswell's *Johnson*, ed. by Birkbeck Hill, 1887, vol. ii, p. 233.
[2] *Ibid.*, p. 378.
[3] *Encyclopédie ou Dictionnaire raisonné des sciences, des arts, et des métiers*, 1751–72. I have used 3rd edition, 1778.
[4] Tome 8, Art. "Comédie," p. 560.
[5] *Ibid.*, Art. "Comique," p. 603.

an idea comes to excite the bodily movements of the laugh.[1]

JOSEPH WARTON, after surveying the whole field of comic literature from Aristophanes to his own times, pronounces the moderns superior to the ancients in humour and ridicule, and Molière matchless among them all. "The arts of civility, and the decencies of conversation, as they unite men more closely, and bring them more frequently together, multiply opportunities of observing those incongruities and absurdities of behaviour, on which Ridicule is founded. The antients had more Liberty and Seriousness; the moderns have more Luxury and Laughter."[2]

Among the many heresies to which JEAN JACQUES ROUSSEAU gave trenchant expression in the famous *Lettre à M. D'Alembert*,[3] not the least disturbing to contemporary men of letters (to Voltaire in especial) was his downright assertion that comedy performed no useful social function even at its best, and might at its worst lead directly to corruption and immorality. "Qu'on n'attribue donc pas au théâtre le pouvoir de changer des sentiments ni des mœurs qu'il ne peut que suivre et embellir. . . . Quand Molière corrigea la scène comique, il attaqua des modes, des ridicules; mais il ne choqua pas pour cela le goût du public, il le suivit ou le développa, comme fit aussi Corneille de son côté."[4] "Or, par une suite de son inutilité même, le théâtre, qui ne peut rien pour corriger les mœurs, peut beaucoup pour les altérer. En favorisant tous nos penchants, il donne un nouvel ascendant à ceux qui nous dominent; les continuelles émotions qu'on y ressent nous énervent, nous affoiblissent, nous rendent plus incapables de résister à nos passions; et le stérile intérêt qu'on prend à la vertu ne sert qu'à

[1] Tome 29, p. 254.
[2] *Adventurer*, No. 133, February 12, 1754. The quotation is interesting when compared with the view of Meredith on comedy; *vide infra*.
[3] 1758. I have used the edition Baudouin Frères, Paris, 1826.
[4] Tome 2, p. 26.

contenter notre amour-propre sans nous contraindre à la pratiquer." [1]

ALEXANDER GERARD says that the object of the sense of the ludicrous "is in general incongruity, or a surprising and uncommon mixture of relation and contrariety in things. More explicity; it is gratified by an inconsistence and dissonance of circumstances in the same object; or in objects nearly related in the main; or by a similitude or relation unexpected between things on the whole opposite and unlike." [2]

HENRY HOME, LORD KAMES, draws logical distinctions between the *ludicrous*, the *risible*, and the *ridiculous*. The ludicrous signifies what is "playsome, sportive, or jocular," the risible is that species of the ludicrous which makes us laugh.[3] "A risible object is mirthful only; a ridiculous object is both mirthful and contemptible," [4] contempt being the only other emotion which will mix with that of laughter. He will not attempt to define the risible in general, for "all men are not equally affected by risible objects; nor the same man at all times" [5]; but he circumscribes it within certain limits by saying that it must be slight, little, trivial, and out of rule. In accounting for the pleasure we take in the ridiculous he falls back upon the Hobbesian theory. "An improper action not only moves our contempt for the author, but also, by means of contrast, swells the good opinion we have of ourselves." [6] Ridicule, being corrective of impropriety, is divinely ordered for the good of mankind. "It is painful to the subject of ridicule; and to punish with ridicule the man who is guilty of an absurdity, tends to put him more on his guard in time coming. It is well ordered, that even the most innocent blunder is not

[1] Page 86.
[2] *An Essay on Taste* (1759), sect. vi, p. 66.
[3] *Elements of Criticism* (1762), 9th edition, 1817, vol. i, p. 245.
[4] *Ibid.*, p. 247.
[5] *Ibid.*, p. 246.
[6] *Ibid.*, p. 311.

committed with impunity; because, were errors licensed where they do no hurt, inattention would grow into habit, and be the occasion of much hurt." [1]

A line or two will suffice for VOLTAIRE. No one doubts, he says, that the laugh is a sign of joy, just as tears are a symptom of pain; and anyone who pushes his curiosity further in the matter is a fool.[2]

"Comedy," wrote LESSING, "corrects by laughter, but not by derision, and it does not correct exactly those failings on which it turns the laugh, nor solely those persons in which it exposes these laughable failings. Rather is its true and general utility to be found in laughter itself, in the exercise it gives to our faculty of seizing upon the ridiculous, noticing it easily and quickly, under the disguises of passion and custom, in all combinations with good and bad qualities, and, what is more, even in the folds of solemn earnestness. . . . A preservative is also a valuable remedy, and morality possesses none more energetic or efficacious than the laughable." [3]

The influence of *The Philosophy of Rhetoric*, by GEORGE CAMPBELL,[4] was considerable in his day. In the first volume he deals at some length with *Wit, Humour*, and *Ridicule*. The characteristics of wit are suddenness, surprise, and contrariety. "It is the design of wit to excite in the mind an agreeable surprise, and that arising, not from anything marvellous in the subject, but solely

[1] *Elements of Criticism* (1762,), 9th edition, 1817, vol. i. p. 312.

[2] "Le Rire," in *Dict. philosophique* (1764), tome 7.

[3] "Die Komödie will durch Lachen bessern, aber nicht eben durch Verlachen; nicht gerade diejenigen Unarten, über die sie zu lachen macht, noch weniger blos und allein Die, an welchen sich diese lächerlichen Unarten finden. Ihr wahrer allgemeiner Nutzen liegt in dem Lachen selbst, in der Uebung unserer Fähigkeit, das Lächerliche zu bemerken, es unter allen Bemäntelungen der Leidenschaft und der Mode, es in allen Vermischungen mit noch schlimmern oder mit guten Eigenschaften, sogar in Runzeln des feierlichen Ernstes, leicht und geschwind zu bemerken. . . . Ein Präservativ ist auch eine schätzbare Arzenei, und die ganze Moral hat kein kräftigeres, wirksameres als das Lächerliche."—*Hamburgische Dramaturgie*, 29th evening, August 7, 1767.

[4] 1776.

from the imagery she employs, or the strange assemblage of related ideas presented to the mind."[1] "It is to the contrast of dissimilitude and likeness, remoteness and relation in the same objects, that its peculiar effect is imputable."[2] "As wit is the painting, humour is the pathetic. . . . A just exhibition of any ardent or durable passion, excited by some adequate cause, instantly attacheth sympathy, the common tie of human souls, and thereby communicates the passion to the breast of the hearer. But when the emotion is not violent or not durable, and the motive not anything real, but imaginary, or at least quite disproportionate to the effect; or when the passion displays itself preposterously, so as rather to obstruct than to promote its aim; in these cases a natural representation, instead of fellow-feeling, creates amusement, and universally awakens contempt. The portrait in the former case we call *pathetic*, in the latter *humorous*."[3]

The longest eighteenth-century essay on Laughter is that by JAMES BEATTIE, entitled *Essay on Laughter and Ludicrous Composition*, published in 1776. He distinguishes, as Kames had done, though not quite in the same way, between the *ludicrous* and the *ridiculous*. The feeling aroused by the former is simple, and admits of no definition,[4] the feeling aroused by the latter is mixed with contempt or disapprobation.[5] Innocent laughter is of two kinds, *animal* (aroused by tickling, etc.) and *sentimental* (aroused by ideas).[6] "Laughter arises from the view of two or more inconsistent, unsuitable, or incongruous parts or circumstances, considered as united in one complex object or assemblage, or as acquiring a sort of mutual relation from the peculiar manner in which the mind takes notice of them."[7] Every ludicrous combination must be incongruous,[8] must be new and surprising,[9] and must not arouse other stronger emotions,

[1] *Op. cit.*, p. 42. [2] *Ibid.*, p. 45. [3] *Ibid.*, pp. 57–8.
[4] *Op. cit.* (3rd edition, 1779), p. 305. [5] Page 302.
[6] Page 303. [7] Page 320. [8] Page 324.
[9] Page 389.

such as anger, pity, or fear."[1] "If, then, it be asked, what is that quality in things which makes them provoke that pleasing emotion or sentiment whereof Laughter is the external sign? I answer: It is an uncommon mixture of relation and contrariety, exhibited, or supposed to be united, in the same assemblage. If again it be asked, whether such mixture will always provoke Laughter? my answer is: It will always, or for the most part, excite the Risible Emotion, unless when the perception of it is attended with some other emotion of greater authority."[2] Such, in outline, is the theory. But some of Beattie's *obiter dicta* deserve quotation. "I know not," he says, "whether the entertainment we receive from the playful tricks of kittens, and other young animals, may not in part be resolved into something like a fellow-feeling of their vivacity."[3] Again: "The theory of Mr. Hobbes would hardly have deserved notice, if Mr. Addison had not spoken of it with approbation."[4] And again: "A thing not ludicrous in itself, may occasion laughter, when it suggests any ludicrous idea related to it by custom, or by any other associating principle."[5]

On the view of JOSEPH PRIESTLEY laughter arises from the perception of contrast.[6] He quotes Hartley's 'nascent cry,'[7] and adds that "almost any brisk emotion or surprise, suddenly checked, and recurring alternately," will result in laughter, and so "at last any strong opposition, or contrast, in things," whether we are personally interested in them or not, from association with others in which we are or have been interested.[8] The *risible* he defines as "anything in which there is perceived a great *incongruity* or *disproportion*, provided that the object, at the same time that it is of some consequence, be not capable of exciting a more serious emotion."[9] But since the most frequent sources of laughter are human improprieties—before an inanimate object can be laughable,

[1] Pages 397–9. [2] Pages 419–20. [3] Page 304.
[4] Page 307. [5] Pages 408–9.
[6] *A Course of Lectures on Oratory and Criticism*, 1777.
[7] *Vide*, p. 238 above. [8] Page 200. [9] Page 205.

he says, it must be personified [1]—it is hardly ever possible to get unmixed laughter. To the merely risible an element of contempt is added, making it the ridiculous. "In reality, *men* can hardly be the object of a laugh that is not more or less a laugh of *derision*, and is excited by the ridiculous strictly so called; because we connect the idea of design with everything belonging to man." [2]

HUGH BLAIR contributed nothing new to the subject, his position being sufficiently indicated by the following quotations. "Comedy proposes for its object, neither the great sufferings nor the great crimes of men; but their follies and slighter vices, those parts of their characters, which raise in beholders a sense of impropriety, which expose them to be censured, and laughed at by others, and which render them troublesome in civil society." [3] "To polish the manners of men, to promote attention to the proper decorums of social behaviour, and above all to render vice ridiculous, is doing a real service to the world." [4]

In a quaint eighteenth-century treatise by POINSINET DE SIVRY,[5] an imaginary dialogue is recorded on the physical and moral causes of laughter, three of the most famous philosophers of the day, Destouches, Fontenelle, and Montesquieu, being supposed to take part. Destouches disagrees with the opinion of Aristotle, and objects to the idea of surprise being the cause of laughter. Laughter, he maintains, has its source in a "reasoned joy."[6] Fontenelle takes an opposite view. According to him, "La Folie est le principe du rire [7] . . . le rire est pour l'ordinaire un symptôme passager de déraison." [8] Montesquieu

[1] Cf. the view of Bergson, p. 269 below.
[2] Page 208.
[3] *Lectures on Rhetoric and Belles-Lettres* (1783), 5th edition, 1793, vol. iii, lect. xlvii, p. 355.
[4] *Ibid.*, p. 356.
[5] *Traité des causes physiques et morales du rire, rélativement à l'art de l'exciter*, Amsterdam, 1778.
[6] Page 25.
[7] Page 64.
[8] Page 75.

agrees with Hobbes; laughter is the expression of pride.[1] What opinion Poinsinet himself held is difficult to determine, though in his introduction to the dialogue he writes, "La comédie, cette source inépuisable de plaisirs utiles, nous divertit par des leçons, et nous instruit par le tableau des défauts et des vices. Le rire est son véritable attribut; et c'est par lui qu'elle marche au but respectable de *corriger l'homme en le divertissant.*"[2]

The whole of what IMMANUEL KANT has to say on laughter, influential though it has been, is contained in a few pages of a 'Remark' in the *Critique of Judgment.*[3] We must distinguish, he says, between gratification which is the bodily feeling of well-being, and satisfaction, which belongs to reason and is equivalent to approbation. "All changing free play of sensations (that have no design at their basis) gratifies because it promotes the feeling of health."[4] Wit is such free play of sensation, and its animation, though excited by ideas in the mind, is merely bodily.[5] "Laughter is an affection arising from the sudden transformation of a strained expectation into nothing."[6] The transformation must be into nothing, not into the positive opposite of expectation.[7] It is not enjoyable to the Understanding directly, but only indirectly, by throwing the organs of the body into a state of oscillation, restoring them to equilibrium, and thus promoting health.

It is with great diffidence that I attempt a summary of HEGEL'S views on laughter and comedy; I cannot pretend that I know exactly what he means.[8] He notes

[1] *Passim.*
[2] Page 8.
[3] 1790.
[4] *Op. cit.*, Bernard's translation, 2nd edition, 1914, p. 221.
[5] *Ibid.*, p. 222.
[6] Page 223.
[7] Page 225.
[8] I think Professor Baillie has borrowed profitably from Hegel in his essay on "Laughter and Tears" (see p. 277 below); reading it has helped me to understand Hegel.

the great variety of different things which may excite laughter, provided notice is taken only of "some entirely unimportant feature, which may conflict with habit and ordinary experience."[1] Laughter consequently is little more than "an expression of self-satisfied shrewdness."[2] "What on the other hand is inseparable from the comic as distinguished from the merely laughable is an infinite geniality and confidence (Wohlgemuthkeit und Zuversicht), capable of rising superior to its own contradiction, and experiencing therein no taint of bitterness or sense of misfortune whatever. It is the happy frame of mind, a hale condition of soul, which, fully aware of itself, can suffer the dissolution of its aims and realization. The unexpansive type of intelligence is, on the contrary, least master of itself where it is in its behaviour most laughable to others."[3] The true comic arises when the individual attempts to realize ends which are at variance with reality—'the substantive being,' 'the realized divine nature of the world,'[4]—but when the contradiction is exposed, feels no serious loss, "because he is conscious that what he strove after was really of no great importance."[5] In the *resolution* of comedy neither the substantive being nor the personal life as such must be abrogated. It is therefore only when the persons in the play are aware that they are comic that we have genuine comedy.[6]

Reviewing Edgeworth's *Essay on Irish Bulls*, the Rev. SYDNEY SMITH, himself a wit of the first order, delivers himself of a few *obiter dicta* on the topic, worthy of preservation for the sake of the author.[7] A bull, he says, is the exact reverse of wit, for the bull suddenly discovers an apparent congruity and a real incongruity of ideas, whereas wit discovers a real congruity, or

[1] *The Philosophy of Fine Art* (c. 1820), English translation, vol. iv, p. 302.
[2] *Loc. cit.*
[3] *Loc. cit.*
[4] Page 294.
[5] Page 303.
[6] Page 328.
[7] In *Edinburgh Review*, 1803. I have used collected edition of Works, 3 vols., London, 1859.

similarity, in an apparent incongruity or dissimilarity.[1] "The essence of every species of wit is surprise; which, *vi termini*, must be sudden; and the sensations which wit has a tendency to excite, are impaired or destroyed, as often as they are mingled with much thought or passion."[2] "The less apparent, and the more complete the relations established by wit, the higher gratification does it afford."[3]

In the main, R. P. KNIGHT follows Hobbes. Laughter is the expression of triumph over new and uncommon combinations of vices, frailties, or errors. "It is something of defect or deformity which pleases us; and consequently, how degrading soever it may be to own it, the passion flattered must be of the malignant kind."[4]

The comic, says JEAN PAUL FRIEDRICH RICHTER, is the opposite of the sublime.[5] The sublime is the infinitely great, which awakens wonder, the comic is the infinitely small, awakening the opposite feeling. But since there cannot be anything small in the moral sphere, the comic is localized only in the realm of the understanding. It is the absurd, as it is perceived in an action or a state.[6] Either an action must be a wrong means towards some end of the understanding, or the situation must have a topsy-turvy meaning. Yet to this objective contrast must be added a subjective contrast, for the comic is never in the object, but always in the subject. The absurdity need not be real, it need only appear.

COLERIDGE delivered one lecture at least on 'The distinctions between the witty, the droll, the odd, and the humorous.'[7] "Generically regarded, wit consists in presenting thoughts or images in an unusual connection

[1] Vol. i, p. 148. [2] *Ibid.*, p. 150, note. [3] *Ibid.*, p. 151.

[4] *Principles of Taste* (1804), 2nd edition, 1805, Part III, chap. ii, p. 417.

[5] *Vorschule der Æsthetik* (1804), sect. 28.

[6] "Das Unverständige, so fern es in einer Handlung oder in einem Zustand sinnlich angeschaut wird."—von Hartmann, *Die deutsche Æsthetik seit Kant*, p. 412.

[7] c. 1818; in *Literary Remains* (1836), vol. i.

with each other, for the purpose of exciting pleasure by the surprise."[1] The positive character of the droll or ludicrous is impropriety, its negative character dangerlessness.[2] The true ludicrous is its own end. Humour depends on some peculiarity of individual temperament, it must be 'growth from within.'[3] The one point common to all examples of the humorous 'consists in a certain reference to the general and the universal, by which the finite great is brought into identity with the little, or the little with the finite great, so as to make both nothing in comparison with the infinite."[4] In another passage he says, "The comic poet idealizes his characters by making the animal the governing power, and the intellectual the mere instrument . . . by contradictions of the inward being, to which all folly is owing."[5]

WILLIAM HAZLITT'S lecture, *On Wit and Humour*, introductory to those on the *English Comic Writers*,[6] contains what he describes as "a desultory and imperfect sketch" of the subject. Laughter and tears arise from our perception of the difference between what is and what ought to be. "We weep at what thwarts or exceeds our desires in serious matters: we laugh at what only disappoints our expectations in trifles."[7] Laughter is a "convulsive and involuntary movement, occasioned by mere surprise or contrast (in the absence of any more serious emotion) before the mind has time to reconcile its belief to contradictory appearances."[8] "The serious is the habitual stress which the mind lays upon the expectation of a certain given order of events, following one another with a certain regularity and weight of interest attached to them. When this stress is increased beyond its usual pitch of intensity, so as to overstrain the feelings by the violent opposition of good to bad, or of objects to our desires, it becomes the pathetic or tragical. The ludicrous, or comic, is the unexpected

[1] Page 131. [2] Page 133. [3] Page 134. [4] Page 136.
[5] *Lectures on Poetry, the Drama, and Shakespeare*, Bohn's Library, 1897, p. 189.
[6] 1818. [7] *Op. cit.*, World's Classics, 1907, p. 1. [8] Page 2.

loosening or relaxing this stress below its usual pitch of intensity, by such an abrupt transposition of the order of our ideas, as taking the mind unawares, throws it off its guard, startles it into a lively sense of pleasure, and leaves no time nor inclination for painful reflections."[1] Hazlitt further distinguishes the *laughable*, the essence of which is the incongruous, "the disconnecting of one idea from another, or the jostling of one feeling against another"[2]; the *ludicrous*, where the contradiction between object and expectation is heightened "by its being contrary to what is customary or desirable;"[3] and the *ridiculous*, where the laughable "is contrary not only to custom, but to sense and reason."[4] The principle of contrast is the same throughout, but the ridiculous is proper to satire, and it would seem, to comedy also in the strict sense.[5] "Someone is generally sure to be the sufferer by a joke."[6] "Humour is the describing the ludicrous as it is in itself; wit is the exposing it, by comparing or contrasting it with something else."[7] Hazlitt has no respect for Locke's distinction between wit and judgment: "The shrewd separation or disentangling of ideas that seem the same, or when the secret contradiction is not sufficiently suspected, and is of a ludicrous or whimsical nature, is wit just as much as the bringing together those that appear at first sight totally different."[8]

"Nothing," says THOMAS BROWN, "is felt as truly ludicrous in which there is not an unexpected congruity developed in images that were before supposed to be opposite in kind, or some equally unexpected incongruity in images supposed to be congruous; and the sudden perception of these discrepancies and agreements may be said to be that which constitutes the ludicrousness; the gay emotions being immediately subsequent to the

[1] Page 4. [2] *Loc. cit.* [3] Page 5. [4] *Loc. cit.*
[5] *Loc. cit.* Cf. Lect. II, where Hazlitt expresses the view that Molière was a greater *comic* genius than Shakespeare, because there was more sting in his laughter.
[6] Page 7. [7] Page 14. [8] Page 19.

mere perception of the unexpected relation."[1] At the same time, the mere suddenness of a newly discovered relation will not excite laughter if the matter in hand is too important, engaging the mind too closely.[2] The general conditions of the ludicrous are the bringing together either of the noble and the mean, the high and the low, or the very great and the very small.[3]

STENDHAL (Henri Beyle) distinguishes 'le ridicule' from 'le plaisant,' greatly preferring the latter, which is open, frank, joyous, harmless, requiring only a society of light and kind-hearted people who search for happiness along all the paths by which it may be found.[4] "Enfin, si l'on veut me faire rire, malgré le sérieux profond que me donnent la bourse et la politique, et les haines des partis, il faut que des gens passionnés se trompent, sous mes yeux, d'une manière plaisante, sur le chemin qui les mène au bonheur."[5] For a theory, the statement is somewhat vague, but significant is the remark: "Il faut que j'accorde un certain degré d'estime à la personne aux dépens de laquelle on prétend me faire rire."[6]

In his essay on Richter,[7] THOMAS CARLYLE says some memorable things on humour. "The essence of humour is sensibility; warm, tender fellow-feeling with all forms of existence. . . . But it is this *sport* of sensibility; wholesome and perfect therefore; as it were, the playful teasing fondness of a mother to her child."[8] "True humour springs not more from the head than from the heart; it is not contempt, its essence is love; it issues not in laughter, but in still smiles, which lie far deeper. . . . It is, in fact, the bloom and perfume, the purest

[1] *Lectures on the Philosophy of the Human Mind* (1820), vol. iii, p. 203.
[2] Page 205.
[3] Page 212.
[4] *Racine et Shakespeare* (1823), chap. ii. I have used a recent but undated reprint.
[5] *Op. cit.*, p. 32.
[6] Page 23.
[7] First printed in *Edinburgh Review*, 1827. I have used collected edition of *Essays*, 3 vols., London, 1869.
[8] *Op. cit.*, p. 15.

effluence of a deep, fine, and loving nature; a nature in harmony with itself, reconciled to the world and its stintedness and contradiction, nay finding in this very contradiction new elements of beauty as well as goodness." [1]

"The natural and proper object of ridicule," says DUGALD STEWART, "is those smaller improprieties in character and manners which do not rouse our feelings of moral indignation, or impress us with a melancholy sense of human depravity." [2] The ridiculous is not always immoral, but it always implies imperfection of some kind, and awakens contempt. It has a salutary effect on mankind.[3]

LAMENNAIS has but a poor opinion of laughter; it is an image of evil, the instinctive expression of the sentiment of individuality, of the joy of belonging to oneself.[4] In all laughter there is secret satisfaction of self love. "Quiconque rit d'un autre se croit en ce moment supérieur à lui par le côté où il l'envisage et qui excite son rire, et le rire est surtout l'expression du contentement qu'inspire cette supériorité réelle ou imaginaire." [5] Nevertheless the *smile* is sometimes tender, expressing a tendency opposite to that of the laugh, a tendency towards others and away from the self.[6]

The problem of the ludicrous, proposed and given up by Cicero, and attempted unsuccessfully by so many writers since Cicero, is finally solved, says ARTHUR SCHOPENHAUER.[7] "The cause of laughter in every case is simply the sudden perception of the incongruity between a concept and the real objects which have been thought through it in some relation, and the laugh itself is just

[1] *Op. cit.*, pp. 15–16.
[2] *Philosophy of the Active and Moral Powers of Man* (1828), vol. i, p. 316.
[3] *Ibid.*, p. 318.
[4] *De l'art et du beau* (1841). I have used an undated reprint.
[5] Page 245.
[6] Page 247.
[7] *The World as Will and Idea* (1844), English translation, 5th edition, vol. ii, chap. viii, p. 271.

the expression of this incongruity."[1] Either two or more objects are brought under one concept (wit), or one object under one concept (folly).[2] "In everything that excites laughter it must always be possible to show a conception and a particular, that is a thing or event, which certainly can be subsumed under that conception, and therefore thought through it, yet in another and more predominating aspect does not belong to it at all, but is strikingly different from everything else that is thought through that conception."[3] Laughter is pleasant, being closely akin to joy, because in any conflict between the perception and the conception the perception is always right; the perception is the more primitive kind of knowledge, attended with less exertion, while reason is an obstruction to primitive desires, and we are therefore glad to see "this strict, untiring, troublesome governess, the reason, for once convicted of insufficiency."[4]

LEIGH HUNT locates the cause of laughter in triumph,[5] but he does not identify this triumph with the 'sudden glory' of Hobbes. We may laugh out of a contemptuous sense of superiority: "but on occasions of pure mirth and fancy, we only feel superior to the pleasant defiance which is given to our wit and comprehension; we triumph, not insolently but congenially; not to any-one's disadvantage, but simply to our own joy and reassurance."[6] Wit and humour challenge us with apparent antagonisms of one sort or another, and we are willing to be so challenged, in order that we may feel ourselves the more alive in the process of overcoming. "Our surprise is the consequence of a sudden and agree-able perception of the incongruous . . . the jar against us is not so violent as to hinder us from recurring to that habitual idea of fitness, or adjustment, by which the shock of the surprise is made easy. It is in these reconcile-ments of jars, these creations and re-adjustments of

[1] *Op. cit.*, vol. i, p. 76.
[2] *Loc. cit.*
[3] Vol. ii, p. 271.
[4] *Ibid.*, p. 280.
[5] *Wit and Humour* (1846), cheap edition, 1910.
[6] Page 7.

disparities, that the delightful faculty of the wit and the humorist is made manifest. He at once rouses our minds to action; suggests, and saves us the trouble of a difficulty; and turns the help into a compliment, by implying our participation in the process." [1]

SIR GEORGE RAMSAY classifies the *Ludicrous Emotion* along with the emotions of Beauty and Sublimity as the object of taste.[2] Like the other two the ludicrous emotion is passive, immediate, temporary, and pleasing, and its cause is a combination of novelty and excessive contrast.

The comic consists of three phases or moments, according to A. ZEISING.[3] The first moment is a shock caused by an object which seems to be something and is really nothing; in the second moment we realize the nothingness of the object, thus obtaining a counter shock; in the third moment we assert our superiority over the nothingness and laugh.

On the whole, ALEXANDER BAIN follows Hobbes. "Not in physical effects alone, but in everything where a man can achieve a stroke of superiority, in surpassing or discomfiting a rival, is the disposition to laughter apparent." [4] "The occasion of the ludicrous is the degradation of some person or interest possessing dignity in circumstances that excite no other strong emotion." [5] Yet the smile accompanies the tender emotion, and is a mode of signifying that emotion to others.[6] So, again, incongruity in itself has nothing to excite laughter: the comic must be approached through the serious. The comic, in fact, represents a breakdown of the "coerced

[1] *Loc. cit.*
[2] *Analysis and Theory of the Emotions* (1848).
[3] *Æsthetische Forschungen* (1855). I have not seen the original, and take my account at secondhand partly from von Hartmann, *Die deutsche Æsthetik seit Kant*, and partly from Eastman, *The Sense of Humor*.
[4] *The Emotions and the Will* (1859), 1st edition, p. 153.
[5] *Op. cit.*, 2nd edition, p. 248.
[6] *Op. cit.*, 1st edition, p. 282.

serious."[1] "The mirthful is the aspect of ease, freedom, abandon, and animal spirits. The serious is constituted by labour, difficulty, hardship, and the necessities of our position, which give birth to the severe and constraining institutions of government, law, morality, education, etc. It is always a gratifying deliverance to pass from the severe to the easy side of affairs, and the comic conjunction is one form of the transition."[2]

According to VICTOR DE LAPRADE[3] laughter has two forms: the laughter of gaiety, and the laughter of irony or raillery. But of the former he has little to say. Without evil in the world there would be neither laughter nor tears.[4] "La comédie est la peinture des travers de toute espèce qui enlaidissent la nature humaine, depuis les grands vices jusqu'aux petits ridicules."[5] But comedy has never performed any valuable corrective function in society: "La réforme de nous-mêmes est chose trop difficile et trop grave pour naître du rire."[6] It is of the essence of laughter eventually to turn against the good itself. "Le sentiment le plus réel que la comédie éveille, c'est donc un sentiment de vanité et d'orgueil."[7]

LÉON DUMONT defines the laughable: "Tout objet à l'égard duquel l'esprit se trouve forcé d'affirmer et de nier en même temps la même chose; c'est en d'autres termes, ce qui détermine notre entendement à former simultanément deux rapports contradictoires."[8] This analysis, he claims, is applicable to all cases of laughter whatsoever.[9] Yet the mental process is so quick that it cannot be measured,[10] and is rather one of feeling than of knowledge.[11] "La connaissance d'un objet donne d'abord à notre entendement une certaine impulsion, et stimule son activité dans une certaine direction; mais immédiatement une impulsion contraire lui vient d'une

[1] *Op. cit.*, 1st edition, p. 283.
[2] *Ibid.*, 1st edition, p. 284.
[3] *Questions d'art et de morale* (1861).
[4] Page 327.
[5] Page 308.
[6] Page 313.
[7] Page 310.
[8] *Des causes du rire* (1862), p. 48.
[9] Page 49.
[10] *Loc. cit.*
[11] Page 55.

autre qualité de ce même objet, et imprime à cette activité, avec une assez forte secousse, la direction contraire." [1] The pleasure of laughter arises from the exercise of the understanding in this double manner.[2] The comic is something permanent, the laughable is something merely momentary and fleeting.[3]

CHARLES LÉVÊQUE,[4] reviewing Dumont's *Des causes du rire,* criticizes his intellectualist definition of the laughable,[5] on the ground that it is simply impossible for the understanding to affirm and deny the same thing simultaneously. Rather there are two moments in the process: "Il y a un moment, si bref que l'on voudra, où l'on connait d'abord la chose dont on ne rit qu'ensuite." [6] "L'objet risible, apparaissant brusquement, tente de séduire la raison, et l'entrainer avec lui. Pour la mieux attirer . . . il feint d'être dans l'ordre ou affirme naïvement y être. . . . De prime abord, la raison le constate, et tout aussitôt l'objet risible, au lieu de l'attirer comme un aimant, la repousse, non violemment, mais d'une poussée prompte, vive, irrésistible, dans les voies où elle se plaît naturellement." [7] The laughable must be distinguished from the comic. The laughable is temporary, the comic has elements of permanence, addresses itself to the intelligence, and calls down upon itself the punishment of being ridiculed. The comic is the disorderly, and in exposing it the comic poet indirectly affirms the eternal order. "C'est parce qu'ils [les poetes comiques] aiment l'ordre moral plus qu'eux-mêmes qu'ils en poursuivent et punissent la négation, même partielle, comme une atteinte à la raison, qu'ils la couvrent de ridicule, et qu'ils réussissent à la faire siffler." [8]

The theory of HERBERT SPENCER is, and professes to be, mainly physiological.[9] He bases it on the axiom:

[1] Page 62. [2] Page 75. [3] Page 124.

[4] "Le rire, le comique, et le risible dans l'esprit et dans l'art," *Rev. des deux mondes*, seconde période, xxxiiime année, 1863.

[5] See previous page. [6] Pages 117–18.

[7] Page 123. [8] Page 139.

[9] "The Physiology of Laughter (1863), in *Essays*, vol. ii.

"Nervous excitation always *tends* to beget muscular motion; and when it rises to a certain intensity, always does beget it."[1] The outflow of nervous energy will follow the paths of least resistance, and the closure of some possible outlets will increase the intensity of the discharge through those that remain open. Unexpressed emotion is "reflected back, accumulates, and intensifies"[2]; conversely, bodily activity deadens emotion. Laughter is a display of muscular excitement due to strong feeling of almost any kind. It is purposeless.[3] The muscles round the mouth, being small and easy to move, will be the first to be innervated; from them the discharge, if intense, will pass to the respiratory muscles, then to those of the upper limbs, then to those of the head and trunk, and so on.[4] We therefore do not laugh at incongruity in general, but only at "a descending incongruity," which leaves a store of emotion ready to be discharged without any *purposeful* channel along which it may be discharged.[5]

According to CHARLES BAUDELAIRE, laughter is the mark of man's primeval fall from grace; "le Sage, par excellence, le Verbe incarné, n'a jamais ri."[6] Until simple innocence is lost, laughter does not occur, for laughter comes from the feeling of superiority over our fellows. "Comme le rire est essentiellement humain, il est essentiellement contradictoire, c'est à dire qu'il est à la fois signe d'une grandeur infinie et d'une misère infinie, misère infinie rélativement a l'Être absolu dont il possède la conception, grandeur infinie rélativement aux animaux. C'est du choc perpétuel de ces deux infinis que se dégage le rire."[7]

CHARLES DARWIN shows a certain catholicity among conflicting theories. In general, he regards laughter as

[1] Page 106. [2] Page 109. [3] Page 111.
[4] *Loc. cit.* [5] Page 115.
[6] "De l'essence du rire," in *Curiosités esthétiques* (1869), p. 362.
[7] Page 370.

the expression of mere joy or happiness.[1] But "something incongruous or unaccountable, exciting surprise and some sense of superiority in the laugher, who must be in a happy frame of mind, seems to be the commonest cause" of laughter.[2]

EWALD HECKER evolves a theory of laughter on the basis of tickling.[3] Tickling is an intermittent excitation of the skin, producing an intermittent excitation in the vaso-motor system, and in respiration, and thus an alternation of agreeable and disagreeable states of feeling. The comic has the same effect, producing an agreeable feeling of superiority, and a disagreeable feeling of contradiction. Laughter has the compensatory function of increasing the blood pressure in the brain.

The laughable may be classified, according to VICTOR COURDAVEAUX, under four main headings: (i) slight imperfections, physical, intellectual, or moral; (ii) slight annoyances; (iii) the unexpected, the surprising, the extraordinary; and (iv) the indecent, the vulgar, the obscene.[4] All these, occurring in life or art, may make us laugh, but our enjoyment of them in art is modified by our appreciation of the ability or cleverness of the artist.[5] The pleasures which give rise to laughter are as diverse as the objects of laughter, and cannot be reduced to any single principle.[6]

EMERSON includes an essay on "The Comic" in *Letters and Social Aims*.[7] "The essence of all jokes, of all comedy," he says, "seems to be an honest or well-intended

[1] *The Expression of the Emotions in Man and Animals* (1872).
[2] *Ibid.*, popular edition, 1904, p. 205.
[3] *Die Physiologie und Psychologie des Lachens und des Komischen* (1873). I have not seen the original, and base my summary on those given by Ribot, *Psychologie des sentiments*, and William James, *Principles of Psychology*, vol. ii, chap. xxv.
[4] *Le rire dans la vie et dans l'art* (1875), p. 27.
[5] Pages 40–1.
[6] Page 157.
[7] 1876. I have used Edina edition of *Works*, 1907.

halfness; a non-performance of what is pretended to be performed, at the same time that one is giving loud pledges of performance. The balking of the intellect, the frustrated expectation, the break of continuity in the intellect, is comedy; and it announces itself physically, in the pleasant spasms we call laughter." [1] Reason does not laugh, for Reason sees the whole; the intellect, isolating the object of laughter, sees in it some discrepancy with the ideal.[2] "In all the parts of life, the occasion of laughter is some seeming, some keeping of the word to ear and eye, whilst it is broken to the soul." [3]

Comedy has for MEREDITH a special limited meaning.[4] It is social in origin, and dependent upon society. The Comic Spirit is the spirit of common sense in society, vigilant but kindly. "If you believe that our civilization is founded in common sense (and it is the first condition of sanity to believe it), you will, when contemplating men, discern a Spirit overhead; not more heavenly than the light flashed upward from glassy surfaces, but luminous and watchful; never shooting beyond them nor lagging in the rear; so closely attached to them that it may be taken for a slavish reflex, until its features are studied. . . . Its common aspect is one of unsolicitous observation, as if surveying a full field and having leisure to dart on its chosen morsels, without any fluttering eagerness. Men's future upon earth does not attract it; their honesty and shapeliness in the present does; and whenever they wax out of proportion, overblown, affected, pretentious, bombastical, hypocritical, pedantic, fantastically delicate; whenever it sees them self-deceived or hoodwinked, given to run riot in idolatries, drifting into vanities, congregating in absurdities, planning shortsightedly, plotting dementedly; whenever they are at variance with their professions, and violate the unwritten but perceptible laws binding them in consideration one

[1] Page 645. [2] Pages 545–6. [3] Page 647.
[4] *An Essay on Comedy, and the uses of the Comic Spirit* (1877), reprint, 1918.

to another; whenever they offend sound reason, fair justice; are false in humility or mined with conceit, individually, or in the bulk—the Spirit overhead will look humanely malign and cast an oblique light on them, followed by volleys of silvery laughter. That is the Comic Spirit."[1] It is to be noted that the comic does not imply even the temporary inhibition of feeling. "You may estimate your capacity for Comic perception by being able to detect the ridicule of them you love, without loving them less."[2] But comedy addresses the wits, it is "the humour of the mind."[3] It does not aim at arousing emotion. Humour is the laugh of heart and mind in one. In satire the kindliness that is of the essence of the comic attitude is chilled: "The Satirist is a moral agent, often a social scavenger, working on a storage of bile."[4] In general, it is the function of the comic poet to teach the world what ails it.

The effect of the ridiculous, says Professor HARALD HÖFFDING, depends on a contrast of feeling, rather than on a contrast apprehended only intellectually.[5] This is shown by the fact that the ridiculous will not stand too frequent repetition, feeling being easily deadened. The simplest mental cause of laughter is the feeling of pleasure, and at the primitive stage it is almost exclusively produced by impressions which satisfy the instinct of self-preservation and appeal to the love of self. Hobbes was right in part, in emphasizing 'sudden glory,' though the feeling expressed is more generally one of salvation or deliverance."[6] "The mere possibility of employing laughter as a weapon shows that it presupposes power."[7] Yet sympathy may be behind laughter, as in humour. "Here there is duality of feeling; the worth of the object is recognized beneath its littleness. In one and the same instant a double standard is applied."[8] The feeling of the ridiculous, like the feeling of the sublime, depends

[1] Pages 88–90. [2] Page 78. [3] Page 88. [4] Page 82.
[5] *Outlines of Psychology* (1882). I have used the English translation, 1896.
[6] Page 293. [7] Page 294. [8] Page 295.

on the fundamental relation between greatness and smallness. "For man's real position is this, that he must bring his force to bear on his surroundings, must overcome and crush resistance, while at the same time he must feel his insignificance in face of the great powers of Nature and history. Only he who neither exults nor fears has won complete victory over himself and over the world. . . . In humour we feel great and small at the same time, and sympathy makes laughter humorous, just as it changes fear into reverence." [1]

LOUIS PHILBERT wrote a very long book to prove the following thesis: "Le plaisant consiste dans le caractère visiblement spécieux d'un désordre non pénible. L'esprit est le plaisant d'idée; le comique est le plaisant moral; la bouffonnerie est le plaisant matériel." [2] Laughter is pleasant, a flash of happiness; and happiness consists in coordination, or the complete development of our physical and moral forces. The amusing has both an intellectual and an emotional effect; it sets up an oscillation in the intelligence between two contrasting ideas; it sets up a similar conflict of an emotional kind, in which "notre malice se délecte pendant que notre conscience applaudit; ce sont deux sentiments, l'un cruel, l'autre pur, tous deux agréables différemment, qui nous agite et nous renvoient de l'un à l'autre." [3]

ALFRED MICHIELS is nothing if not controversial. In his *Monde du comique et du rire* [4] he belabours everyone who differs from him (Philbert particularly) with a virulence which is apt to obscure what he has to say on his own account. In general, his thesis is: "Tout ce qui est contraire à l'idéal absolu de la perfection humaine excite le rire et produit un effet comique." [5] But a deviation from the ideal is comic only "lorsqu'elle ne fait pas souffrir le sujet et ne met en péril ni son existence,

[1] Page 298.
[2] *Le rire, essai littéraire, moral et psychologique* (*c.* 1882), 2me édition, 1883, pp. 401–2.
[3] Page 390. [4] 1886. [5] Page 6.

ni celle d'autrui."[1] He classifies the sources of the comic under four main categories: (1) Organic vices or perturbations, (2) rupture of equilibrium among human faculties, (3) maladaptation of man to the external world, and (4) maladaptation of man to his own kind. Each category is subdivided again into four parts, according as the failure of the ideal relates to (1) the animal functions, (2) the intellectual faculties, (3) the emotions and sentiments, or (4) the will and moral life. The comic contains four elements, or moments; (i) the perception of an imperfection; (ii) a rapid and very lively intuition of the ideal principle against which the imperfection offends ("Cette perspective lumineuse . . . nous cause une vive émotion de plaisir: elle nous entraîne dans le monde des vérités absolues, des idées éternelles."[2]); (iii) a disdain, secret or open, for the imperfection ("C'est ce dédain qui produit l'acre sentiment de blessure causé par le rire à ceux qu'il atteint"[3]); and (iv) a secret satisfaction with ourselves, in that we believe ourselves exempt from the imperfection in question. "Ainsi, pour résumer en une seule phrase notre solution du problème, la perception d'une difformité, d'une erreur, d'un vice, d'un malentendu ou d'une contrariété, ranime dans notre esprit la notion du type absolu de la perfection humaine, nous inspire un sentiment de dédain pour les choses, les pensées, les actions et les situations en désaccord avec ce type general, un sentiment d'approbation pour nous-mêmes, et ces quatre causes réunies font éclater la joie bruyante du rire, ou donnent naissance à la joie plus discrète du sourire."[4]

On the problem of the comic C. C. EVERETT proclaims himself a follower of Schopenhauer.[5] "The ludicrous is simply the incongruity between the elements which we bring under a single generalization, or the incongruity of any one fact with the generalization under which we

[1] *Passim.*
[2] Page 164.
[3] Page 165.
[4] Page 166.
[5] *Poetry, Comedy, and Duty,* Boston and New York, 1888.

would bring it." [1] The tragic also is the incongruous,[2] the difference between the tragic and the comic lying "in the fact that the comic is found in an incongruous relation, considered merely as to its *form*, while the tragic is found in an incongruous relation taken as to its *reality*. By the *form* I mean the simple relation of incongruity. By the *reality* I mean the elements that enter into the relation, the causes that produced it, and the effects which result from it." [3] The tragic has objective existence, the comic is purely subjective. The pleasure which we take in the comic is probably due to the freedom we find in it; it brings us "emancipation from reason even while we are using the forms of reason." [4]

The essence of laughter is freedom, says A. PENJON.[5] "La spontanéité, ou mieux la liberté même, telle est en effet l'essence de l'agréable et du risible sous toutes leurs formes, et le rire n'est que l'expression de la liberté ressentie ou de notre sympathie pour certaines manifestations, réelles ou imaginaires, d'une liberté étrangère: toujours et partout il est comme l'écho naturel en nous de la liberté." [6] Any release from restraint, any break down of the monotonous regularity of the outside world, which does not frighten us, or do us or others any harm, makes us laugh or disposes us thereto. "Le plaisir qui nous fait rire est la satisfaction de nos inclinations, et, comme nous l'avons dit, nait de la suppression par une cause ou par une autre de tout obstacle." [7]

H. R. MARSHALL's theory of wit and the ludicrous depends entirely on his general theory of pleasure and pain.[8] In his opinion, "pleasure and pain are determined by the relation between the energy given out and the energy received at any given moment by the physical organs which determine the content of that moment.

[1] Page 177. [2] Page 166.
[3] Page 188. [4] Page 200.
[5] "Le rire et la liberté," in *Revue philosophique*, August 1893.
[6] Page 113. [7] Page 139.
[8] *Pain, Pleasure, and Æsthetics* (1894).

Pleasure is experienced whenever the physical activity coincident with the psychic state to which the pleasure is attached involves the use of surplus stored force—the resolution of surplus potential into actual energy—or, in other words, whenever the energy involved in the reaction to the stimulus is greater in amount than the energy which the stimulus habitually calls forth." [1] Accordingly, much of the effect of the *ludicrous* results from sudden transitions from mental processes involving effort to others involving much less effort because more habitual.[2] The relaxation of attention allows a powerful overflow. The wit, on the other hand, artificially prepares for his effects. He " plays around his subject, avoiding the more usual outcome of the train of his thought, but leading that of his hearer close to this normal resultant, until, when it may be supposed that all the organs connected with the normal outcome are fully prepared for action, he turns the thought train in the direction which is effective for pleasure. The stimulation of the well-nourished organs, which is thus involved, is followed by the burst of pleasure-giving activity which irradiates the system and expands its surplus energy in the pleasurable exercise of laughter." [3]

The subject of laughter is treated incidentally by Professor JOHN DEWEY in an article on "The Theory of Emotion." [4] Laughter is not, he says, to be viewed from the standpoint of humour, its connection with humour being secondary. The laugh is of the same general character as the sigh of relief. " It marks the ending (that is, the attainment of a unity) of a period of suspense, or expectation, an ending which is sharp and sudden." [5]

C. MÉLINAUD, after criticizing Penjon, Dumont, and Bain, maintains that all laughter implies a certain double-

[1] Page 221. [2] Page 329. [3] Pages 330–1.
[4] In *Psychological Review*, vol. i, No. 6, November 1894.
[5] *Op. cit.*, p. 558.

ness of view.[1] The odd or singular (le baroque) is not comic in itself, but only when it is both odd and natural at the same time, and from different points of view. "Partout on retrouvera le même élément : quelque chose de surprenant et d'absurde qui, d'un autre côté est naturel et banal."[2] When a comic personage makes an amusing statement, it is absurd from our point of view, but inevitable from his, and unless we can grasp both points of view, it is not comic.

RIBOT considers the two main theories of laughter, the incongruity theory and the superiority theory, and admits both as partially true.[3] But in general he thinks that the attempt to reduce laughter to one cause, rather than to many causes, is vain. "Pour conclure, le rire se manifeste dans des circonstances si hetérogènes et si multiples—sensations physiques, joie, contraste, surprise, bizarrerie, étrangeté, bassesse, etc.—que la reduction de toutes ces causes à une seule reste bien problématique. Après tant de travaux sur un fait aussi banal, la question est loin d'être complètement élucidée."[4]

Though I have read, several times, the sections on the comic, wit, humour, and the grotesque, in Mr. GEORGE SANTAYANA'S *Sense of Beauty*,[5] I still doubt if I understand what he would be at. It would seem that he considers the essentially fictitious nature of the comic as the important matter. "The excellence of comedy," he says, "lies in the invitation to wander along some by-path of the fancy, among scenes not essentially impossible, but not to be actually enacted by us on account of the fixed circumstances of our lives. If the picture is agreeable, we allow ourselves to dream it true."[6] But

[1] "Pourquoi rit-on ? Étude sur la cause psychologique du rire," in *Revue des deux mondes*, February 1895.
[2] Page 621.
[3] *Psychologie des sentiments* (1896), p. 344.
[4] Page 348.
[5] 1896. I have used the reissue dated 1904.
[6] Page 245.

fiction is unstable and contradictory, and our pleasure in it is not pure. Comic effects are mainly those of incongruity and degradation [1]: these are not pleasant in themselves, for "we are in the presence of an absurdity; and man, being a rational animal, can like absurdity no better than he can like hunger or cold." [2] "The pleasure comes from the inward rationality and movement of the fiction, not from its inconsistency with anything else. . . . We enjoy the stimulus and the shaking up of our wits. It is like getting into a new posture, or hearing a new song." [3] It is not disorder which we like, but expansion [4]; we put up with the disorderliness of the comic for the sake of the freedom to which it stimulates us. Wit is purer amusement, and can dispense with absurdity. "Unexpected justness makes wit." [5] "The essence of what we call humour is that amusing weakness should be combined with an amicable humanity." [6]

Careful reading of the article on "Tickling, Laughter, and the Comic" [7] by President G. STANLEY HALL (with the collaboration of ARTHUR ALLIN) has failed to show what theory (if any) it is designed to support on laughter in general. On the one hand laughter would seem to be regarded as "an atavistic reverberation," [8] and on the other, as practice for the superman that is to be, something like "the first expression of a higher potentialization of the human race." [9]

Writing "On the Philosophy of Laughing," PAUL CARUS finds the secret of the problem in triumph.[10] "We laugh only at petty triumph." [11] And again: "Nothing is in itself ridiculous, but anything will become so as soon as it serves to secure a harmless triumph." [12] "Every joke must have a point; it must be directed against someone or something; otherwise there is nothing at

[1] Page 247. [2] Page 248. [3] Page 249.
[4] Page 250. [5] Page 250. [6] Page 254.
[7] *American Journal of Psychology*, October 1897
[8] *Op. cit.*, p. 25. [9] *Ibid.*, p. 30.
[10] In *Monist*, vol. viii, 1897-8. [11] Page 261. [12] Page 264.

which we may laugh."[1] But the triumph must be sudden.[2]

One of the most famous modern theories of laughter is that developed by THEODOR LIPPS in his *Komik und Humor* and *Grundlegung der Æsthetik*.[3] Lipps brings together Kant, Jean Paul, and Herbert Spencer. In his view, the comic is something little masquerading as something big. It is "the little, the less impressive, the less significant and weighty (and therefore not sublime), which steps into the place of the relatively large, impressive, weighty, and sublime. It is the little behaving as the big, puffing itself out and playing the role of the big, and then on the contrary appearing as the little, and dissolving into nothingness."[4] There are two moments in the comic, first a moment of confusion (Verblüffung), and then a moment of enlightenment (Erleuchtung). The feeling of the comic is unique, not to be confused with any other emotion; it is not joy, but diversion (es erfreut nicht . . . sondern es 'belustigt'), and remains light, superficial, poor in content, a surface tickling which does not touch the heart. In so far as it is pleasant, the pleasure depends on there being a surplus of prepared psychical energy over what is actually needed. We adjust ourselves to comprehend something relatively significant and weighty; what we are actually confronted with, in the comic situation, is something relatively insignificant and light. The parturient mountain produces a mouse.

CH. RENOUVIER and L. PRAT, joint authors of *La nouvelle monodologie*,[5] follow Schopenhauer in the main.

[1] Page 265. [2] Page 263. [3] 1898 and 1903.

[4] "Komisch ist das Kleine, minder Eindrucksvolle, minder Bedeutsame, Gewichtige, also nicht Erhabene, das an Stelle eines relativ Grossen, Eindrucksvollen, Bedeutsamen, Gewichtigen, Erhabenen tritt. Es ist das Kleine, das sich wie ein Grosses gebärdet, dazu aufbauscht, die Rolle eines solchen spielt, und dann doch wiederum als ein Kleines, ein relatives Nichts erscheint, oder in ein solches zergeht." *Grundlegung*, p. 575.

[5] 1899.

According to them, incoherence is fundamental in the amusing and the comic.[1] The feelings of the sublime and the laughable are both among the disinterested passions, and are alike in that thought is thrown out of its habitual orderliness. The sublime surpasses expectation by grandeur and power, the laughable deceives expectation by an abrupt contradiction between a concept and a representation.[2] "Le franc rire, chez un sujet favorablement disposé, exempt de préoccupations, éclate quand vient à lui être réprésentée quelque chose ou quelque idée dans lesquelles il rencontre inopinément de l'inattendu, de l'anormal, de l'incohérent, ou du contradictoire, sans que cependant, il entre rien du nuisible, odieux, ou intéressé dans l'image . . . il sent que ce n'est pas le moment de *faire le raisonnable,* et se *détend.* Cette détente de la raison se traduit physiologiquement par le rire. Mentalement c'est un mode de jeu."[3] In addition there is laughter of another kind, the smile and the laugh of friendship and sympathy.[4]

Of all recent works on Laughter that of M. HENRI BERGSON is probably the best known.[5] The Comic, he says, always lodges in something directly or indirectly human. If any animal other than man, or any lifeless object, arouses laughter, "it is always because of some resemblance to man, of the stamp he gives it, or the use he puts it to."[6] Secondly, the Comic appeals to pure intelligence, and inhibits feeling. "The comic demands something like a momentary anæsthesia of the heart."[7] Thirdly, laughter is social; it is always "the laughter of a group."[8] Now life and society demand from man tension and elasticity, alertness and adaptability. Life sets a lower standard than society. A moderate degree of adaptability enables one to live; to live well, which is the aim of society, requires much greater flexibility. Society is compelled to be suspicious of all tendencies

[1] Page 215. [2] Page 187.
[3] Page 214. [4] Page 215.
[5] *Le rire* (1900). I have used the English translation (1911).
[6] Page 4. [7] Page 5. [8] Page 6.

towards the inelastic, and for this purpose has devised a social gesture, laughter, as a corrective of all unsocial aberrations. The comic is always something rigid, inelastic, inflexible, usurping the place in human affairs of the fine tension and adjustment that society needs. It is always "something mechanical encrusted on the living."[1] Laughter is, consciously or unconsciously, corrective in aim. "In laughter we always find an unavowed intention to humiliate and consequently to correct our neighbour, if not in his will, at least in his deed."[2] Comedy therefore stands midway between art and life, in the zone of artifice. On the one hand, the comic in life appeals to us because we watch it detachedly; on the other hand, comedy is not, like art, disinterested; it has a social function. This social function must not be confounded with morality, and it is a failure to distinguish the immoral from the unsocial that has, according to M. Bergson, misled those thinkers who have localized the comic in the trifling faults of men. A virtue as well as a vice may be comic, for the comic depends on the conventions or prejudices of a particular group or society, and not upon any more stable moral standard. Laughter is the revenge of society upon the unsocial. It is not kindly, nor is it strictly just; it breaks out spontaneously, and is just only in the rough, punishing certain failings as disease punishes others, not always distinguishing the innocent from the guilty, but aiming at an average result. "Laughter is a froth with a saline base. Like froth it sparkles. It is gaiety itself. But the philosopher who gathers a handful to taste may find that the substance is scanty, and the after-taste bitter."[3]

M. L. Dugas professes in the opening chapters of his book,[4] to follow Ribot in believing that it is impossible to reduce all forms of laughter to one principle. None the less, in the progress of the work, he does put forward

[1] Page 37. [2] Page 136. [3] Page 200.
[4] *Psychologie du rire* (1902). I have used the second revised and augmented edition of 1910.

a theory, namely, that the point of view from which people, things, or events appear laughable is the point of view of play. The laughable is the imaginary: "rire, c'est se dégager de la réalité, plâner au-dessus d'elle." [1] "Imaginaire est donc synonyme de ridicule." [2] The imaginary is in *contradiction* with reality, and the pride or superiority of the laugher is really his sense of freedom from the limitations of the external world. "Le rieur est orgueilleux sans doute en ce sens qu'il s'arroge le droit ou s'octroie la permission de juger toutes choses au gré de sa fantaisie et les juge volontiers extravagantes ou absurdes." [3] And so he concludes: "Tous les caractères du rire trouvent ainsi leur explication dernière dans cet état de notre esprit, dans cette forme de notre humeur, qu'on appelle l'*enjouement*, ou, plus generalement, le *jeu* (*ludus*, jeu et plaisanteries, en français, *badinage*)." [4] On this basis, M. Dugas cannot admit any function in laughter. [5] Laughter is a-social and a-moral, an accident, an epiphenomenon, neither good nor evil in itself, though it may accidentally appear either as a good or an evil from its association with certain psychical states, some of which are moral, some immoral.

Like M. Dugas, Professor JAMES SULLY makes the principle of play fundamental in his theory of laughter.[6] Much of the laughable, he says, "may be regarded as an expression in persons or things of the play-mood which seizes the spectator by way of a sympathetic resonance." [7] "Even if the laughable spectacle does not wear the look of a play-challenge . . . it may so present its particular feature as to throw us off our serious balance, and by a sweet compulsion force us to play with it rather than to consider it seriously." [8] Laughter arises, in the first place, "from a sudden accession of happy consciousness." [9]

[1] Page 105. [2] Page 109. [3] Page 114.
[4] Page 116. [5] Pages 156 ff.
[6] *An Essay on Laughter* (1902), reissue, 1907. It is impossible to do justice to this admirable book in any summary. The mere theory it happens to contain is the least valuable thing in it.
[7] Page 149. [8] Page 150. [9] Page 72.

This may be either through the release from external constraint, or through "the sudden transformation of one's world, from the arrival of some good thing which is at once unexpected and big enough to lift us to a higher level of happiness."[1] The feeling out of which laughter comes is highly complex, "containing something of the child's joyous surprise at the new and unheard of; something, too, of the child's gay responsiveness to a play-challenge: often something also of the glorious sense of expansion after compression which gives the large mobility to freshly freed limbs of young animals and children."[2]

Reviewing Professor Sully's book,[3] Mr. ARTHUR ALLIN, no longer in collaboration with President Stanley Hall, maintains that the real causal ground for laughter must be found in physiological processes. He suggests that the smile betokens an attitude of the whole organism in which the inception of food is the most striking characteristic, and that "the laugh is the rehabilitation of function, the rebound to increased metabolism."[4] "The sense of joy present in the feeling of *bien-être*, in the witticism, in the wild atmosphere of humour, is evidently due to vaso-motor phenomena and a discharge of surplus stored energy where the discharge does not involve too much strain, effort, or lesion."[5]

Professor J. R. ANGELL notes that the typical expression of joy is laughter, but that laughter is also typical of surprise, derision, contempt, and even paroxysmal forms of grief.[6] "In all these cases the laugh is the motor activity which inevitably accompanies the explosive release from sustained tension, with its suspended breathing."[7]

M. PAUL GAULTIER is concerned not so much with laughter in general as with the laughter occasioned by

[1] *Loc. cit.* [2] Page 153.
[3] In *Psychological Review*, vol. x, 1903. [4] Page 310.
[5] Page 312. [6] *Psychology* (2nd edition, 1905), p. 333. [7] *Loc. cit.*

caricature.[1] The most accusatory caricatures are, he says, the most laughable: "Nous aurons vîte fait de constater que les plus chargées sont les plus amusantes, et qu'à l'inverse, les plus véridiques sont les moins gaies."[2] The only cause of laughter is exaggeration towards the ugly: "Pour faire naître le rire, l'exagération est . . . obligée d'enlaidir et de rabaisser la nature."[3] Yet ugliness is not sought for its own sake, but by contrast to show up the ideal. Caricature is "la protestation de ce qui devrait être contre ce qui est."[4]

It is a mistake to take Professor SIGMUND FREUD'S theory of wit, as developed in his *Wit and its Relation to the Unconscious*,[5] for a complete theory of laughter, though this mistake is often made, even by his followers.[6] For Freud, wit is one thing, the comic another, and humour a third; and though he suggests similar formulæ for all three, namely: "The pleasure of wit originates from *an economy of expenditure in inhibition*, of the comic from an *economy of expenditure in thought*, and of humour from an *economy of expenditure in feeling*,"[7] it is only of wit that he speaks with any confidence. Wit is analogous to the dream. In the dream the unconscious, which is the infantile, transforms a remnant of the thoughts left over from the day before, so as to secure fulfilment of a repressed wish, by eluding, or deluding, the 'censor' of conscious wishes making up the character of the dreamer in his waking moments. Wit is a convenient, though on the whole less effective, way of doing the same thing without the necessity of going to sleep. Freud subdivides it into 'harmless' and 'tendency' wit. In the former, apart from the thought expressed, which may be either profound or trivial, we obtain a feeling of

[1] *Le rire et la caricature*, 2me edition, 1906.
[2] Page 8.
[3] Page 34.
[4] Page 38.
[5] 1905. I have used the English translation, 1916.
[6] Cf. E. B. Holt, who seems to me to make this mistake; *The Freudian Wish*, pp. 17 ff.
[7] Freud, *op. cit.*, p. 384.

pleasure simply from the form or technique of the witticism. This technique takes many shapes, such as condensation, displacement, unification, representation through the opposite, etc., all of which have in common the character of 'economy.' One word, or similar words, are made to do duty to cover diverse ideas, and psychic energy is saved; or by witty conjunctions of words we discover the familiar when we expected to discover the new, and again save psychic expenditure. We regress to infantile states of mind, and play, avoiding the restrictive and fatiguing rules of logic or reason. In tendency wit, our pleasure in the economical technique is supplemented by our pleasure in being able, again with very little expenditure of energy, to gratify a sexual or an aggressive wish, in an indirect way. Culture puts hindrances in the way of our openly satisfying hostile or obscene desires; but these, if restricted, are not eliminated, and by enlisting the services of the technique of wit, they avoid the hindrances, and obtain momentary satisfaction. As to the comic: this arouses in us a comparison between two expenditures of psychic energy. Either we are led to expect a heavy expenditure and find less necessary, or we are led to expect a slight expenditure and find more necessary. In either event the difference between the two expenditures must be isolated and not *used*: it is *discharged* in laughter. Humour again results from an economy of affect. We are prepared to react emotionally to a situation, and then some of the emotion is diverted, the psychic energy thus set free being discharged as before in laughter. Humour is the highest of the 'defence' processes. "It disdains to withdraw from conscious attention the ideas which are connected with the painful affect . . . as repression does, and thus it overcomes the defence automatism. It brings this about by finding the means to withdraw the energy resulting from the liberation of pain, which is held in readiness, and through discharge changes the same into pleasure." [1]

[1] Page 380.

OTTO SCHAUER [1] links up all comedy with teasing. He divides the comic into the objective-comic and the subjective-comic, according as we triumph or are triumphed over. Yet the pleasure felt in successful teasing is the pleasure of play, and this can be enjoyed " not only when others are hoodwinked and overcome, but also in the cases when one must himself play the rôle of the hoodwinked and overcome." [2]

The essential principle in laughter and comedy, according to Dr. HORACE M. KALLEN, is the overcoming of disharmony.[3] In the laughable we have " an inversion of the ordinary—an inversion, shocking, fresh, and unexpected." [4] The prime source of comedy is malproportion of character,[5] though " the range of the comic scene . . . is no less than the cosmos itself." [6] The outcome of laughter, however, is a re-establishment of harmony; " the disintegration which is the object of laughter leads to re-distribution, re-adjustment, harmony, not to real human loss." [7] " The first laughter is life's earliest cry of victory over the elemental world-wide enemy that wages the titanic battle with it. . . . It is the frustrated menace in things,—personal, social, or cosmic—that moves men merrily, when their power for evil is turned to emptiness." [8]

Dr. BORIS SIDIS claims that his " view of the comic includes all the other theories proposed since the time of Aristotle for the explanation of the ludicrous, the funny, and the comic." [9] It is not surprising, therefore, that it is a little difficult to state shortly this comprehensive view. Laughter belongs to the emotion of joy, and " all unrestrained spontaneous activities of normal functions " [10]

[1] " Ueber das Wesen der Komik," in *Archiv für die gesamte Psychologie*, 1910.
[2] Quoted by Eastman, *The Sense of Humor*, p. 143.
[3] " The Æsthetic Principle in Comedy," in *Amer. Journ. Psychology*, vol. xxii, 1911.
[4] Page 146.
[5] Page 149.
[6] Page 152.
[7] Page 153.
[8] Pages 156–7.
[9] *The Psychology of Laughter*, 1913, p. 65.
[10] Page 3.

give rise to this emotion. Laughter appears to take two main forms: *ascending* laughter, in proportion as the difficult becomes easy for the laugher, and *descending* laughter, or the laughter of derision, in proportion as the easy appears difficult for other people.[1] "We laugh from strength, and we laugh at weakness."[2] Although Sidis objects to Freud's idea that economy is at the root of all laughter, he adopts a view of laughter as a discharge of surplus energy which is very similar, in appearance at least. "The superabundant, spontaneous overflow of unused energies gives rise to joy and its accompaniment, laughter. When we expect the normal and are adjusted to respond to it by an amount of energy, and then the subnormal is discovered, the amount of energy that is left over goes into the overflow, giving rise to laughter. . . . In fact, we may say that any *release of reserve energy is the source of all laughter.*"[3]

At the annual meeting of the British Association in 1913, Professor WILLIAM McDOUGALL delivered a paper on Laughter, of which all I have been able to discover is the short summary printed in *Nature*.[4] According to this summary, he reduces the conditions which excite laughter to (i) situations that are mildly unpleasant, except in so far as they are redeemed by laughter; and (ii) those things which would excite a feeble degree of sympathetic pain, if we did not actually laugh at them. He accordingly argues that laughter has been evolved in the human race as an antidote to sympathy, or a protective reaction shielding us from the depressive influence of the shortcomings of our fellow-men.

In an article on "The Origin of Laughter,"[5] Miss SILVIA H. BLISS sets out a theory which she claims to have developed independently of Freud's theory of wit. "The

[1] Page 23.
[2] Page 80.
[3] Page 68 (italics in text).
[4] Vol. xcii.
[5] In *Amer. Journ. Psychology*, vol. xxvi, April 1915.

secret of laughter," she says, "is in a return to Nature."[1] Man being only partially civilized, "the human being, from childhood up, must curb, repress, skulk, hide, control,"[2] and "laughter is the result of suddenly released repression, the physical sign of sub-conscious satisfaction."[3]

In the last chapter of his *Studies in Human Nature*[4] Professor J. B. BAILLIE gives a fresh twist to the intellectualist theory of laughter. A situation is *judged* to be ludicrous, and this judgment represents a different attitude of mind from mere apprehension or comprehension, even in a child. "We 'understand' it if we know how its parts are connected and the laws that control its being: we 'appreciate' it when we relate it to some end and we express this appreciation when we judge its value."[5] Undue fixity of the attention in the first attitude, that of apprehension, inhibits laughter: we must not try to *explain* a joke. "Laughter arises when the character or process of an object, which is considered to refer to an end, real or supposed, is judged to be partially or wholly incongruent or incoherent with the end in view. It is important to note that the end must not be given up, but must hold good in spite of the incongruity; and also that the object laughed at must not give way and must be none the worse for its incoherence with the end."[6] Thus, neither mere incongruity nor mere contrast is enough to occasion laughter. Any end whatever may be made the subject of laughter. In contrast to laughter, the end with tears is always really or apparently defeated.[7]

The latest full discussion on the subject of Laughter is contained in Mr. MAX EASTMAN'S *The Sense of Humor*.[8]

[1] Page 240. [2] Page 238. [3] Page 239. [4] 1921.
[5] Page 257. [6] Page 259. [7] Page 273.
[8] 1921. I had already written most of my book, and sketched out the remainder, when Mr. Eastman's book reached me. I disagree altogether with his fundamental idea that humour is an instinct on its own, so to speak. I disagree also with many of the incidental opinions put forward in his book. He appears to me to have followed too trustfully the leading—the misleading, as I believe it to be on only too many occasions—of Professor William McDougall. At the same

Humour, according to Mr. Eastman, is a human *element*, an instinct, not to be analysed further. And it is a play instinct. "The sense of humor is a primary instinct of our nature, functioning originally only in the state of play, and related not remotely in its development to that gregarious instinct of which smiles and smiling laughter appear to be an inherent part."[1] "Play is an attitude in which we exercise our instincts and experience our emotions superficially, as though tasting or smelling of them, but not drinking them down."[2] The instinct of humour is an instinct to take a shock or disappointment playfully, "a very inward indispensable little shock-absorber—an instinct, as we might call it, for making the best of a bad thing."[3] It is "a simple emotional mitigation"[4] of failure. In adults, humour has two currents, a negative and a positive. "The negative current is a discommoding of some light or playful interest that has been specifically aroused, the position a gratification of some interest which, if it has not been specifically aroused, may at least be assumed to have a general existence in the hearts of those who are to laugh."[5] The positive current may be hostility,[6] sexuality,[7] or the love of truth, blunt and unconcealed,[8] or there may be, apparently, no positive current at all, so that "we are simply tripped up, or dropped into a trap, or left staring at nothing."[9] In accordance with the theory above outlined, Eastman formulates eight laws for jokes. These are: (i) "There must be a real engagement of the interest of the person who is expected to laugh"[10]; humour is not purely intellectual, but emotional. (ii) "The feelings aroused in the person who is expected to laugh must not be too strong and deep"[11]; we must be able to take *playfully* the matter at which we are to laugh. (iii) "Both the negative and the positive current

time I should like to say, if I may without impertinence, that *The Sense of Humor* is the best written book on Laughter I have yet read, and I have read a good many. It is full of good things. And it is full of true things, aptly said.

[1] Pages 226–7. [2] Page 11. [3] Page 21. [4] Page 24.
[5] Page 30. [6] Chap. v. [7] Chap. vi.
Chap. vii. [9] Page 58. [10] Page 88. [11] Page 92.

of feeling must be simply and naturally induced "[1]; there is no forcing of a joke. (iv) " The identity of the positive current with the negative must be immediate and perfect "[2]; there is no explaining a joke, it must flash. (v) " Practical jokes should not be poetically told, nor poetic jokes practically told."[3] (vi) " The disappointment involved in a practical joke should be genuine "[4]; a joke must be fresh. (vii) " The interest satisfied must not be too weak in proportion to the interest disappointed."[5] (viii) " The interest disappointed must not be too strong in proportion to the interest satisfied."[6]

[1] Page 96. [2] Page 99. [3] Page 104.
[4] Page 106. [5] Page 111. [6] Page 116.

BIBLIOGRAPHY

List I comprises works which I have consulted.

List II comprises works of which I have heard, but which, for one reason or another, I have been unable to consult.

LIST I.

1. ADDISON, JOSEPH. *The Spectator,* Everyman's Library, 8 vols., London, 1909.
2. AKENSIDE, MARK. *Pleasures of the Imagination,* in Johnson's Poets, vol. xiv, London, 1810.
3. ALLIN, ARTHUR. "On Laughter," *Psychological Review,* vol. x, No. 3, May 1903.
   See also under HALL, G. STANLEY.
4. ANGELL, J. R. *Psychology,* 2nd edit., London, 1905.
5. APULEIUS. *The Golden Ass,* Adlington's translation, reprint, London, 1913.
6. ARISTOPHANES. *The Comedies,* translated by B. B. Rogers, 6 vols., London, 1902–16.
7. *The Comedies,* translated by W. J. Hickie, 2 vols., Bohn's Classical Library, London, 1873, 1875.
8. *The Acharnians, The Knights, The Birds, The Peace,* translated by J. Hookham Frere, Everyman's Library, London, 1911.
9. *The Frogs, The Trial of Euripides, The Clouds, The Wasps,* translated by J. Hookham Frere and others, Everyman's Library, London, N.D.
10. *The Frogs,* translated by Gilbert Murray, London, 1908.
11. ARISTOTLE. *The Poetics,* translated by S. H. Butcher, 4th edit., London, 1907.

12. ARISTOTLE. *The Nicomachean Ethics*, translated by F. H. Peters, 10th edit., London, 1906.

13. BAILLIE, J. B. *Studies in Human Nature*, London, 1921.

14. BAIN, ALEXANDER. *The Emotions and the Will*, London, 1859.

15. BALDWIN, J. M. *Mental Development in the Child and the Race*, London, 1895.

16. BALFOUR, SIR G. *The Life of Robert Louis Stevenson*, 14th (abridged) edit., London, 1914.

17. BARROW, ISAAC. "Sermon against Foolish Talking and Jesting," extract in Hunt's *Wit and Humour*, q.v

18. BAUDELAIRE, CH. *Curiosités esthétiques*, Paris, 1869.

19. BAUDOUIN, CH. *Suggestion et autosuggestion*, 2me édit., Neuchatel et Paris, 1921. English translation, London: George Allen & Unwin, Ltd.

20. BAWDON, H. H. "The Comic as illustrating the summation-irradiation theory of pleasure-pain," *Psychological Review*, vol. xvii, 1910.

21. BEATTIE, JAMES. "Essay on Laughter and Ludicrous Composition," in *Essays*, Edinburgh, 1776.

22. BÉDIER, JOSEPH. *Les Fabliaux*, 2me édit., Paris, 1895.

23. BELL, SIR C. *The Anatomy and Philosophy of Expression*, 7th edit., London, 1890.

24. BELL, S. "Preliminary Study of the Emotion of Love between the Sexes," *American Journal of Psychology*, July 1902.

25. BÉNARD, CH. "La théorie du comique dans l'esthétique allemande," *Revue philosophique*, tomes x et xii, 1880, 1881.

26. BERGSON, HENRI. *Creative Evolution*, English translation, London, 1911.

27. *Laughter*, English translation, London, 1911.

28. BLAIR, HUGH. "Lectures on Rhetoric and Belles-Lettres, 3 vols., 5th edit., London, 1793.

29. BLISS, SILVIA H. "The Origin of Laughter," *American Journal of Psychology*, vol. xxvi., April 1915.

30. BOSWELL, JAMES. *Life of Samuel Johnson*, edited by Birkbeck Hill, 6 vols., Oxford, 1887.

31. BRADLEY, F. H. "On Floating Ideas and the Imaginary," *Mind*, N.S., vol. xv, October 1906.

32. BRILL, A. A. "Freud's Theory of Wit," *Journal of Abnormal Psychology*, vol. vi, October–November 1911.

33. BROWN, THOMAS. *Lectures on the Philosophy of the Human Mind*, 4 vols., Edinburgh, 1820.

34. BRUHL, LÉVY. *Les fonctions mentales dans les sociétés inférieures*, Paris, 1910.

35. *Primitive Mentality*, London, G. Allen & Unwin, Ltd.

36. BULLOUGH, EDWARD. "'Psychical Distance' as a factor in Art and an æsthetic principle," *British Journal of Psychology*, vol. v, June 1912.

37. BURTON, ROBERT. *The Anatomy of Melancholy*, London, 1859.

38. BUTCHER, S. H. *Aristotle's Theory of Poetry and the Fine Arts*, 4th edit., London, 1907.

39. BUTLER, SAMUEL. *Poetical Works*, 2 vols., Edinburgh, 1854.

40. BUTLER, SAMUEL. *The Note-Books*, edited by H. Festing Jones, London, 1919.

41. *Unconscious Memory*, London, 1910

42. *Life and Habit*, London, 1917.

43. *Erewhon*, London, 1919.

44. *Erewhon Revisited*, 1916.

45. *The Way of all Flesh*, London, 1919

46. CALVERLEY C. S. *Fly Leaves*, Cambridge and London, 1883.

47. CAMPBELL, GEORGE. *The Philosophy of Rhetoric*, London, 1776.

48. CARLYLE, THOMAS. *Sartor Resartus*, Edinburgh edition, London, 1905.

49. "Jean Paul Friedrich Richter," in *Critical and Miscellaneous Essays*, 3 vols., London, 1869.

50. CARUS, PAUL. "On the Philosophy of Laughing," *Monist*, vol. viii, 1897–8.

51. *The History of the Devil and the Idea of Evil*, Chicago and London, 1900.

52. CARVER, A. "The Generation and Control of Emotion," *British Journal of Psychology*, vol x, November 1919.

53. CASTIGLIONE, B. "The Book of the Courtier," done into English by Sir Thomas Hoby, anno 1561, reprinted in *Tudor Translations*, London, 1900.

54. CERVANTES, M. DE. *The Adventures of Don Quixote de la Mancha*, English translation, Nelson, London, 1906.

55. CHAMBERS, E. K. *The Mediæval Stage*, 2 vols., Oxford, 1903.

56. CHAPIN, HAROLD. *Comedies*, London, 1921.

57. CHARAUX, CH. *L'ombre de Socrate*, Paris, 1878.

58. CHESTERFIELD, EARL OF. *Letters to His Son*, edited by C. Strachey, 2 vols., London, 1901.

59. CHESTERTON, G. K. *Twelve Types*, London, 1910.

60. CICERO. *De Oratore*, Clarendon Press Series, Oxford, 1881.

61. COLERIDGE, S. T. *The Literary Remains*, edited by H. N. Coleridge, 4 vols., London, 1836.

62. *Biographia Literaria*, Everyman's Library, London, 1906.

63. *Lectures and Notes on Shakespeare and Other English Poets*, Bohn's Library, London, 1897.

64. COMPAYRÉ, GABRIEL. *The Intellectual and Moral Development of the Child*, Part I, English translation, New York, 1901.

65. CONGREVE, WM. *The Comedies*, Mermaid Series, London, 1887.

66. "Essay upon Humour in Comedy," in Spingarn's *Critical Essays of the Seventeenth Century*, q.v.

67. COUAT, A. *Aristophane et l'ancienne comédie attique*, Paris, 1902.

68 COURDAVEAUX, VICTOR. *Le rire dans la vie et dans l'art*, Paris, 1875.

69. DARWIN, CHARLES. *The Descent of Man*, 2 vols., London, 1871.

70. *The Expression of the Emotions in Man and Animals*, popular edition, London, 1904.

71. "A Biographical Sketch of an Infant," *Mind*, 1877.

72. DEKKER, THOMAS. *The Comedies*, Mermaid Series, London, 1887.

73. DESCARTES, RÉNÉ. *Passions de l'âme,* Œuvres, publiées par Charles Adam et Paul Tannery, t. x, Paris, 1909.
74. DEWEY, JOHN. "The Theory of Emotion," *Psychological Review,* vols. i and ii, 1894-5.
75. D'ISRAELI, ISAAC. *Curiosities of Literature,* London, 1866.
76. DOSTOEVSKY, FYODOR. *The Idiot,* translated by Mrs. Garnett, London, 1913.
77. *The Brothers Karamazov,* translated by Mrs. Garnett, London, 1912.
78. DREVER, JAMES. *Instinct in Man,* Cambridge, 1917.
79. "Instinct and the Unconscious," *British Journal of Psychology,* vol. x, November 1919.
80. DRYDEN, JOHN. *The Poems,* Oxford, 1910.
81. *The Essays,* 2 vols., edited by W. P. Ker, Oxford, 1900.
82. DUGAS, L. *Psychologie du rire,* 2me édit., Paris, 1910.
83. "La fonction psychologique du rire," *Revue philosophique,* tome 62, 1906.
84. DUMONT, LÉON A. *Des causes du rire,* Paris, 1862.
85. EASTMAN, MAX. *The Sense of Humor,* New York and London, 1922.
86. ELLIS, HAVELOCK. *Man and Woman,* 5th edit., London, 1914.
87. *Studies in the Psychology of Sex,* 6 vols., Philadelphia, 1902-14. Vol. i: "The Evolution of Modesty, etc." Vol. ii: "Sexual Inversion, etc." Vol. iii: "The Sexual Impulse, etc." Vol. iv: "Sexual Selection in Man." Vol. v: "Erotic Symbolism, etc." Vol. vi: "Sex in Relation to Society."
88. EMERSON, R. W. "Letters and Social Aims," *Works,* Edina edition, Edinburgh, 1907.
89. EVERETT, C. C. *Poetry, Comedy, and Duty,* Boston and New York, 1888.
90. FIELD, G. C. "Faculty Psychology and Instinct Psychology," *Mind,* N.S., No. 119, July, 1921.
91. FIELDING, HENRY. *Joseph Andrews,* Hutchinson, London, N.D.
92. *Tom Jones,* 2 vols., Bell, London, 1905.
93. FIGGIS, DARRELL. *Shakespeare: a Study,* London, 1911.
94. FITZGERALD, PERCY. *Principles of Comedy and Dramatic Effect,* London, 1870.

95. FLÜGEL, J. C. "On the biological basis of sexual repression and its sociological significance," *British Journal of Psychology*, Medical Section, vol. i, July 1921.

96. FRANCE, ANATOLE. *L'île des pingouins*, Paris, 1908.

97. *La rotisserie de la reine pédauque*, 125me édit., Paris, N.D.

98. *La révolte des anges*, Paris, 1914

99. *Les contes de Jacques Tournebroche*, 11me édit., Paris, 1921.

100. *Le puits de Sainte-Claire*, Paris, N.D.

101. FRAZER, SIR J. G. *The Golden Bough*, 3rd edit., 12 vols., London, 1911–15. Vols. i–ii: "The Magic Art and the Evolution of Kings. Vol. iii: "Taboo and the Perils of the Soul." Vol. iv: "The Dying God." Vols. v–vi: "Adonis, Attis, Osiris." Vols. vii–viii: "Spirits of the Corn and of the Wild." Vol. ix: "The Scapegoat." Vols. x–xi: "Balder the Beautiful." Vol. xii: Bibliography and General Index.

102. FREUD, SIGMUND. *Selected Papers on Hysteria and other Psychoneuroses*, 2nd edit., translated by A. A. Brill, Nervous and Mental Diseases, Monograph Series, No. 4, New York, 1912.

103. *Three Contributions to the Theory of Sex*, 2nd edit., translated by A. A. Brill, Nervous and Mental Diseases, Monograph Series, No. 7, Washington, 1920.

104. *The Psychopathology of Everyday Life*, translated by A. A. Brill, London, 1914.

105. *The Interpretation of Dreams*, translated by A. A. Brill, 2nd edit., London, Geo. Allen & Unwin, Ltd., 1921.

106. *Totem and Taboo*, translated by A. A. Brill, London, 1919.

107. *Wit and its Relation to the Unconscious*, translated by A. A. Brill, London, 1916.

108. *Introductory Lectures on Psychoanalysis*, translated by Mrs. Joan Rivière, London, Geo. Allen & Unwin, Ltd., 1922.

109. FROEBEL, F. *The Education of Man*, English translation, New York, 1892.

110. FRY, ROGER E. "An Essay in Æsthetics," *New Quarterly*, April 1909.

111. GAULTIER, PAUL. *Le rire et la caricature*, 2me édit., Paris, 1906.

112. GERARD, ALEXANDER. *An Essay on Taste*, London, 1759.

113. GILBERT, W. S. *Fifty Bab Ballads*, Routledge, London, N.D.

114. GOETHE. *Literary Essays*, selected and arranged by J. E. Spingarn, Oxford, 1921.

115. GOGOL, NICOLAI V. *The Inspector-General*, English translation, London, 1892.

116. GOLDSMITH, OLIVER. *Inquiry into the Present State of Polite Learning*, Works, edited by Spalding, London and Glasgow, 1858.

117. *Poems and Plays*, Everyman's Library, London, N.D.

118. GREEN, GEORGE H. *Psychanalysis in the Class-room*, London, 1921.

119. GREGORY, J. C. "The relation between the word and the Unconscious," *British Journal of Psychology*, vol. x, November 1919.

120. GROOS, KARL. *The Play of Animals*, translated by Elizabeth L. Baldwin, London, 1898.

121. *The Play of Man*, translated by Elizabeth L. Baldwin, London, 1900.

122. HALL, G. STANLEY. *Adolescence*, 2 vols., New York and London, 1904.

123. "The Psychology of Tickling, Laughing, and the Comic" (with Arthur Allin), *American Journal of Psychology*, vol. ix, 1897.

124. HAMILTON, WALTER. *Parodies of the Works of English and American Authors*, edited by Walter Hamilton, 6 vols., London, 1884–9.

125. HANKIN, ST. JOHN. *Dramatic Works*, 3 vols., London, 1912.

126. HANNAY, DAVID. "Humour," *Encyclopædia Brittanica*, 11th edit., Cambridge, 1910.

127. HARRINGTON, SIR JOHN. "A Brief Apology for Poetry," in Smith, *Elizabethan Critical Essays*, q.v.

128. HARRISON, JANE E. *Ancient Art and Ritual*, Home University Library Series, London.

129. HART, BERNARD. *The Psychology of Insanity*, Cambridge, 1916.

130. HARTLEY, DAVID. *Observations on Man*, 2 vols., 5th edit., Bath, 1810.

131. VON HARTMANN, E. *Die deutsche Æsthetik seit Kant*, Berlin, 1886.

132. HAZLITT, WILLIAM. *Lectures on the English Comic Writers*, World's Classics, London, 1907.

133. HAZLITT, W. C. *Shakespeare's Jest Books*, reprint, edited by W. C. Hazlitt, London, 1881.

134. HEGEL, G. W. F. *The Philosophy of Fine Art*, English translation, 4 vols., London, 1920.

135. HIRN, Y. *The Origins of Art*, London, 1900.

136. HOBBES, THOMAS "Human Nature" and "Leviathan," *Works*, edited by Molesworth, 11 vols., London, 1840.

137. HÖFFDING, HARALD. *Outlines of Psychology*, English translation, London, 1896.

138. HOLLINGSWORTH, H. L. "Experimental Studies in Judgment: Judgments of the Comic," *Psychological Review*, vol. xviii, March 1911.

139. HOLT, EDWIN B. *The Freudian Wish*, London, 1915.

140. HOOD, THOMAS. *Poems*, World's Classics, Oxford, 1907.

141. HOUGHTON, STANLEY. *Dramatic Works*, 3 vols., London, 1914.

142. HUGO, VICTOR. *William Shakespeare*, Paris, 1864.

143. HUNT, LEIGH. *Wit and Humour*, reprint, London, 1910.

144. HUTCHESON, FRANCIS. *Reflections upon Laughter*, Glasgow, 1750.

145. JAMES, WILLIAM. *Principles of Psychology*, 2 vols., London, 1918.

146. JANET, P. *Les médications psychologiques*, 3 tomes, Paris, 1919.

147. "La tension psychologique," *British Journal of Psychology*, Medical Section, vol. i, 1920–1.

148. JOHNSON, SAMUEL *Rambler*, No. 125, in *British Essayists*, vol. xxi, London, 1802.

149. *The Lives of the Poets*, 2 vols., World's Classics, London, 1906.

150. JONES, ERNEST. *Papers on Psycho-Analysis*, 2nd edit., London, 1920.

151 JONSON, BEN. *Works*, edited by Gifford, 9 vols., London, 1816.

152. JUNG, C. G. *Analytical Psychology,* English translation, London, 1916.

153. *The Psychology of the Unconscious,* English translation, London, 1916.

154. "Instinct and the Unconscious," *British Journal of Psychology,* vol. x, November 1919.

155. JUSSERAND, J. J. *The English Novel in the Time of Shakespeare,* English translation, London, 1908.

156. *English Wayfaring Life in the Middle Ages,* English translation, 2nd edit., London, 1920.

157. KALLEN, HORACE M. "The Æsthetic Principle in Comedy," *American Journal of Psychology,* vol. xxii, April 1911.

158. KAMES, LORD. *Elements of Criticism,* 9th edit., 2 vols., Edinburgh, 1817.

159. KANTOR, J. R. "An attempt towards a naturalistic description of emotions, *Psychological Review,* vol. xxviii, 1921.

160. KANT, IMMANUEL. *Critique of Judgment,* Bernard's translation, 2nd edit., London, 1914.

161. KIMMINS, C. W. "Visual Humour: Sights that Children Laugh at," *Strand Magazine,* April 1922

162. KLINE, L. W. "The Psychology of Humor," *American Journal of Psychology,* vol. xviii, 1907.

163. KNIGHT, R. P. *An Analytical Enquiry into the Principles of Taste,* 2nd edit., London, 1805.

164. KWANG LAI LOU. "Theories of Laughter," *The Chinese Student's Monthly,* vol. xvii, 1921.

165 LABICHE, EUGÈNE. *Théâtre complêt,* 9 tomes, Paris, N.D.

166. LAMB, CHARLES. *Essays of Elia,* Paterson, Edinburgh, 1885.

167 LAMENNAIS, F. *De l'art et du beau,* Paris, N.D.

168. LANGFELD, H. S. *The Æsthetic Attitude,* New York, 1920.

169. LAPRADE, VICTOR DE. *Questions d'art et de morale,* Paris, 1861.

170 LEACOCK, STEPHEN. *Literary Lapses,* 6th edit., London, 1914.

171. *Further Foolishness,* London, 1917.

172. LEE VERNON. *The Beautiful,* Cambridge, 1913.

173. LEE VERNON. *Beauty and Ugliness, and other Studies in Psychological Æsthetics* (with C. Anstruther Thompson), London, 1912.

174. LESAGE. *Histoire de Gil Blas de Santillane,* 2 tomes, édition Lutetia, Paris, N.D.

175. LESSING, E. G. *Hamburgische Dramaturgie,* Werke, 7ter Theil, Gustav Hempel, Berlin.

176. *Ibid.*, French translation, Paris, 1869.

177. LÉVÊQUE, CHARLES. "Le rire, le comique, et le risible, dans l'esprit et dans l'art," *Revue des deux mondes,* 2me période, tome 47, 1863.

178. LILLY, W. S. "Theory of the Ludicrous," *Fortnightly Review,* May 1896.

179. LIPPS, THEODOR. *Komik und Humor,* Berlin, 1898.

180. *Grundlegung der Ästhetik,* Hamburg und Leipsig, 1903.

181. LOCKE, JOHN. *An Essay concerning Human Understanding,* edited by A. C. Fraser, 2 vols., Oxford, 1894.

182. LOTZE, HERMANN. *Outlines of Æsthetics,* translated and edited by George T. Ladd, Boston, 1886.

183. MACNAUGHTAN, S. "Humour," *Nineteenth Century and After,* 1913.

184. McDOUGALL, WILLIAM. *An Introduction to Social Psychology,* 15th edit., London, 1920.

185. *Psychology, the Study of Behaviour,* Home University Library Series, 2nd edit., London, 1921.

186. "Instinct and Intelligence," *British Journal of Psychology,* vol. iii, October 1910.

187. "Instinct and the Unconscious," *British Journal of Psychology,* vol. x, November 1919.

188. DE MARMONTEL. "Comédie" and "Comique," in *Encyclopédie ou Dictionnaire raisonné des sciences, des arts, et des métiers,* 3me édit., Genève, 1778.

189. MARSHALL, H. R. *Pain, Pleasure, and Æsthetics,* London, 1894.

190. MARTIN, LILLIEN J. "Psychology of Æsthetics: Experimental Prospecting in the Field of the Comic," *American Journal of Psychology,* vol. xvi, 1905.

191. MÉLINAUD, C. "Pourquoi rit-on? Étude sur la cause psychologique du rire," *Revue des deux mondes,* February 1895.

192. MEREDITH, GEORGE. *An Essay on Comedy and the Uses of the Comic Spirit*, reissue, London, 1918.

193. MICHIELS, ALFRED. *Le monde du comique et du rire*, Paris, N.D.

194. MOLIÈRE, J. B. P. DE. *Œuvres*, 7 tomes, Didot, Paris, 1817

195. MORGAN, C. LLOYD. "Instinct and Intelligence," *British Journal of Psychology*, vol. iii, October 1910.

196. *Instinct and Experience*, London, 1912.

197. "Laughter," in *Encyclopedia of Religion and Ethics*, vol. vii, Edinburgh, 1914.

198. MORGANN, MAURICE. *An Essay on the Dramatic Character of Sir John Falstaff*, reprint, London, 1912.

199. MURRAY, MARGARET A. *The Witch Cult in Western Europe*, Oxford, 1921.

200. MYERS, C. S. "Instinct and Intelligence, *British Journal of Psychology*, vol. iii, October 1910.

201. "Instinct and the Unconscious," *British Journal of Psychology*, vol. x, November 1919.

202. PALMER, JOHN. *Comedy*, Art and Craft of Letters Series, London, N.D.

203. *The Comedy of Manners*, London, 1913.

204. PATER, WALTER. *Appreciations*, London, 1898.

205. PATRICK, G. T. W. *Psychology of Relaxation*, Cambridge, U.S.A., 1916.

206. PENJON, A. "Le rire et la liberté," *Revue philosophique*, 1893.

207. PEREZ, BERNARD. *Les trois premières années de l'enfant*, 5me édit., Paris, 1892.

208. *L'enfant de trois à sept ans*, 3me édit., Paris, 1894.

209. *L'education morale dès le berceau*, 3me edit., Paris, 1896.

210. PHILBERT, L. *Le rire : Essai littéraire, moral et psychologique*, Paris, 1883.

211. PLATO. *Philebus*, Jowett's translation, 3rd edit., Oxford, 1892.

212. *Poems from "Punch,"* 1909–20, with introductory essay by W. B. Drayton Henderson, London, 1922.

213. POINSINET DE SIVRY. *Traité des causes physiques et morales du rire, relativement à l'art de l'exciter*, Amsterdam, 1778

214. POPE, ALEXANDER. *Poetical Works.*

215. PRAT, L. See under RENOUVIER, CHARLES.

216. PREYER, W. *The Mind of the Child*, English translation: Part I: "The Senses and the Will," New York, 1892. Part II: "The Development of the Intellect," New York, 1890.

217. *Mental Development in the Child*, English translation, New York, 1897.

218. PRIESTLEY, JOSEPH. *A Course of Lectures on Oratory and Criticism*, London, 1777.

219. PRINCE, MORTON. *The Dissociation of a Personality*, London and New York, 1906.

220. "My Life as a Dissociated Personality," *Journal of Abnormal Psychology*, vol. iii, 1908–9.

221. *The Unconscious*, New York, 1914.

222. PYCRAFT, W. P. *The Courtship of Animals*, London, 1913.

223. QUINTILIAN. *De Institutione Oratoria*, London, 1714.

224. RABELAIS, FRANÇOIS. *Gargantua and Pantagruel*, Urquhart's translation, reprint, 2 vols., London, 1904.

225. RALEIGH, SIR WALTER. *The English Novel*, 5th edit., London, 1907.

226. *Shakespeare*, English Men of Letters Series, London, 1907.

227. RAMSAY, SIR GEORGE. *Analysis and Theory of the Emotions*, London, 1848.

228. RASMUSSEN, VILHELM. *Child Psychology.* Part I, "Development in the First Four Years," English translation, London, 1920.

229. RAULIN, J. M. *Le rire et les exhilarants*, Paris, 1899.

230. READ, CARVETH. *The Origin of Man*, Cambridge, 1920.

231. REANEY, MABEL JANE. "The Psychology of the Organized Group Game," *British Journal of Psychology*, Monograph Series, Cambridge, 1916.

232. RENOUVIER, CH. *La nouvelle monodologie* (with L. Prat), Paris, 1899.

233. RIBOT, TH. *Psychologie des sentiments*, Paris, 1896.

234. RICHTER, JEAN PAUL. *Vorschule der Æsthetik,* French Translation, Paris, 1862.

235. RIVERS, W. H. R. "Instinct and the Unconscious," *British Journal of Psychology,* vol. x, November 1919.

236. *Instinct and the Unconscious,* 2nd edit., Cambridge, 1922.

237. ROBINSON, E. S. "The Compensatory Function in Make-believe Play," *Psychological Review,* vol. xxvii, November 1920.

238. ROBINSON, LOUIS. "Ticklishness," in Tuke's *Dictionary of Psychological Medicine,* London, 1892.

239. ROSTAND, EDMOND. *Cyrano de Bergerac,* Paris, 1916.

240. ROUSSEAU, J. J. *Lettre à M. d'Alembert,* Œuvres, édit. Baudouin Frères, 25 tomes, Paris, 1826.

241 ROY, DENNIS-PRUDENT. *Dissertation médico-chirurgicale sur le rire, considéré comme phénomène sémiologique,* Paris, 1812.

242. RUSSELL, BERTRAND. *The Analysis of Mind,* London, 1921.

243. SAINTE-BEUVE, C. A. *Nouveaux portraits et critiques litéraires* (article on Molière), tome 2, Brussels, 1836.

244. *Causeries du Lundi* (article on Rabelais), October 7, 1850.

245. SANTAYANA, GEORGE. *The Sense of Beauty,* New York, reissue, 1904.

246. SCHOPENHAUER, ARTHUR. *The World as Will and Idea,* translated by Haldane and Kemp, 5th edit., London, 1906.

247. SCOTT, COLIN A. "Sex and Art," *American Journal of Psychology,* vol. vii, January 1896.

248. SEMON, RICHARD. *The Mneme,* English translation, London, 1921.

249. SHADWELL, THOMAS. Preface to "The Sullen Lovers," in Springarn, *Critical Essays of the Seventeenth Century,* q.v.

250. Preface to "The Humorists," in Springarn, *op. cit.,* q.v.

251. SHAFTESBURY, EARL OF. *Characteristics of Men, Manners, Opinions, Times*, 3 vols., 6th edition., London, 1737.

252. SHAKESPEARE, WILLIAM. *Works*, Eversley edition, 10 vols., London, 1899.

253. *Shakespeare's Jest Books*. See under HAZLITT, W. C.

254. SHAND, A. F. *The Foundations of Character*, London, 1914.

255. SHAW, G. BERNARD. *Unpleasant Plays*: "Widowers' Houses," "The Philanderer," "Mrs. Warren's Profession," London, 1898.

256. *Pleasant Plays*: "Arms and the Man," "Candida," "The Man of Destiny," "You Never Can Tell," London, 1898.

257. *Three Plays for Puritans*: "The Devil's Disciple," "Cæsar and Cleopatra," "Captain Brassbound's Conversion," London, 1901.

258. *Man and Superman*, London, 1903.

259. *John Bull's Other Island*, London, 1904.

260. *The Doctor's Dilemma*, London, 1906.

261. *Misalliance, The Dark Lady of the Sonnets, Fanny's First Play*, London, 1910.

262. *Androcles and the Lion, Overruled, Pygmalion*, London 1912.

263. *Back to Methuselah*, London, 1920.

264. SHERIDAN, R. B. *Plays*, Everyman's Library, London, 1906.

265. SHINN, MILLICENT W. *Notes on the Development of a Child*, University of California publications in Education, vols. i and iv, 1893–9 and 1907.

266. SIDIS, BORIS. *The Psychology of Laughter*, New York, 1913.

267. SIDNEY, SIR PHILIP. "An Apology for Poetrie," in Smith *Elizabethan Critical Essays*, q.v.

268. SMITH, GREGORY. *Ben Jonson*, English Men of Letters Series, London, 1909.

269. SMITH, GREGORY. *Elizabethan Critical Essays*, edited by Gregory Smith, 2 vols., Oxford, 1904.

270. SMITH, SYDNEY. *Works*, 3 vols., London, 1859.

271. SPENCER, HERBERT. *Principles of Psychology*, 2 vols., London, 1872.

272. "The Physiology of Laughter," in *Essays*, 2 vols., London, 1863.

273. SPINGARN, J. E. *Literary Criticism in the Renaissance*, 3rd edit., New York, 1912.

274. *Ibid.*, Italian translation, with additions, 1905.

275. *Critical Essays of the Seventeenth Century*, edited by J. E. Spingarn, Oxford, 1908.

276. DE STENDHAL. *Racine et Shakespeare*, Paris, N.D.

277. STERNE, LAWRENCE. *The Life and Opinions of Tristram Shandy, Gentleman*, World's Classics, Oxford, 1903.

278. *A Sentimental Journey through France and Italy*, Gibbings, London, 1903.

279. STEVENSON, R. L. *Virginibus Puerisque*, London, 1909.

280. *Moral Emblems*, London, 1921.

281. STEWART, DUGALD. *The Philosophy of the Active and Moral Powers of Man*, 2 vols., Edinburgh, 1828.

282. STOUT, G. F. *Manual of Psychology*, 3rd edit., London, 1913.

283. "Instinct and Intelligence," *British Journal of Psychology*, vol. iii, October 1910.

284. STUBBES, PHILIP. *Anatomy of Abuses in England*, reprint by New Shakspere Society, London, 1877–9.

285. SULLY, JAMES. *Studies of Childhood*, 2nd edit., London, 1896.

286. *An Essay on Laughter*, reissue, London, 1907.

287. SYNGE, J. M. *The Playboy of the Western World*, Dublin, 1907.

288. TANSLEY, A. G. *The New Psychology and its Relation to Life*, London, 1920.

289. *Tarleton's Jests and News out of Purgatory*, edited for the Shakspeare Society, by J O. Halliwell, London, 1844.

290. TAYLOR, H. O. *The Mediæval Mind*, 2 vols., London, 1911.

291. TEMPLE, SIR WM. "Of Poetry," in *Works*, 2 vols., Edinburgh, 1764.

292. THOMSON, J. ARTHUR. *Heredity*, London, 1911.

293. *The System of Animate Nature*, 2 vols., London, 1920.

294 THORNDIKE, E. L. *The Original Nature of Man*, being vol. i of *Educational Psychology*, London, 1919.

295 Titchener, E. B. *Experimental Psychology of the Thought Processes*, New York, 1909.

296. *Townley Plays*, Early English Text Society, London, 1897.

297. TROTTER, W *Instincts of the Herd in Peace and War*, London, 1916.

298 TYLOR, E. B. *Primitive Culture*, 4th edit., 2 vols., London, 1903.

399. TWAIN, MARK. *Tom Sawyer*, Nelson, London, N.D.

300. *Huckleberry Finn*, Nelson, London, N.D.

301. VASEY, GEORGE. *The Philosophy of Laughter and Smiling*, London, 1875.

302. VOLTAIRE. *Candide, ou l'optimisme*, Œuvres, tome xxiii, édition Lefèvre, Paris, 1829.

303. *Zadig, ou la Destinée*, tome xxiii.

304. "Le rire," in *Dictionnaire philosophique*, tome xxxii.

305. *Lettre sur la comédie*, tome xxxvii.

306. *Mémoire sur la satire*, tome xxxviii.

307. WARD, SIR A. W. *A History of English Dramatic Literature*, 2nd edit., 2 vols., London, 1899.

308. WARD, JAMES. *Psychological Principles*, Cambridge, 1919.

309. WARTON, JOSEPH. *Adventurer*, No. 133, in *British Essayists*, vol. xxv, London, 1802.

310. WALKLEY, A. B. *Pastiche and Prejudice*, London, 1921.

311. WALLAS, GRAHAM. *Human Nature in Politics*, London, 1908.

312. *The Great Society*, London, 1914.

313. *Our Social Heritage*, London, 1921.

314. "Instinct and the Unconscious," *British Journal of Psychology*, vol. x, November 1919.

315. WATSON, JOHN B. *Psychology from the Standpoint of a Behaviorist,* Philadelphia and London, 1919.

316. WHETSTONE, GEORGE. Dedication to "Promos and Cassandra," in Smith, *Elizabethan Critical Essays,* q.v.

317. WILSON, THOMAS. *The Art of Rhetorique,* reprint, Oxford, 1909.

318. WINCH, W. H. "The Psychology and Philosophy of Play," *Mind,* N.S., vol. xv, 1906.

319. WOHLGEMUTH, A. "Pleasure-Unpleasure," *British Journal of Psychology,* Monograph Series, Cambridge, 1919.

320. WOODWORTH, R. S. *Psychology, a Study of Mental Life,* London, 1922.

321. WRIGHT, THOMAS. *A History of Caricature and Grotesque in Literature and Art,* London, 1865.

322. WYCHERLEY, WILLIAM. *Comedies,* Mermaid Series, London, 1893.

LIST II.

1. ALBERT. *Dissertatio de Risu commodo et incommodo in œconomia vitali,* Halle, 1746.

2. ANONYMOUS. *Physiologie du Ridicule,* Paris, 1833.

3. LE BATTEUX. *Théorie des Belles-Lettres.*

4. BELLEGARDE. *Réflexions sur le Ridicule et sur les moyens de l'éviter,* Paris, 1696.

5. BERRELARIUS. *Tractatus de Risu,* Florence, 1603.

6. BOHTZ. *Ueber das Komische und die Komoedie,* 1844.

7. BOUTERWECK. *Æsthetik,* 1806.

8. BRUCE, H. A. "Why do we laugh?" *Outlook,* August 1913.

9. CAZAMIAN, L. "Pourquoi nous ne pouvous définir l'humour," *Revue germanique,* 1906.

10. CROCE, BENEDETTO. "L'Umorismo," *Journal of Comparative Literature,* vol. i, No. 3.

11 DUCLOS. *Considérations sur les mœurs,* 1750.

12. ESCHENBURG. *Collection de modèles pour servir à la théorie et à l'histoire des Belles-Lettres,* 1788–95.

13. FISCHER, KUNO. *Über den Witz*, 1889.

14. FRACASTOR. *Naugerius, sive de Poetica, dialogus*, Venice, 1555.

15. FRANCUS. *Dissertatio de Risu sardonico*, Heidelberg, 1683.

16. FLEURY, JULES. *Histoire de la caricature sous la république, l'empire, et la restauration, par Chamfleury*, 1874.

17. FLOEGEL, C. F. *Geschichte der Komischen Litteratur*, Leipsig, 1784.

18. GOCLENIUS, R. *Physiologia Crepitus ventris, item Risus et Ridiculi et elogium Nihili*, Frankfurt, 1607.

19. GROOS, KARL. *Einleitung in die Æsthetik*, 1892.

20. HECKER, E. *Die Physiologie und Psychologie des Lachens und des Komischen*, Berlin, 1873.

21. HERCKENRATH. *Problèmes d'esthétique et de morale*, 1897.

22. JOSSIUS, N. *Opuscula de Voluptate et Dolore, de Risu et Fletu, de Somnio et Vigilia, de Fame et Siti*, Frankfurt, 1603.

23. JOUBERT, LAURENT. *Traité du Ris*, Paris, 1579.

24 KAISIN. *Dissertatio de Risu*, Lyons, 1733.

25. LEVI, GIULIO A. *Il Comico*, 1913.

26. LUPICHIUS, J. S. F. *Dissertatio inauguralis physico-medica de Risu*, Bale, 1738.

27. MAPPUS, MARCUS. *De Risu et Fletu*, Strasburg, 1684.

28. MITCHELL, SIR ARTHUR. *Dreaming, Laughing and Blushing*.

29. MOESER. *Harlequin, oder Vertheidigung des Groteske-Komischen*, 1761.

30. MÜNSTERBERG, H. *Principles of Art Education.*

31. PLATNER, J. Z. *Dissertatio de Risu a splene*, Leipsig, 1738.

32. POLITIEN, A. L. *Dialogu pulcherrimus et utilissimus des Risu, ejusque causis et consequentibus, dilucide ac philosophice tractatus, inque libros duos divisus*, Frankfurt, 1603.

33. ROSENKRANTZ. *Æsthetik des Hässlichen*, Koenigsberg, 1853.

34. SCHAUER, OTTO. "Über das Wesen der Komik," *Archiv für gesamte psychologie*, xviii, 1910.

35. Schmid. *Dissertatio de Risu*, Jena, 1630.

36. Schütze. *Versuch einer Theorie des Komischen*, 1815 (? 1817).

37. Simon, L. *De naturali et præternaturali Risu*, Messina, 1656.

38. Smith, W. "Comedy," *Psychological Bulletin*, 1910.

39. Vavassor, Franz. *De ludicra Dictione, in quo tota jocandi ratio ex Veterum scriptis affirmatur*, Leipsig, ? 1722.

40. Vischer, Theodor. *Ueber das Erhabene und Komische* 1837.

41. Zeising, Adolf. *Æsthetische Forschungen*, 1855.

NOTES.

In addition to the above, practically all German works on Æsthetics (e.g. those of Trahndorff, Schleiermacher, Kirchman. Weisse, Fechner, Wundt, Kräpelin, Zimmermann) treat incidentally the subjects of Laughter and Comedy.

J. M. Raulin, in his *Le rire et les exhilarants*, gives a fairly full bibliography of medical and semi-medical works on Laughter, But Raulin is so grossly inaccurate throughout that I have hesitated to cite any works from his list which I have been unable to trace through other sources.

INDEX